Music Cognition

This is a volume in

ACADEMIC PRESS
SERIES IN COGNITION AND PERCEPTION

A Series of Monographs and Treatises

A complete list of titles in this series appears at the end of this volume.

Music Cognition

W. JAY DOWLING

*Program in Human Development
and Communication Sciences
University of Texas at Dallas
Richardson, Texas*

DANE L. HARWOOD

*Situation Management Systems, Inc.
Plymouth, Massachusetts*

1986

ACADEMIC PRESS, INC.

(Harcourt Brace Jovanovich, Publishers)

Orlando   San Diego   New York   London
Toronto   Montreal   Sydney   Tokyo

Passages from the following are reprinted by permission of the publishers:

Denes, P. B., & Pinson, E. N., *The Speech Chain*. Copyright © 1963 by Bell Telephone Laboratories, Incorporated. Reprinted by permission of Doubleday & Company, Inc.

Granit, R., *The purposive brain*. Copyright © 1977 by The Massachusetts Institute of Technology.

Jairazbhoy, N. A., *The rāgs of North Indian Music*. Copyright © 1971 by N. A. Jairazbhoy. Reprinted by permission of Weslayan University Press.

Jones, M. R., Only time can tell: On the topology of mental space and time, *Critical Inquiry, 7*, 557–576. © 1981 by The University of Chicago.

Locke, D. Principles of offbeat timing and cross-rhythm in southern Eve dance drumming, *Ethnomusicology, 26*, 217–246. © Copyright 1982 by the Society for Ethnomusicology, Inc. Used by Permission.

Lomax, A. *Folk song style and culture*, AAAS Pub. No. 88. Copyright 1968, by AAAS.

Meyer, L. *Emotion and meaning in music*. © 1956 by The University of Chicago.

Rosen, C. Battle over Berlioz: Review of J. Rushton *The musical language of Berlioz, The New York Review of Books, 31*(7), 40–43. Reprinted with permission from *The New York Review of Books*. Copyright © 1984 Nyrev, Inc.

ACADEMIC PRESS, INC.
Orlando, Florida 32887

United Kingdom Edition published by
ACADEMIC PRESS INC. (LONDON) LTD.
24–28 Oval Road, London NW1 7DX

LIBRARY OF CONGRESS CATALOGING IN PUBLICATION DATA

Dowling, W. Jay.
    Music cognition.

    (Academic Press series in cognition and perception)
    Includes index.
    1. Music—Psychology.   2. Cognition.   3. Perception.
I. Harwood, Dane L.   II. Title.   III. Series.
ML3838.D73   1985   781'.15   85-7541
ISBN 0-12-221430-7 (alk. paper)

PRINTED IN THE UNITED STATES OF AMERICA

86 87 88 89   9 8 7 6 5 4 3 2 1

To Darlene
and
to Gail and Caren

Contents

Preface

This book focuses on the perception and cognition of music. The point of view we take toward psychology is what is generally called information processing. We view the music listener as a gatherer and interpreter of information from the environment, and we believe that is possible to study the separate component processes by which the listener accomplishes this gathering and interpreting. In studying the component processes, we believe that it is important to remain continually cognizant of the way those components fit into the whole process of understanding music. The musical information processing we discuss in this volume is called *cognitive* because it focuses on the mental activities involved. Not all the cognitive processes we describe are explicit ones, accessible to conscious awareness. In fact, most of the processes involved in hearing and comprehending music are implicit and unconscious. Many of the experiments we discuss show that even inexperienced listeners are able to make sophisticated judgments concerning the music of their culture but are not able to state explicitly the psychological or musical basis for those judgments. This should not be surprising, since native speakers of a language are also rarely able to verbalize the grammatical and semantic rules governing their language use or to describe how they go about producing sentences.

There are a number of reasons why we enjoy studying the psychology of music, some of them having more to do with psychology and others having more to do with music. Both of us (and we hope many readers, too) have a lifelong interest in music that is continually renewed by exciting encounters with music when we perform and listen. A psychologist who has an exciting experience tends to ask, "Why did I have that experience? Where did it come from?" (Some may consider that an occupational hazard.) Music is ephemeral, and when it departs, the psychologist is left reflecting on the sources of its effects. These reflections lead in two directions: toward the musical and toward the psychological. The musical and the psychological are mutually illuminating: The study of musical patterns tells us something about the mind, and the study of the mind tells us something about the forms of music. Musical form illumines our understanding of the mind because all people everywhere seem always to have had music, and so music takes its place beside language as a basic and universal cultural pattern. Not only are the behaviors of singing and listening found worldwide, but music everywhere has structure. The variety of structure found in the world's musics provides some idea of the limits of human mental capacity—of possible mental organizations. That which is musically possible, which the ear can hear and the mind can grasp, is the province of cognitive psychology.

THE ORGANIZATION OF THIS BOOK

We begin our presentation of music cognition with seven chapters devoted primarily to the investigation of musical behavior in the psychological laboratory. The laboratory is a highly constrained cultural context for gathering data on human capacities and habits with considerable precision. The supposition underlying laboratory experimentation is that the same component processes of cognition continue to operate out in the world in real-life situations. We strive to relate information gathered from laboratory studies to behavior in the world outside and, in the process, to extend our discussion beyond the borders of western European culture.

All music is transmitted through sound waves. Chapter 2 begins with a description of the physical properties of sound, followed by a description of the relationships between those physical properties and the psychological dimensions of what we hear. The most basic psychological dimensions—pitch, loudness, and duration—appear to function in all cultures. It is in the use to which those dimensions of sound are put in the construction of complex and meaningful musical patterns that cultures differ. Thus our hearing of a piece of music can be described partly in terms of the way our auditory system processes the basic dimensions of sound, but to that partial description must be added a description of how our cultural learning and our familiarity with a particular style of music leads us to hear it in a certain way. In the course of this and the following chapters, we point out instances in which a listener's expectations, conditioned by cultural learning, lead to auditory experiences different from those of the naïve listener. Knowing what to expect in a piece leads one to hear it differently.

The following chapters explore the various dimensions of sound and how they are used in musical contexts. Chapter 3 is concerned with timbre (tone color) and consonance versus dissonance. The auditory dimension Westerners label consonant versus dissonant provides a good illustration of the cultural use of an auditory dimension. Though it is present in musical sounds all over the world, the musical functions of those sounds implied by the label pertain only to certain cultural contexts, most especially Western music of the eighteenth and nineteenth centuries. That type of Western music uses the consonance–dissonance dimension as one of the bases of functional harmony, but in other cultures, the same auditory dimension is put to other uses.

Chapter 4 explores the dimension of pitch as it is used in musical scales. Nearly all cultures have scales in the sense of stable sets of pitch relationships, and nearly all use the auditory feature of octave similarity as a basis for scale organization. But the way scales are organized within the octave and the functional relationships of the pitches differ from culture to culture. Chapter 5 continues the discussion of the pitch material of music in considering perception and memory for melodies. Considerations that pervade our discussion here and throughout the book are the questions, What dimensions of the musical stimulus are psychologically relevant? How fine a grain of perceptual discrimination is relevant for the composer and performer? and, Which physical dimensions of the auditory signal make a difference to the listener's perceptions?

The organization of melodies results in patterns in the dimensions of pitch and time. Chapters 6 and 7 consider melodic organization as extended in time. Chapter 7 is concerned in particular with rhythm and temporal organization, especially as they relate to the basic problem of the relationship between memory and musical form. Chapter 8 examines several perspectives on emotion and meaning in music and explores possible relationships between musical structure and emotional response.

Having discussed the notions of meaning and cultural relativism in the first seven chapters, we turn our attention in the last chapter to the social contexts of music performance. In the first eight chapters, we bring in cross-cultural examples whenever possible. In Chapter 8, we move more directly toward providing the listener with a complex cultural environment. Chapter 9 focuses on the importance of cross-cultural studies of musical behavior. We examine Lomax's provocative attempt to relate song-style to social-psychological behavior as well as alternative approaches to the study of music in its cultural context. We conclude by examining cross-cultural universals.

A tape recording of examples is included with this book. Many of the chapters refer to the recorded examples, and those references are indicated by notations in the margins (see also the list of Recorded Examples, p. xvii). Longer recorded examples cited in the text include references to easily available recordings, and we recommend them to the interested reader.

There are three books that form a nucleus of what we consider most important in the psychology of music: Helmholtz's *On the Sensations of Tone* (1877/1954), Francès's *La Perception de la Musique* (1958), and Meyer's *Emotion and Meaning in Music* (1956). These works define three focal dimensions of our field: Helmholtz establishes the empirical investigation of the elements of music, Francès shows how the cognition of more elaborate musical structures can be investigated, and Meyer points the way to an understanding of the interrelationships of cognition and affect underlying musical meaning. Over our twenty-some years of studying in this area, these are the books we have kept closest to hand as indispensible. In the process of writing our own book, we went back to them often to verify a quotation or trace the background of an idea. In so doing, we were often drawn into rereading passages we had not looked at for years, rereading with even greater pleasure passages whose meaning we had at first only dimly grasped but now better understood. We recommend them most heartily to the reader who wishes to pursue our subject into broader and deeper regions than we present here.

OTHER APPROACHES

There are several approaches clustered around the psychology of music that this book does not explore. For the reader's convenience we list them here with suggestions about where to find further reading.

Music Therapy.   We are not directly concerned with the use of music as a tool for achieving psychotherapeutic goals, though we hope some of the material we have assembled here may be of use to those who wish to do that. The interested reader may wish to consult Gaston (1968) or Anderson (1977).

Testing.   We are interested in individual differences in musical behavior, and many of the studies we discuss address those issues. We do not discuss, however, assessment and testing per se. We highly recommend Shuter-Dyson and Gabriel (1981).

Philosophy and Aesthetics.   While on occasion we take up issues relevant to various philosophical positions, we do no attempt to develop a rigorous aesthetic theory. We do hope that aestheticians find the research and discussions we present to be both interesting and useful. But our aim is empirical, not normative. To readers who wish to pursue aesthetic questions further we recommend Dewey (1934), Goodman (1968), Hanslick (1957), Langer (1953), Levinson (1980), Meyer (1956, 1967), Peckham (1965), Stravinsky (1956), and Wollheim (1968).

Acoustics. Our discussion of musical acoustics is introductory and meant to serve as background for our discussion of perceptual and cultural issues that could not be well understood without it. An excellent and highly readable discussion of general acoustics may be found in Feather (1964). Two classic texts on musical acoustics are Backus (1969) and Benade (1976). Hunt's (1978) engaging *Origins in Acoustics* contains much historical material to interest the musician. And in architectural acoustics the works of Beranek (1962) and of Knudsen and Harris (1980) are standard.

Audition. The purpose in our overview of auditory physiology is likewise to provide the reader with an indispensible minimum of background. A very accessible discussion, especially related to speech perception and production, is provided by Denes and Pinson (1973). Green's (1976) text on hearing is a good, more advanced source. And for the latest developments in both acoustics and audition, readers are directed to the *Journal of the Acoustical Society of America,* which successfully covers a wide range of fields, reporting work of uniformly high quality.

Anthropology and Ethnomusicology. Ethnomusicology for us has been a rich source of anthropological theories, methods, and descriptions of musical experience. We believe there is a need to extend the study of music cognition to a range of the world's cultures wider than those of western Europe. The approach to anthropology we find most congenial is perhaps best represented by a collection of articles by Geertz (1973). Among ethnomusicological texts, Hood (1971) states the problems and prospects of the discipline most eloquently and sympathetically. Malm (1977), Nettl (1973), and Wade (1979) also present good overviews. In this field, the journal *Ethnomusicology* is indispensible.

Acknowledgments

Many individuals helped make this book a reality, contributing encouragement, advice, and comments. In particular, we thank Edward C. Carterette for his long-standing commitment and enthusiasm and for his editorial and scholarly guidance. Judith Becker, Donald T. Campbell, and Donald A. Norman were additional sources of inspiration, and they strongly influenced our thinking. Kelyn Roberts and James Bartlett were unwavering sources of intellectual stimulation and constructive commentary. Ellen April, Christopher Frederickson, Kathryn King, Darlene Smith, and Andrew Toth also offered suggestions and support. The University of Michigan Society of Fellows supported Dane Harwood at a key stage in this book's development.

Recorded Examples

SIDE A

1

The Sense of Sound

Take care of the sense, and the sounds will take care of themselves.

(Lewis Carroll, 1865–1871/1944, p. 133)

Music exists only in the moment of its performance, for if one were ever so skillful in reading notes and had ever so lively an imagination, it cannot be denied that it is only in an unreal sense that music exists when it is read. It really exists only in being performed.

(Kierkegaard, 1843/1959, p. 67)

BACKGROUND

Some years ago, one of us (DLH) joined a newly formed university musical ensemble whose purpose was to play a newly acquired set of Javanese *gamelan* instruments. I was told that the easiest instrument to learn was the largest gong, the *gong ageng*, since it sounded least frequently in every piece. One had only to strike its center boss in such a way as to produce a "good sound" on the right beat. By good sound I assumed was meant a sound with no distortion, and for the next 2 years proceeded on that assumption whenever I was asked to play the gong. Eventually, I found myself a member of a *gamelan* ensemble including three native Indonesian musicians, each of whom indicated to me that the sound I was producing on the gong was not quite right. At separate times, each of these musicians was able to demonstrate for me the appropriate way of striking the instrument. At first, I failed to hear a difference, and so I asked for verbal clarification. I was told that striking exactly on the correct beat was not always appropriate, even if formally correct. "When

1

is it appropriate, and when not?'' I asked and received no clear answer. Instead, I was told I would learn through observation. And, indeed, over the next few months I began to realize that for some musical structures, a delay in striking the gong brought smiles to the faces of the Javanese; for other musical structures, a delay in striking brought polite frowns. Indeed, the distinctions were quite systematic, and I was able to confirm my hypothesis by asking.

I thought my problems with playing the gong were over, but not so. Over time I came to understand that manner of striking was important and that tempo, musical genre, and even the acoustic characteristics of the individual gong determined how and precisely when it should be played. None of this information was ever conveyed to me verbally, but rather through example and observation in the course of many rehearsals and performances. In the years that have followed, I have studied many other *gamelan* instruments and have found that each has a body of implicit knowledge of performance practice. To make that knowledge explicit, I could not ask the native musician for a theoretical explanation. Often, there was none. I watched, and played, and allowed myself to be guided by the numerous subtle cues concerning the appropriateness of my behavior. Visiting Indonesia, I found that the extent of implicit knowledge of performance practice was quite large. In fact, there were differences, all unverbalized, from one native teacher to the next. Writing a theory of *gamelan* music that incorporates all this information would be an unending and probably impossible task. But while the musical knowledge of the native musician may often be tacit, it is not inaccessible. As outsiders to the tradition, we found ourselves learning as children in traditional cultures learn—through observation, imitation, and experimentation.

What is true of Indonesian music is equally true of the western European music more familiar to most readers: that much of our knowledge is also tacit—not bounded by the explicitly verbalized or by textbooks on music theory. But in thinking and talking about music; we tend to overlook what is implicit and tacit and therefore, overlook the psychological and cultural processes that underlie the acquisition and transfer of such knowledge. My interest in and study of a musical tradition very different from my native ones raised the issue for me and made me aware that I had been implicitly learning my own traditions as well.

This book grows out of our attempts to understand the psychological processes underlying human cognition of music—processes involved in perceiving, learning, and remembering music. Music is a universal human mode of behavior and cognition. This book is concerned with how music is comprehended: Experience demonstrates that the process of comprehension is not immediately obvious. We do not want to take away the music lover's experience of music, but rather provide the music lover with a psychological explanation of certain parts of his or her experience. Furthermore, we do not intend to provide composers with new rules to follow, but rather to understand what composers have been doing out of good musical sense for centuries. We aim at an explication of good musical sense.

MUSIC, COGNITION, AND CULTURE

The experience of listening to two people conversing in a language we do not know is both fascinating and frustrating. Not only do we fail to grasp the content of the discussion, we even have a difficult time deciding where words and sentences begin and end. We cannot break the stream of sound into meaningful units, which would seem to be a first step toward understanding. Knowing a language means knowing (implicitly) an elaborate rule structure for the interpretation of speech sounds—parsing them into temporal units and interpreting their meaning.

It should come as no surprise that understanding a musical performance from an unfamiliar tradition leads to analogous difficulties of perception. A Westerner's first experience of Japanese *gagaku*, Balinese *gamelan*, or Persian *dastgah* improvisation is perhaps "ear opening." We may even think we hear structural units and relationships. But just as with our perception of an unknown language, our perceptual structuring of the music of an unfamiliar tradition is fraught with difficulty. Elements are there, of course, but they are not the ones we thought were there. Accurate interpretation of music, as of language, requires appropriate mental structures. As the Duchess suggested to Alice in the quotation at the beginning of this chapter, the "sense" of a musical language—the high-level structure that allows us to interpret its meanings—is prerequisite to hearing the sounds.

Every culture studied by anthropologists has some organized behavior that could be labeled music, even though the society might not have a term for such behavior. And musical behavior must be performed in real time. Performers can rarely afford to sit back and think about what comes next—all thinking must be "thinking ahead" during the ongoing performance. Musical performance, then, must simultaneously involve thinking, listening, remembering, acting, and even feeling. Is it possible to formulate a psychological theory that explains how people develop and apply musical knowledge processes?

Here we adopt an information-processing approach to understanding musical knowledge and behavior. This approach suggests that the brain can perform many complicated operations simultaneously, not all of which are accessible to conscious experience. Our sensory systems receive information about the world. Sensations are filtered through perceptual processes that direct attention to important events. But even important signals—those that might deserve our attention—are often too numerous to handle. Processes for remembering, for labeling, for integration with other information in memory, help us to handle the incredible amount of stimulation we face each moment of our lives, making action in the environment possible. Musical sounds and the musical actions of others are environmental stimuli that are important—that have meaning for us—sensed by our ears and eyes and interpreted in the context of our memories.

Studies of musical perception and memory suggest that the information processing involved is flexible and context sensitive. It depends greatly on how familiar we are with the information to be understood, what task it is we are trying to do, and how complicated the sensory information is. And much of it goes on subconsciously. The ultimate result of our ability to perceive, remember, conceptualize, and act on musical information is the formation of internal frameworks, or schemata, for representing and reproducing more complex musical knowledge. Schemata, too, are flexible. They certainly change as we get older and as our familiarity with musical traditions grows.

The flexibility and context sensitivity of music cognition extends to the rich variety of musical behavior found across cultures. There are pronounced cross-cultural differences in melodic and rhythmic organization and in performance practices. A psychological theory of musical behavior must be applicable across these differences. We argue that cultural variability is constrained by some underlying properties of the human information-processing system. Among these universals built into the world's musics are (1) the use of discrete pitch intervals, (2) octave equivalence, and (3) the presence of four to seven focal pitches in an octave. We return to questions of cross-cultural universals in Chapter 9.

MUSIC MATERIALS

This book is addressed to readers approaching the psychology of music from the directions of both music and psychology. Psychological theories and methods are usually explained in the text as they become relevant. However, for our nonmusician readers, we present a short introduction to what is commonly called music theory—an account of the use of the pitch, duration, loudness, and timbre of sounds in European music over the past 400 years with particular attention to the notation by which those sounds are represented. Readers familiar with the materials of European music can skip immediately to Chapter 2. For afficianados who read our short introduction anyway, we caution them that this is not intended to be a definitive outline of musical organization, but merely something useful, and not too misleading, to the musically naîve reader. We return in subsequent chapters to a detailed discussion of the pschological aspects of most of the topics covered briefly here.

Dimensions of Sounds

There are four psychological qualities of sounds that are especially important in music: pitch, duration, loudness, and timbre. Those are the main perceptual qualities that composers and performers control and listeners attend to. These sound qualities are organized in terms of psychological dimensions. Pitch, loudness, and duration seem at first sight to be unidimensional qualities, while timbre is multidimensional. Pitch is the quality that differentiates high and low sounds—men's voices are usually lower pitched than women's. Loudness and duration function in much the same way as in nonmusical contexts. Timbre (or tone color), which is the most complicated, refers to the differences of sound quality among various musical instruments, as well as among the various syllables of speech (*hah* vs. *goo,* for example). Sounds vary in timbre along several dimensions, just as the syllables *pah, poh, tah,* and *toh* differ on at least two dimensions. We will see that timbre distinctions for speech sounds are fundamentally the same as those required for musical sounds.

In what follows, we concentrate on pitch and duration and their notational representation. Loudness is notated simply by abbreviations of the Italian words for loud (*forte,* f), soft (*piano,* p), and medium (*mezzo,* m). This gives a scale with the gradations: pp–p–mp–mf–f–ff. Timbre is usually notated at the start of the line by indicating the instrument to be played. (Some non-Western notations, for example Chinese, indicate timbral variations for individual notes; Needham, 1962.)

Pitch

Pitch is organized in terms of scales made up of discrete steps. The scales consist of a limited number of pitches selected from the infinity of possibilities. The scales used in familiar melodies are called *tonal,* meaning that there is a *tonic,* or most important pitch, with which a melody usually starts and, even more often, ends. Think of a familiar melody—"Frère Jacques," "Twinkle, Twinkle, Little Star," or "My Country, 'Tis of Thee." Even better, sing one of those softly to yourself—loudly if no one is around. Notice that the pitch of the last note you sang is the same as the first—you could begin singing the same melody again starting with the same note and return to the same pitch at the end. That pitch is the tonic. It serves as a reference point in the pitch scale to which the other pitches are related. With the scale, it defines a musical *key*.

For the most part, melodies move along the scale by single steps between neighboring pitches. The first three phrases of "My Country, 'Tis of Thee" ("God Save the Queen") illustrate that very well. The up and down motion of the melody (its contour) moves always to the neighboring scale step. Figure 1.1 shows "My Country, 'Tis of Thee" as represented in European musical notation. Notice that the ups and downs of the contour (indicated by pluses and minuses) are represented by movement

Figure 1.1 Notation of (A) My Country, 'Tis of Thee," and (B) "Frère Jacques." Melodic contour is indicated by + (upward) and − (downward).

of the notes up and down the musical staff. Each line and each space between lines represents a different pitch in the scale. Figure 1.1 also shows the notation for "Frère Jacques," in which you can see skips from one pitch to another across intervening neighboring steps.

We do not say much about the notation of time and rhythm in this brief introduction, but notice as you sing "Frère Jacques" that the notes are of three different lengths. The basic beat is represented as quarter notes (filled symbols with stems). Half notes, as on the word *vous*, are twice as long as quarter notes and are represented by open symbols with stems. Eighth notes, as on *sonnez*, are half as long as quarter notes and are represented as quarter notes with flags on the stems. Each additional flag divides, the duration in half: sixteenths, thirty-seconds, and so on. Whole notes, not shown here, are (logically enough) equal in length to four quarters (or two halves) and are represented by open symbols without stems. A dot adds half again the value of the note to which it is attached. Thus the dotted quarter note on *'tis* in "My Country, 'Tis of Thee" is equal in length to three eighth notes. It is followed by one eighth note (on *of*). Thus the total time taken by *'tis of* is equal to four eighths, or two quarters, but with the time distributed unequally between the two syllables. (The fractional number $\frac{3}{4}$ at the start of the line indicates that time is organized into three quarter-note values per *measure*, or space between *bar* lines. The $\frac{4}{4}$ in "Frère Jacques" denotes four quarter-note values per measure.)

Pitches eight tonal scale steps apart are said to be an octave apart. When men and women sing together, they sing the same melody with pitches separated by an octave. The pitches they sing are functionally equivalent in the musical system. Thus, each scale has seven functionally distinct pitches. Tonal scales are cyclical. After seven notes in either direction, the pattern repeats. The names given the pitches reflect this. In English, we usually use the first seven letters of the alphabet, A through G. For obscure historical reasons, the tonic of the most basic tonal scale is called C. The melodies in Figure 1.1 have C as the tonic—the second space down in what is called the *treble* staff. The "curlicue" at the start of the staves in Figure 1.1 (the clef) is actually a stylized *G*, and it curls around the line representing the pitch G. (In Bach's time, the G clef could be placed on any line on the staff, and musicians knew that that line represented the G; but now musicians are not so flexible, and the treble G always falls on the second line from the bottom.) Figure 1.2 shows the note names across the four octaves most often used in music. The lower pitches are represented on the *bass* staff, which has an F clef (a stylized *F*) designating the fourth line as F. Note that extra ledger lines can be added when the pitch goes beyond the confines of the staff. Note also that

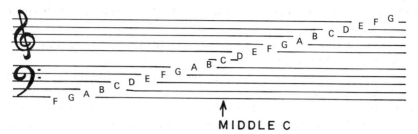

MIDDLE C

Figure 1.2 Grand staff with treble (G) and bass (F) clefs. Middle C falls on the additional ledger line between the two staves.

one such ledger line falls between the two staves. That pitch is called middle C and is a useful reference point to remember.

Major and Minor Modes

Within the octave, the pattern of pitch distances—*intervals*—between adjacent scale steps is not uniform. The steps between neighboring pitches are of two sizes: large and small. The large and small scale steps are not physically equal in any sense, and they are psychologically equal only in the sense of being steps of a tonal scale. A scale constructed with two sizes of intervals is called *diatonic*. The pattern of large and small intervals in the scale used for the melodies in Figure 1.1 is shown in Figure 1.3. That pattern of intervals defines a scale in what is called the

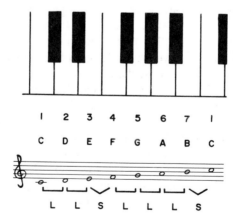

Figure 1.3 Pattern of large and small steps in the C-major diatonic scale, as represented in music notation and on the piano keyboard. The scale notes numbered 1–7 are also called do, re, mi, fa, sol, la, and ti.

major mode. Since the tonic here is C, this scale is called C major; that is its *key*.

Figure 1.3 also shows the pattern of keys on the piano. Notice that the large intervals between scale pitches contain a black key between the white keys, while the small intervals contain no intervening pitch. Since 1600, a common system for making sense of the pattern of large and small steps in the diatonic scale takes all small intervals between adjacent keys, black and white, as equal along the whole keyboard and all large steps as equal to two small steps. This system is called *equal temperament*. (Actually the small steps are physically equal steps along a logarithmic frequency scale, as explained in Chapter 2.) Thus, the octave of eight diatonic steps contains 12 small intervals. The succession of the 12 small steps is called the *chromatic* scale. The large steps are commonly called *whole* steps, and the small steps are called *half* steps or *semitones*. The intermediate pitches in the large intervals are designated by a sharp (♯), denoting a half step higher than the notated pitch––the adjacent white note—or by a flat (♭), denoting a half step lower.

If we used the same pattern of large and small intervals but took A as the tonic, we would have the other mode commonly used in European melodies, the *minor mode*. Figure 1.4 shows that interval pattern along with two melodies in the key of A minor: "God Rest Ye Merry, Gentlemen" and "Greensleeves" (called "What Child Is This?" at Christmas). (Notice the altered pitches in "Greensleeves," preceded by ♯.)

Transposition

The greatest advantage of the equal-temperament system of 12 equal half steps underlying all the intervals is that a melody can be shifted along the chromatic scale—transposed—without distortion. (One reason to do that is that a melody might make excessive demands on the average singer's range of comfortable pitches; for example, "The Star-Spangled Banner" goes too high for most people when sung in the key of C major.) Transposition is accomplished by shifting the tonic to the desired pitch and then generating the scale pattern of whole and half intervals around that tonic. Figure 1.5 illustrates the shifting of the major-scale interval pattern from Figure 1.3 to a variety of different pitches. The C-major scale from Figure 1.3 appears at the top. In the first new case shown, the scale beings on G. The pattern goes up by one whole step to A, by another large step to B, then by a half step to C. (We know from Figure 1.3 that the half step between B and C is built into the system.) From C to D is a whole step, and so is the step from D to E. But now we run into a problem. Figure 1.3 indicates that from E to F is a half step, but the scale pattern

Figure 1.4 (A) "God Rest Ye, Merry Gentlemen," and (B) "Greensleeves," with the minor diatonic scale.

demands a whole step. Therefore, we raise the F to F♯ using the neighboring black note. E to F♯ is two half steps, or one whole step, as the scale pattern requires. Nicely enough, from F♯ to G is a half step and fits the pattern. Shifting the tonic from C to G requires the alteration of one pitch in the scale by one semitone, namely, from F to F♯. (Thus, musicians say, "The key of G has one sharp in it.")

The next line in Figure 1.5 applies the same principles to the generation of a scale beinning on D. Notice that now two sharps are required: F♯ and C♯. The fourth line starts on A, and three sharps are required: F♯, C♯, and G♯. The important thing to remember when working out where the pitches should be altered is that the intervals in the unaltered (C major)

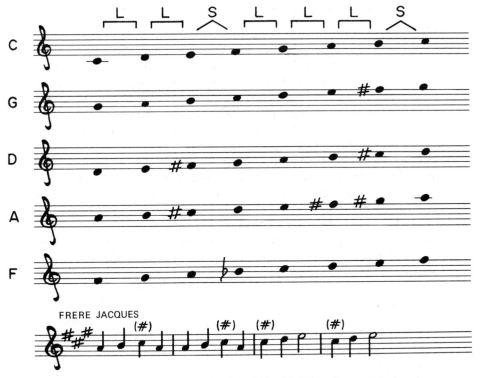

Figure 1.5 Major scales in C, G, D, A, and F, with "Frère Jacques" in A major.

pattern are all whole steps except for those between E and F, and B and C. The bottom line of Figure 1.5 illustrates the application of transposition to the melody "Frère Jacques" to the key of A major. For convenience the three sharps are placed on the staff at the start of the line, where they are called the key signature. They apply to all F's, C's, and G's in the line, unless canceled by a *natural sign* (♮).

The fifth line of Figure 1.5 applies transposition of the major scale pattern to a key requiring a flat (♭) instead of sharps. When starting on F, B must be altered to B♭ to create a half step between the third and fourth degrees of the scale and a whole step between the fourth and fifth degrees. This pattern could be continued by starting on B♭, where E must be flatted to produce the same result. The key of B♭ has two flats in it: B♭ and E♭. In this way, one could generate major scales starting on each of the 12 different pitches in the chromatic scale, using up to six flats or sharps in the different patterns.

Dynamic Tendencies and Stability

The seven pitches in the scale differ in stability. The more stable pitches can function best as ends of phrases and melodies. Less stable pitches seem to "pull" in the direction of more stable ones. The ends of the first two phrases in "My Country, 'Tis of Thee" are relatively unstable, and we can tell that the melody needs to continue. The end of the third phrase is more stable and provides a point of relative relaxation within the melody. The tonic is the most stable pitch, followed by the third and fifth degrees of the scale (C, E, and G in C major). Scale degrees 7, 2, 4, and 6 (B, D, F, A) are less stable, and tend to pull toward the neighboring stable ones (their dynamic tendencies). A cadence involves the resolution of a succession of dynamic tendencies ending on a stable pitch, usually the tonic.

In any key, there are seven pitches used in the tonal scale, leaving five unused "foreign" notes out of the 12 pitches available. Those foreign notes are the least stable of all the pitches in the context of the key. In C major and A minor, they always appear as added sharps or flats. Sometimes, as in "Greensleeves" (Figure 1.4), they simply function as *passing tones* in phrases that stay within the same key as the overall melody. A more elaborate use is to take advantage of their instability within the original key to lead the melody into another key; for example, the pitch F♯ could be used to lead from C major into G major. Such a change of key is called *modulation*.

Harmony

Chord refers to the simultaneous sounding of different pitches. A unique trait of European music since 1600 is the development of a system of chord relationships based on the relative stability of their component tones. The common chords in the key of C major are shown in Figure 1.6. The most stable chord is the triad consisting of the first, third, and fifth degrees of the scale (C–E–G in C major), called the tonic triad since it is built by two successive skips up from the tonic (1–3–5) and symbolized with the Roman numeral I. The least stable chord (symbolized VII$_7$) consists of all the other notes (7–2–4–6, or B–D–F–A in C major) and is best thought of as built by three successive skips up from the seventh degree, the least stable pitch in the scale.

Next in stability to the tonic triad are triads built from skips on the fifth and fourth degrees of the scale, called *dominant* (5–7–2, or G–B–D; symbolized V) and *subdominant* (4–6–1, or F–A–C; symbolized IV).

Note that among them, the tonic, dominant, and subdominant triads contain all the degrees of the scale. That means that any melody using the pitches of the scale can be harmonized using just those chords. *Harmonizing* a melody means selecting chords that go well with the melody notes— usually chords that contain the melody notes, especially if a melody note falls on a rhythmic accent. These three triads—tonic, dominant, and subdominant—are all called *major* triads in that the lower skip in their construction contains four half steps, and the upper skip, three half steps (these skips correspond to the first two skips in the major scale).

The three most stable triads are shadowed by three less stable triads, each positioned a scale skip below, that share two pitches with them and that can be used as substitutes for them to produce varied harmonic patterns. To the tonic 1–3–5 there corresponds 6–1–3 (VI). To the dominant 5–7–2 there corresponds 3–5–7 (III). To the subdominant 4–6–1 there corresponds 2–4–6 (II). These three triads are called *minor* and, in fact, constitute the three principal triads of the minor mode (based as it is on the sixth degree of the major scale). *Minor* here means that the lower skip is small—three small steps—and the upper is larger—four small steps.

The three major triads and three minor triads account for six of the possible triads built on scale degrees. The seventh triad is the one built on the seventh degree of the scale: 7–2–4 (VII). From what we said above, this is the least stable, consisting as it does of three unstable pitches. It consists of two small skips, each three semitones in extent and so is called *diminished* (in contrast to major or minor). Notice that it shares two pitches with the dominant triad. The dominant triad often precedes the tonic triad in cadences. The effect of motion from instability to stability is often heightened by combining the dominant and seventh-degree triads in a single chord: 5–7–2–4—the *dominant seventh* chord (V_7). It is called a seventh chord because 4 is the seventh scale degree above 5 if you start counting on 5: 5, 6, 7, 1, 2, 3, 4. The subscript 7 on the chord label indicates a seventh chord.

Note that the chords are labeled with Roman numerals referring to the scale degree on which they are based. The scale degree on which triad is based is called the *root*. Chords may be arranged with their pitches distributed in any order throughout the pitch range—the root need not be the lowest pitch. Such rearrangements, called *inversions*, affect the chord's function to some extent and definitely affect the way it sounds. For example, a less stable variant of the tonic (I) triad that is often used in the intermediate stages of a cadence pattern has the fifth degree of the scale on the bottom.

Dissonance

Notice that the dominant seventh chord contains two adjacent scale notes, 4 and 5 (F and G in C major—they are considered functionally adjacent even if they fall in different octaves). Those adjacent notes, only a step apart, are called *dissonances*. They represent maximally unstable points in the chord sequence and in the classical style, must be *prepared* and *resolved*. Rosen puts the rules for preparation and resolution of dissonances very well:

> The countermelody [a harmonizing part] must not often leap into a dissonance and never out of it, but the dissonance must be approached and, above all, resolved in stepwise motion directly and simply to the nearest consonance—this last is a rule for making dissonant movement graceful and beautiful, and is central to all tonal music. (Rosen, 1984, p. 42)

More elaborate dissonances can arise from the use of pitches foreign to the scale. Consider the chord B–D–F–A^b, shown at the end of the top line and the start of the bottom line in Figure 1.6. The A^b is equivalent in pitch to a G . Those four notes are all separated by small skips of three half steps each. Taking into account the fact that the very same pitches can have either "flat" names or "sharp" names, this chord consists of highly unstable pitches in four different major keys: C (in which it is B–D–F–A^b), E^b (D–F–A^b–C^b=B), G^b (F–A^b–C^b–E^{bb}=D), and A (G$^\sharp$

Figure 1.6 (A) Chords based on the scale degrees of C major, and (B) diminished-seventh chords in 12 keys.

=A♭–B–D–F). It is called a *diminished seventh* chord and is obviously highly ambiguous. (The small circle next to the subscript 7 indicates diminished.) It could lead into any of the four keys mentioned. As the bottom line of Figure 1.6 shows, there are just three possible diminished seventh chords using the 12 pitches of the chromatic scale, each leading to 4 of the 12 possible keys.

As noted above, foreign pitches can be used to modulate to other keys. The instability introduced by a foreign tone can be resolved by modulation to a key in which that tone is no longer foreign. As you might have supposed, modulation between keys is simplest when the two keys share most of their pitches. When only one pitch must be altered in order to modulate, the two keys are as close as possible. For example, to move from C major to G major requires only the change of F to F♯. The modulation can be accomplished smoothly if the F♯ can be introduced into the key of C in an unobtrusive way and then resolved to the G in the new key. Similarly, the move from C major to F major requires only the change of B to B♭. From F to G requires two changes: B♭ to B and F to F♯. Keys in the pairs C–G and F–C are very closely related, sharing six out of the seven pitches in the scale. Keys in the pair F–G are less closely related, sharing only five of their seven pitches.

The Circle of Fifths

In fact, all 12 possible major keys can be arranged according to this relationship of key distance, with adjacent keys sharing all but one pitch, keys two steps apart sharing all but two pitches, and so on. Such a spatial representation of key relationships is shown in the circle of fifths (Figure 1.7). Comparison with Figure 1.5 shows that as we add sharps to the key

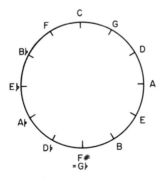

Figure 1.7 The circle of fifths. G♭ is the enharmonic equivalent of F♯; that is, they refer to the same note on the piano.

signature, we move clockwise around the circle: C, G, D, A, E, B, F♯.
Adding flats (or subtracting sharps) leads us counterclockwise: C, F, B♭,
E♭, A♭, D♭, G♭. This process results in a circle because in the equal-
tempered system, G♭ is the same pitch as F♯. This diagram is called the
circle of fifths because adjacent tonics are five diatonic scale steps apart if
you count beginning with the first step: C, D, E, F, G (that is, using the
same counting method as with the seventh chords, described above).

Distance around the circle of fifths represents distance between keys in
terms of shared pitches. Keys directly across the circle from each other
are maximally distant—C and G♭, G and D♭, and so on. (Note that it is
also true that the interval between the tonics of such distant keys is the
maximally unstable interval of 6 semitones formed by the two 3-semitone
skips that occur in the unstable VII triad.) In constructing chord progres-
sions involving changes of key, composers often move around the circle
of fifths one notch at a time and rarely jump across it. An abrupt shift to a
distant key can be startling, and the clumsy remote key shift is a stock
joke in the parodies of Hoffnung Festival and P. D. Q. Bach.

Example from J. S. Bach

At this point the reader may wish to proceed to Chapter 2, since we
have now presented enough background material for the purposes of this
book. In case the reader wishes still more details of music theory, we here
present a brief analysis of a piece of music. The reader may prefer to
return to this analsis later, after becoming more comfortable with the
basic concepts employed. The principles of chord structure and harmonic
progression we have been discussing are well illustrated in the first Prelude from Bach's *Well-Tempered Clavier,* a set of pieces in all 24 major
and minor keys, demonstrating the viability of the even-tempered tuning
system using twelve half steps to the octave. The beginning of Bach's
score is shown in Figure 1.8 with a schematic indication of the harmonies
for the whole piece. The scale degrees on which the chords are based are
1a   indicated under the music. The piece can be heard in Example 1a (a
complete list of recorded examples can be found on p. xvii). The entire
piece consists of chords broken up into arpeggio (harp-like) patterns. It
begins with the tonic triad in C major. In the second measure it moves to
II_7, here serving as a substitute for the subdominant (IV). Next it goes to
the dominant seventh (V_7) and then back to the tonic in the fourth measure. That standard progression, tonic–subdominant–dominant–tonic (I–
IV–V–I), serves to establish the key very firmly. Notice that all the
pitches of the C major scale have appeared somewhere in the progression.
In the fifth measure, the harmony wanders further, to the VI triad. Then,
instead of continuing to a chord in C major, it moves to the dominant

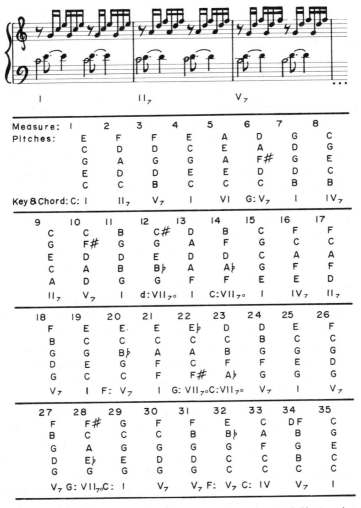

I   II$_7$ V$_7$

Measure:	1	2	3	4	5	6	7	8
Pitches:	E	F	F	E	A	D	G	C
	C	D	D	C	E	A	D	G
	G	A	G	G	A	F#	G	E
	E	D	D	E	E	D	D	C
	C	C	B	C	C	B	B	B
Key & Chord:	C: I	II$_7$	V$_7$	I	VI	G: V$_7$	I	IV$_7$

9	10	11	12	13	14	15	16	17
C	C	B	C#	D	B	C	F	F
G	F#	G	G	A	F	G	C	C
E	D	D	E	D	D	C	A	A
C	A	B	Bb	A	Ab	G	F	F
A	D	G	G	F	F	E	E	D
II$_7$	V$_7$	I	d:VII$_7^\circ$	I	C:VII$_7^\circ$	I	IV$_7$	II$_7$

18	19	20	21	22	23	24	25	26
F	E	E.	E	Eb	D	D	E	F
B	C	C	C	C	C	B	C	C
G	G	Bb	A	A	B	G	G	G
D	E	G	F	C	F	F	E	D
G	C	C	F	F#	Ab	G	G	G
V$_7$	I	F: V$_7$	I	G: VII$_7^\circ$	C:VII$_7^\circ$	V$_7$	I	V$_7$

27	28	29	30	31	32	33	34	35
F	F#	G	F	F	E	C	DF	C
B	C	C	C	B	Bb	A	B	G
G	A	G	G	G	G	F	G	E
D	Eb	E	D	D	C	C	B	C
G	G	G	G	G	C	C	C	C
V$_7$	G: VII$_7^\circ$	C: I	V$_7$	V$_7$	F: V$_7$	C: IV	V$_7$	I

Figure 1.8 Prelude in C Major from J. S. Bach's *Well-Tempered Clavier*, showing the first three measures of Bach's score with a schematic plan of the harmonies for the whole piece. Each measure contains two iterations of the arpeggio pattern on the same chord.

seventh in G major. Notice that the dissonant note, C, is prepared by being present in the preceding chord. The F# signals the shift to the key of G, and we arrive at the tonic triad in G in measure 7. The next several measures go through a variant of the I–IV–V–I pattern in G, using seventh chords and using both IV and II in the subdominant role.

Next, Bach quickly moves back to C major, using the ambiguous diminished-seventh chords discussed above. C#–E–G–Bb in measure 12 functions as the VII$_{7°}$ in D minor (and the D-minor triad serves as a subdominant substitute in C). And B–D–F–A$^\flat$ is the VII$_{7°}$ in C (a dominant substitute). Measure 15 starts another I–IV–V–I sequence in C major. Then, at measure 20, the tonic chord in C becomes the dominant-seventh chord in F by the addition of a B$^\flat$. This leads to the tonic in F major—the subdominant of C major. The next chord is an ambiguous diminished seventh that can be interpreted as leading to G, the dominant of C. But then there is a complicated collection of pitches, perhaps best interpreted as the VII of C, used as a dominant substitute: B–D–F–A$^\flat$, with the dissonant C as a passing tone. That leads to a clarifying dominant seventh in C and finally to the tonic of C in measure 25. (Notice that the overall pattern of modulations in measures 19–25 follows the cadential pattern I–IV–V–I.)

But the tonic in measure 25 is in an unstable inversion: The pitches are arranged with the root not on the bottom. This propels us on into a dominant seventh in which the C has been held over from the preceding chord—a dissonant *suspension*. The C moves to B in the next measure, resolving the dissonance and leaving a plain dominant seventh. Next, there is a diminished seventh in G, with the dissonant low G held over (a *pedal point*). Then there is a return to the C-major tonic in unstable distribution and a repetition of the progression of measures 25–27. But when the tonic arrives in measure 32, it is unsatisfying as an end because of the dissonant B$^\flat$. It is really functioning as the dominant in F major, and leads to the F triad, the subdominant of C. The piece ends with the standard cadence IV–V–I.

All of this illustrates the range of harmonic possibilities that can be explored even within the confines of a brief piece using stylized rhythmic and melodic patterns. Notice that Bach never moves far around the circle of fifths from the key of C major. Also notice that passages of wandering away from the original key are interspersed with variants of the prototypical cadence IV–V–I, reestablishing the main key. This also illustrates the type of musical structure that is implicitly comprehended by the brain when we listen to music. The average listener cannot explicitly verbalize the harmonic relationships just described but is nevertheless quite aware when the harmonies arrive at stable points of rest and when they need further resolution. It is this type of implicit knowledge that we wish to understand and explain.

2

The Perception of Sound

Music alone finds an infinitely rich but totally shapeless plastic material in the tones of the human voice and artificial musical instruments, which must be shaped on purely artistic principles, unfettered by any reference to utility as in architecture, or . . . to the existing symbolic meaning of sounds as in poetry.

(Helmholtz, 1877/1954, p. 250)

BACKGROUND

Helmholtz implies that the principle constraints on the form music takes are psychological. The music of each of the cultures of the world is put together in a different way from the music of the others. Cultural rules determine the selection of instruments, characteristic shapes of melodies, complexity of rhythms, and so on. But underneath all their differences, these structures combine sounds that are similar in some fundamental respects. Certain kinds of sound are used almost universally in the music of the world—the sounds of the human voice, of flutes, of strings that are plucked or bowed, of drums. Further, nearly all cultures split up the pitch continuum into discrete pitch levels arranged in regular patterns that cycle at octave intervals, namely, scales.

The main psychological dimensions along which sounds differ are pitch, loudness, duration, and timbre. The most fundamental problems in the study of the perception of music are concerned with how these basic psychological dimensions are related to the physical sound waves produced by musical instruments and the voice. The first three of these psychological dimensions function more or less independently of one an-

19

other and are relatively unambiguous in their relationships to physical variables. Pitch is usually related directly to frequency of sound vibration, loudness to intensity of sound, and duration to the time through which a sound is heard. Timbre, or tone color, which is more complicated in its relationships to physical variables, is complexly related to the other psychological dimensions.

SOUND WAVES

Since pitch corresponds in general to frequency, we need to introduce some ways of talking about the frequency of sound waves. Sound waves consist of vibrations, which exert variations of pressure on the ear. These variations of pressure cause the eardrum to vibrate in and out, and that vibration is transmitted to the inner ear where sense receptors can encode it in neural form and send its message to the brain. The simplest kind of sound waves have all their energy concentrated at just one frequency and are called simple harmonic vibrations, pure tones, or sine waves. Such sinusoidal vibrations are produced by very simple physical systems such as the one shown in Figure 2.1. If you push down on the mass and then suddenly let go, the mass will bobble up and down for a while. The up and down motion of the mass over time describes a sine wave. If a strip of paper were to move by the mass while it was vibrating and a pencil attached to the mass were set to write on the paper, a sine wave such as that in Figure 2.2 would be drawn.

The vibration in Figure 2.2 can be described completely by two numbers giving amplitude and frequency (setting aside the wave's starting point for the moment). Amplitude is the maximum displacement up or down of the mass from its resting position; with sound, it is the maximum pressure change produced in the surrounding air. Frequency is the number of vibrations per second. Frequency is usually given to Hertz, abbreviated Hz, which means cycles per second (named in honor of the physicist Heinrich Hertz). The frequency (in Hz) is the reciprocal of the period, the time taken by one cycle (in sec). If each cycle of a sine wave takes $\frac{1}{100}$

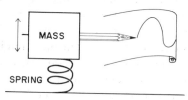

Figure 2.1 Mass–spring vibrating system generating a sine wave.

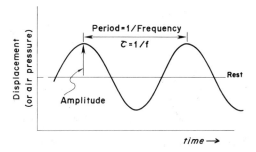

Figure 2.2 A sine wave.

sec—that is, if the time from peak to peak is 0.01 sec—then the frequency
of the wave is 100 Hz. The period is usually symbolized by the Greek
letter tau (τ).

If the mass is rather small and the spring rather tight, the vibrations
transmitted to the air by the mass can be in the frequency range of 20–
20,000 Hz (20 kHz), which is roughly the range picked up by the human
auditory system. In that case you would hear a sound like that of a tuning
fork. (The sound you would actually hear would not be that of a pure sine
wave, since with a mechanism like that of Figure 2.1, there would undoubtedly be noise arising from sources other than the top surface of the
mass—the coils of the spring, for example.) A pure sine wave sounds like
a whistle. The sound of a flute is as close to it as any musical instrument.
Recorded Example 2a presents some electronically produced sine waves.
The first has a frequency of 262 Hz, which gives it the pitch of middle C on   **2a**
the piano. Changing the physical parameters amplitude (A) and frequency
(F) of the sine wave results in changing its perceptual properties. Increasing the aplitude makes it sound louder. The second tone of Example 2a
has the same frequency as the first but has a greater amplitude. Notice
that the pitch remains unchanged by this moderate change of amplitude.
Changing the frequency results in changes in pitch. The third tone of
Example 2a starts with a frequency of 262 Hz and then gradually changes
in frequency until it reaches 524 Hz, having vibrations twice as rapid as
when it started. The pitch is heard as rising through this change of frequency—a glissando—and the ending pitch is that of C one octave higher
than middle C. Doubling the frequency of a sine wave typically results in
the perception of a pitch change of about one octave. Figure 2.3 displays
graphically the tones of Example 2a.

The vibration of the mass–spring system shown in Figure 2.1 would
eventually die out because friction in the spring would lead to dissipation
of energy in the form of heat and noise. However, if we assume that the

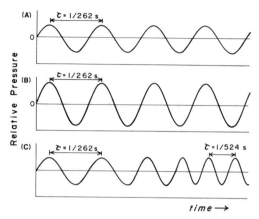

Figure 2.3 Sine waves varying in amplitude and frequency: (A) sine wave of 262 Hz; (B) more intense sine wave of 262 Hz; (C) glissando of sine wave from 262 Hz to 524 Hz, foreshortened in time from recorded Example 2a.

vibration continues indefinitely in time, a very convenient way of representing the wave in Figure 2.2 is available to us. This assumption is often a very practical one to make if the time over which a sound continues unchanged, repeating the same cycle, is long relative to its period (τ). Since the sine wave of Figure 2.2 can be described completely by its amplitude and frequency, we can represent it simply by plotting A and F on a graph. This is done in Figure 2.4. It is no longer necessary to include time as a dimension in Figure 2.4 since we have assumed that the situation in Figure 2.2 will remain the same indefinitely. The height of the line in Figure 2.4 represents the amplitude of the sine wave, and the position of the line on the horizontal axis represents its frequency. Note that the sine wave represented in Figures 2.2 and 2.4 has all its energy concentrated at

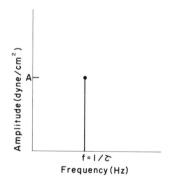

Figure 2.4 Fourier spectrum of a sine wave.

just one frequency. Graphic representations of sound waves usually deal with air pressure and its amplitude (in dyne/cm², for example) rather than displacement, and that is how the ordinate of Figure 2.4 is expressed. Amplitude is a measure of sound intensity. Later we introduce another measure of sound intensity, decibels, as being more convenient for certain purposes. The decibel is a logarithmic transform of amplitude.

The process of translating between pressure versus time graphs like Figure 2.2 and amplitude versus frequency graphs like Figure 2.4 is called Fourier analysis, after the mathematician who developed it during the first part of the nineteenth century. Fourier analysis is especially useful in translating very complex periodic pressure–time waveforms into amplitude–frequency Fourier transforms, which are easier to comprehend at a glance. For example, in discussing the waveforms produced by different musical instruments we will usually deal with graphs of their Fourier spectra, since similarities and differences among their sounds are much easier to discern that way.

Figure 2.5 shows the Fourier spectra of the waveforms in Figure 2.3. Notice the regular way in which changes in amplitude and frequency are represented. Notice also that in Figure 2.3C, when the frequency changes, there is a spread of energy represented as a smear in Figure 2.5C. Only when the sound remains at a steady amplitude and frequency does the Fourier spectrum show a single line, as at the start of the glissando.

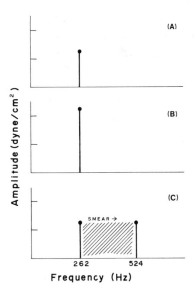

Figure 2.5 Fourier spectra of the waveforms in Fig. 2.3.

Complex Waves

In actual music, we never hear single sine waves in isolation. The nearest thing to a sine wave in music is produced by a flute, but you can see from the Fourier spectrum of a flute tone shown in Figure 2.6 that even the sound of a flute consists of more than one sine wave. In fact, it consists of a whole series of sine waves. The lowest component (in this example, 524 Hz) is called the fundamental frequency. The pitch of such a complex tone generally corresponds to the frequency of the fundamental, and it is this fundamental that is represented in musical notation. The other component sine waves (called harmonics) have frequencies that are two, three, four, five, and so on times the frequency of the fundamental. (Harmonics are also called overtones or partials.) The pattern as a whole is called a harmonic complex tone. The sustained tones of most musical instruments, including the human voice, consist of harmonic complexes in which the upper sine-wave components are integer multiples of some fundamental frequency. The whole complex tone blends together perceptually into one sound—the listener is not usually directly aware of the separate harmonics. The listener can sometimes distinguish the first few harmonics from each other by listening attentively. As Helmholtz (1877/1954) points out, playing a tone beforehand having a fundamental frequency (pitch) the same as that of the harmonic to be distinguished helps one focus attention on it. In this way, Helmholtz himself was able to hear out as many as 17 harmonics.

Sounds produced by acoustic musical instruments such as the flute come with their sine-wave components already blended into a complex wave. We would need electronic equipment to analyze the complex as in Figure 2.6. But if we were producing such a tone with a digital computer, one way to do it would be to start with the separate components and add them together to get the waveform of the complex. By way of example, let **2b** us take the simpler case of a two-component complex as in Example 2b.

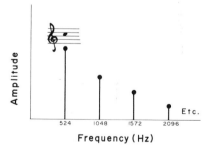

Figure 2.6 Fourier spectrum of a flute tone at C above middle C.

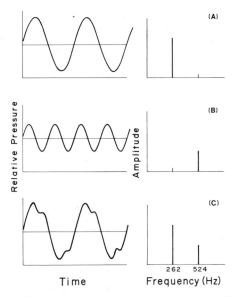

Figure 2.7 Waveform (left) and spectra (right) of two sine waves (A and B), combining into a complex wave (C).

The first sound in Example 2b is composed of a sine wave at 262 Hz and another sine wave at half the amplitude of the first but vibrating twice as rapidly (524 Hz). These two components can be heard separately as the second and third tones of Example 2b and are shown graphically in Figure 2.7A and B. Their combination is shown in Figure 2.7C. The waveform in Figure 2.7C is constructed by adding together the ordinates of the waveforms of Figures 2.7A and B at each point in time. The Fourier spectra of these three sounds are shown to the right of their waveforms in Figure 2.7. Notice that the spectrum of Figure 2.7C contains simply the same components as are shown separately in the first two graphs. The fourth sound in Example 2b starts with the 262 Hz component and then adds the 524 Hz component to it to produce the complex tone. Notice that adding the second component does not change the pitch. When the components are combined, they blend together into one sound, and it is difficult to hear them as separate pitches anymore. This is especially true where there are many components, as with a vowel sound or musical instrument. (Notice also that we are dealing here with the special case in which the component sine waves in Figure 2.7 are sychronized with each other at some point in time; for example, they both cross the zero line (resting pressure) going in the positive direction every one or two cycles and so are said to be *in phase* with each other. The perceived pitch could be different if this phase relationship were allowed to vary over time.)

In order to convince yourself that combining the components of Figure 2.7 yields the appropriate complex waveform, it will be useful to actually carry out the arithmetic involved. To do this easily, let us use a digitized, stair-step version—the way the waveforms would be stored in a digital computer. The computer stores a waveform as a series of numbers representing the waveform ordinates, one number for each point in time. If the points in time are sufficiently close together (say 0.00002 sec) the roughness introduced by the stair steps in the digitized version becomes imperceptible. Figure 2.8 shows digitized versions of the waveforms of Figure 2.7. (In order to simplify the calculations, we have made the time intervals at which ordinates can change rather longer than the computer would.) Every point in Figure 2.8C is the sum of the corresponding points directly above it in Figures 2.8A and B. For example, in the first column on the graph, the ordinate of the first component is 1 and the ordinate of the second component is 1. $1 + 1 = 2$, so the corresponding ordinate of the complex waveform is 2. For the next column, the component ordinates are 3 and 2, respectively, giving a sum of 5 for the complex. You can continue this way across the graphs, adding the ordinates of the components at each point to get the ordinate of the complex tone. As an exercise, you might try adding a third component to Figure 2.8, vibrating three times as fast as the fundamental frequency. Such a component is shown in

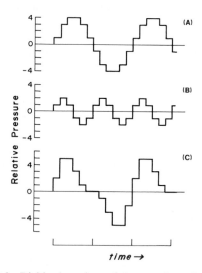

Figure 2.8   Digitized versions of the waveforms in Fig. 2.7.

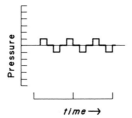

Figure 2.9 Digitized version of a waveform with three times the frequency of Fig. 2.8(a).

Figure 2.9, having three times the frequency and one-third the amplitude of the fundamental in Figure 2.8A. Another exercise you might try is to construct a harmonic complex with a series of components that are all odd-number multiples (3, 5, 7, etc.) of some fundamental frequency and that have proportionally decreasing amplitudes ($\frac{1}{3}$, $\frac{1}{5}$, $\frac{1}{7}$, etc., of the fundamental's amplitude). You will find this last exercise simpler if you avoid digitizing the components at first and just sketch the smooth curves on graph paper. Then add them up at intervals across the paper every $\frac{1}{4}$ inch, for example.

Example 2c is like example 2b only with more harmonic components. **2c** First, you hear a fundamental frequency at 262 Hz. Then we add a second harmonic at 524 Hz, then a third at 786 Hz, a fourth at 1048 Hz, and so on, until eight components are present in the complex wave. The Fourier spectrum of the completed wave is shown in Figure 2.10. Note that the pitch of the complex remains unchanged by the addition of upper harmonics but that the timbre, or tone color, does change. (We discuss timbre in Chapter 3.) In the second part of Example 2c the lower harmonics are removed one by one, beginning with the fundamental. Notice again that timbre is altered while the pitch remains unchanged. In fact, the end of Example 2c has only the three highest harmonics left (Figure 2.11) but still

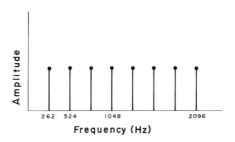

Figure 2.10 Complex tone with eight harmonic components (Example 2c).

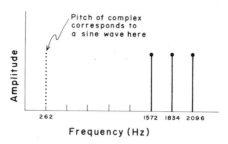

Figure 2.11   The missing fundamental (end of Example 2c).

has the same pitch—that of a sine wave at 262 Hz. This is referred to as the *missing fundamental,* or *residue, phenomenon.* The pitch of a harmonic complex generally corresponds to the pitch of a sine wave equal in frequency to its fundamental, even if the fundamental component itself should be absent from the spectrum. One limitation on this generalization is that in order to be perceived as a pitch, the missing fundamental must fall within a frequency range of about 20–2000 Hz for reasons to be explained shortly. Actually, this phenomenon is quite a common one in our everyday experience, since telephones do not transmit fundamental frequencies of male speakers, and yet that has no effect on the perceived pitches of their voices over the phone.

The missing fundamental has been investigated extensively by Schouten (1938, 1940; Schouten, Ritsma, & Cardozo, 1962) and is important to the theory of pitch perception because some theorists (for example, Helmholtz, 1877/1954; Békésy, 1960) once thought that the pitches we hear all correspond to sine-wave components in the Fourier spectrum. According to these theorists, sine waves of different frequencies produce excitation at different places along the basilar membrane in the inner ear, and the different places of stimulation give rise to different sensations of pitch. This *place* theory of the operation of the inner ear is well established, especially for frequencies greater than 200 Hz. But it is also well established that we can hear pitches where there are no sine-wave components in the spectrum. Therefore, we need other theoretical approaches besides the place theory to explain the origins of pitch sensations.

The principal alternative to a place theory that has been proposed to explain pitch perception is based on the periodicity of the sound wave. The nerves are thought of as simply transmitting the frequency of sound vibration directly to the brain. There is an upper limit to the frequencies that can be transmitted by nerve tracts, owing to the fact that once a neuron fires, it takes some time to recover before it is ready to fire again. Bundles of neurons can act together, taking turns in firing, but as a practical matter, the upper limit for direct neural transmission of auditory frequencies is about 2000 Hz. This leaves us with two mechanisms for the coding of pitch in the nervous system with an overlap in their viable frequency ranges: a place mechanism that operates between 200 and 20,000 Hz and a periodicity mechanism that operates from 20 to 2000 Hz. It is perhaps not surprising that our best performance in discriminating one frequency from another is in the frequency range where the two mechanisms overlap: 200–2000 Hz. Recent evidence forces us to consider theories of pitch perception more complicated than just a combination of place and periodicity mechanisms, though those two mechanisms are fundamental to later theoretical developments. Further exploration of these theories requires a closer look at the structure of the auditory system, which we now take.

THE EAR

Place theories of pitch perception are very attractive because several lines of physiological evidence converge in suggesting that place of stimulation in the inner ear corresponds to perceived pitch for a great variety of stimulus types. Furthermore, if the extraction of separate pitches is not performed by the sorting out of different frequencies to different places along the cochlea, where else in the nervous system could it be so easily performed? Consider how the ear is constructed (Figure 2.12). Sound waves, which are rapid variations in air pressure, push the eardrum in and out. The vibration of the eardrum is transmitted to the inner ear by a series of levers made of bone, the ossicles of the middle ear. The last in the series of ossicles, the stapes (so called because of its shape; Latin *stapes,* "stirrup"), transmits the sound vibration to the oval window of the cochlea, the inner ear. The cochlea is a spiral enclosure filled with lymph and divided lengthwise by the basilar membrane and its attendant structures. It is within the cochlea that sound waves are converted into nerve impulses. Once inside the cochlea, the sound waves travel along the partition that divides it down the middle. Figure 2.12C shows the cochlea "unrolled" for simplicity. The sound waves travel from the oval window down the basilar membrane to the helicotrema, where they are absorbed without bouncing back. As they travel down it, the sound waves make the basilar membrane vibrate. There are sensitive hair cells all along the basilar membrane that are stimulated by this vibration, exciting auditory neurons at the bases of the hair cells. Patterns of hair-cell excitation are thus translated into patterns of neural excitation, which form the basis of our sensation of sound.

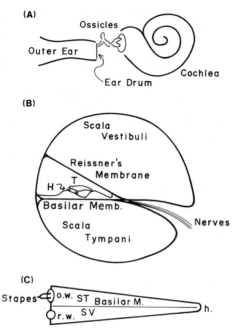

Figure 2.12 The structure of the ear. (A) The outer, middle, and inner ear. (B) Cross-section of the inner ear; T, Tectorial Membrane; H, Hair Cells. (C) The inner ear unrolled; o.w., oval window; r.w., round window; ST, Scala Tympanum; SV, Scala Vestibuli.

Helmholtz (1877/1954) was among the first to emphasize a place mechanism for pitch perception. He supposed that the inner ear performed a continual Fourier analysis on the incoming sound wave, sorting out the separate sine-wave components to different places along the basilar membrane. These sine waves were supposed to stimulate different places on the basilar membrane depending on their frequency. Higher frequency waves excite the region of the basilar membrane nearer the stapes because the membrane is narrower there and naturally vibrates easily at higher frequencies. Lower frequencies excite regions nearer the helicotrema. Helmholtz thought of the basilar membrane as functioning as a series of resonators, each rather precisely tuned to a different frequency. He had noticed that the hair-cell receptors were spread out rather evenly along the length of the membrane and so came to the very plausible (but erroneous) conclusion that each receptor is stimulated by a separate fiber of the membrane and is responsible for signaling the brain upon the occurrence of that fiber's frequency. Helmholtz thought of the membrane as composed of a set of fibers that were to function somewhat like the set of

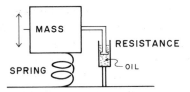

Figure 2.13 A mass–spring vibrating system with damping (resistance).

strings on a piano, the long fibers near the helicotrema resonating to lower notes and the shorter fibers near the stapes resonating to higher notes.

You can demonstrate the phenomenon of resonance in piano strings the next time you are near a piano. Hold down the right-hand pedal tightly with your foot. This lifts the dampers off the strings and leaves them free to vibrate. Then shout very loudly and crisply, "Ha!" You will hear the strings that are tuned to the frequencies of your voice continue ringing after your shout has ended. You can make a different set of strings vibrate by shouting, "Hee!" Notice that the strings continue to ring for several seconds after your shout. They are only slightly damped, and so their vibration dies out very slowly. Unlike piano strings, the structures of the inner ear stop vibrating very soon after a sound stimulus ends, because they are heavily damped. Otherwise, we would have an incessant ringing in our ears from past sounds whose effects in our ear have not yet died away. Vibrations on the basilar membrane are close to what is called being critically damped, which means that hardly any vibration continues after the stimulus ceases. But this damping presents a problem for a place mechanism of pitch perception. To see why, we need to look more closely at the physical nature of damping.

Let us return to the analogy of the mass–spring system of Figure 2.1. In Figure 2.13, this system is reproduced with the addition of a damper—a shock absorber consisting of a piston moving back and forth in oil, which resists its progress. Needless to say, this resistance will cause any vibration of the mass to die out rather quickly, tracing a graph like that of Figure 2.14. The importance for present purposes of adding this damping

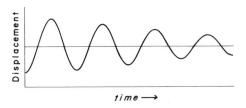

Figure 2.14 A damped sine wave.

is the change it produces in the precision of tuning of the system—in the
range of frequencies at which the system will resonate. An ideal mass–
spring system (Figure 2.1) without damping (friction) will resonate at just
one frequency and no others. Any actual physical system has some friction and resistance and so is somewhat damped. The greater the damping,
the greater the spread of frequencies to which the system will respond,
and the quicker that response will die out once started. This is the reason
for shock absorbers in the automobile. Your car's suspension system is
very similar to the mass–spring-resistance system in Figure 2.13. If there
was no damping—no shock absorbers adding friction—the car would not
bounce unless road vibration happened to stimulate it at just that frequency to which the mass (car) and springs were tuned. If hit by just that
frequency, it would bounce wildly. (In fact, it is by such occasional wild
bouncing that you learn that your shock absorbers are worn out.) The
presence of shock absorbers reduces the car's wild response at any one
frequency at the expense of allowing a little responsiveness spread over a
wide range of frequencies. This is illustrated in Figure 2.15, which shows
the relative response of physical systems with different degrees of damping to stimulation at various frequencies. Note that with no damping, the
system is responsive at just one frequency, and its response at that frequency is quite strong. With greater damping, there is a greater range of
frequencies at which the system will respond, but the response at any one
frequency is subdued.

Now we can see a problem for Helmholtz's theory. If the hypothesized
resonators of the basilar membrane were precisely enough tuned to respond only to very narrow frequency ranges, then they could not be
sufficiently damped to stop vibrating immediately when stimulation
ceased. If the resonators were damped enough to arrest vibration, then
they could not be finely enough tuned. In fact, vibrations along the membrane are heavily damped, and so no part of it acts as a sharply tuned

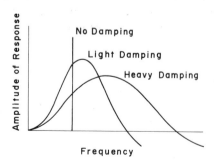

Figure 2.15 Fourier spectra of damped sine waves.

Figure 2.16   Progress of a traveling wave along the basilar membrane. The dotted line that is drawn through the peaks of the wave is called the envelope.

resonator. In the 1920s, Georg von Békésy (1960) made some important observations on the patterns of vibration of the basilar membrane. The membrane does not behave like a series of independent fibers, but is strongly interconnected. As a wave travels along the membrane, it grows in amplitude as it approaches the region of the membrane tuned to its frequency. The maximum response of the membrane occurs at that point, and from there on, the wave diminishes in amplitude until it dies away completely at the helicotrema. Figure 2.16 shows a succession of instants in the progress of a traveling wave on the basilar membrane. A line called the waveform envelope is drawn through the peaks of the traveling wave; this envelope indicates the relative amount of stimulation produced at each point along the membrane. Note that although there is a point of maximum stimulation for a wave of this frequency, such a maximum is rather broadly tuned—many nearby points on the membrane are stimulated almost as much. Figure 2.17 shows traveling-wave envelopes for sine waves of different frequencies. Each wave produces a different point of maximum stimulation, depending on its frequency, with higher frequencies toward the stapes and lower frequencies toward the helicotrema.

From Figure 2.17 it is clear that the inner ear is performing a sort of running Fourier analysis on the incoming waveform, directing stimulation from sine waves of different frequencies to different places along the basilar membrane. Thus, one principal aspect of Helmholtz's place theory of pitch perception is substantiated by more recent work. Receptors at different places are stimulated differently depending on the frequency of the stimulus. But the patterns of stimulation for the different frequencies overlap considerably, and this poses a serious problem. Why do we hear a single, clear pitch when presented with a sine wave, instead of a fuzzy

HIGH   LOW

Figure 2.17   Patterns of stimulation (traveling-wave envelopes) for sine waves of different frequencies on the basilar membrane.

sound image overlapping with the perceptions of other frequencies? Various answers have been proposed. In his later work, Békésy (1967) calls attention to patterns of neural interconnection in the retina of the eye and the touch-reception system of the skin that use lateral inhibition to reduce the fuzziness of percepts, enhancing contrast and reducing overlap of response in adjacent areas. Direct evidence of such neural networks has proved elusive, however. An alternative explanation of perceptual sharpening, based on the mechanical operation of the cochlea, is proposed by Zwislocki (Zwislocki & Kletsky, 1979). Figures 2.16 and 2.17 describe the vertical pattern of basilar membrane motion (that is, motion perpendicular to the membrane surface). Zwislocki points out that the effective stimulus for the hair cells is the "shearing" motion of the tectorial membrane against the tips of the hairs (Figure 2.12). The mechanical description of that shearing motion, taken in conjunction with the fact that the hair cells only respond to bending in one direction (and thus to the approaching but not the departing wave) leads to a much narrower spatial pattern of actual stimulation for a given frequency than was previously supposed. This result makes the place model more viable for pitch coding in the upper frequency ranges.

A remaining problem with the place theory is that it does not work in the lower frequency ranges. Békésy (1960) showed that below about 100 Hz, the basilar membrane vibrates as a whole and separate envelope maxima because different frequencies no longer exist. Below about 200 Hz, what maxima there are overlap too much for the sharpening mechanisms discussed above to sort them out. Therefore, the response of the auditory system to frequencies below about 200 Hz must be based on neural transmission of the periodicity of the incoming stimulus, rather than on mechanical Fourier analysis. As we discuss below, there is good evidence that periodicity mechanisms of pitch perception operate up to frequencies of about 2000 Hz. This leaves us with a picture of overlapping functions of these two mechanisms: a periodicity mechanism from 20 to 2000 Hz and a place mechanism from 200 to 20,000 Hz. Now we are ready to provide an explanation of the phenomenon of the missing fundamental. In order to do that, let us look more closely at the physical stimuli producing the effect.

Beats

One way pitch sensations corresponding to missing fundamentals arise is from physical interactions among the remaining harmonics. In order to see these interactions clearly, let us take the case in which there are just two sine-wave components present in a complex tone. Figure 2.18 shows

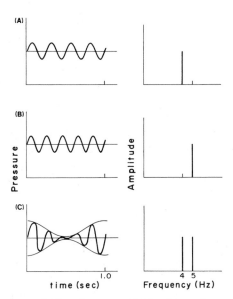

Figure 2.18 Waveforms (left) and spectra (right) of two sine waves individually (A and B) and combined, causing beats (C).

waveforms and spectra of two components separately and then combined. To simplify the calculations, we have made one of the components vibrate four times and the other five times during the 1-sec time period. These two waves are added together just as in Figures 2.7 and 2.8 to obtain the complex waveform. At the start of the time period, the two component waves are crossing zero going in a positive direction—they are in phase. At that point, both have peaks and valleys at roughly the same times and thus reinforce each other. Toward the middle of the time period, the 4 Hz wave has fallen behind the 5 Hz wave, and the two cancel each other out—they are out of phase. At the end of the period, the waves become synchronized again—they are again in phase and reinforce each other. The result of this alternate reinforcement and cancellation is a complex waveform whose amplitude varies over time. This variation is clearly seen in a line drawn through the peaks of the waveform in Figure 2.18C—a waveform envelope fluctuating in time. The rate of fluctuation of this envelope is called the *beat rate* and is equal to the difference between the two component frequencies (1 beat/sec in Figure 2.18). This is because the difference between the two frequencies gives the number of times per second the two waves will come out even with each other and be in phase.

When the beat rate is slow, the beats are heard as variations in the loudness of the sound, corresponding to variations in the amplitude of the complex wave. This effect occurs in the region of beat rates up to about 16 or 20 per second. As beats increase in rate beyond 20 per second, they are too rapid to be heard as separate pulses. In the region of 20 to 50 per second, they contribute to sensations of consonance and dissonance, discussed in Chapter 3. From about 50 to about 2000 per second the beats, if strong enough, are heard as separate pitches. It is these beats that cause the sensation of the missing fundamental. The auditory system responds to the rapid fluctuations of the waveform envelope just as it would to fluctuations in a sine wave of the same frequency. That is, it is the periodicity of the waveform envelope of the complex tone that gives it its pitch. Above about 2000 Hz, the nerves can no longer fire fast enough to follow the periodicity of the stimulus, and so beat rates above that region do not lead to pitch sensations.

2d   Example 2d starts with pure tones at 522 and 526 Hz, beating four times per second. The beats are slow enough that you can count the separate pulses. The pitch of the complex is about the same as that of a sine wave at 524 Hz—C above middle C. After a gap in the sound, the lower component begins to descend slowly. As the difference between the two frequencies becomes greater, the beat rate increases until the separate pulses are no longer distinguishable. At around 40 beats per second, the sound is very rough and dissonant. There is another gap in the sound at this point. By this time, you can hear the pitches of the two pure tones separately. Their frequency separation of 40 Hz/486 Hz = 8% corresponds to a pitch separation of a little more than a musical semitone. As the example continues, the lower tone descends even further in frequency. As it descends, listen for a third pitch rising out of the very low register. This third pitch is a *difference tone,* corresponding to the beat rate. It is coded by the auditory system from the periodicity of the complex waveform envelope and is a special case of the missing fundamental. The lower component in the example stops its descent when it reaches 263 Hz, one octave below the upper component. At this point, the beat rate coincides with the lower frequency, and the pitch of the complex corresponds to that frequency as well. It is as if the two components were the first two harmonics of a harmonic complex tone. Beat rates between adjacent harmonics in a complex tone always have the periodicity of the fundamental.

Beat phenomena have numerous musical applications, of which we discuss three here: difference tones, Balinese vibrato production, and various tuning practices.

Difference Tones.   The lower the pitch, the longer the organ pipe required to produce it. One technique used by organ designers to produce pitches lower than those available from the given lengths of pipe is to produce difference tones. These are typically produced by pipes having a frequency ratio of 2 to 3. This interval is a musical fifth, and so the combination is called a quint. Suppose the designer wants to produce a pitch corresponding to that of a sine wave at 55 Hz (the A below the bass staff) but has only stopped pipes up to 1.5 m long, which produce fundamentals only down to 110 Hz (the A at the bottom of the bass staff). The designer can produce the lower pitch with a combination of a 1.5 m pipe with a fundamental of 110 Hz and a 1.0 m pipe at 165 Hz. The resultant beat rate is 55 per second, and the corresponding periodicity pitch will be perceived, that is, the A an octave below the fundamental of the lowest single pipe. The organ can be constructed so that with the selection of the right stop corresponding pairs of pipes sound in tandem upon the depression of the appropriate key.

Balinese Vibrato Production.   Balinese *gamelan* music has a unique "shimmering" quality achieved by using beats in the range of 7 per second to produce vibrato. A *gamelan* is an orchestra made up largely of percussion instruments, such as gongs and bronze-keyed marimbas. (A marimba is a xylophone with tuned resonator tubes extending down from each tuned key. American marimbas usually have wooden keys.) Example 2e gives you an idea of the sound quality produced by the Balinese *gamelan*. The instruments are tuned in pairs about 7 Hz apart, so that when both instruments in the pair play the same note at the same time, beats are produced at a rate of about 7 per second. Balinese musicians are conscious of this process and have a word for it (*penyorog*). The tuning differences of the pairs are quite precise (Hood, 1966). The vibrato effect of the beats is similar to what is achieved in the West by putting a rotating vane in the resonator pipes of a marimba to make the vibraphone, or "vibes." That the Indonesian process requires two perfectly synchronized performers to produce each note reflects an aspect of the social organization of Indonesian music to which we return in Chapter 9.

2e

Various Tuning Practices.   A third use of beats is in the tuning of instruments. If two musicians play the same note simultaneously and hear beats between the two frequencies, they know that they are not quite in tune—that the frequencies they are playing are slightly different. They adjust their tuning until the beats disappear. Another use of beats in tuning, in which beats are sought rather than avoided, is in establishing an equal-tempered scale on the piano. As we see in Chapter 4, equal-tempered scales result from compromises in the tuning of various notes so that they will be equally suitable in whatever key (tonality) is required. Rather than being tuned so as to coincide in frequency with the harmonics of the other notes, each note is tuned so as to differ from them just a little.

Piano tuners use the beat rates between the harmonics of the note they are adjusting and the harmonics of the other notes in the scale to achieve the correct compromise in tuning.

Periodicity Mechanisms for Pitch

Now we can explain better what is happening in the case of the missing fundamental. In Figure 2.11, even though the fundamental is missing, the remaining components are beating with each other at rates equal to the differences among their frequencies: $2096 - 1834 = 262$ and $1834 - 1572 = 262$. Every pair of adjacent harmonics beats at the fundamental frequency. Provided the components are in phase with each other, those beats will reinforce each other and will appear as the periodicity of the waveform envelope. And it is the periodicity of the waveform envelope that the auditory system codes as pitch. This effect works for any three or more successive harmonics so long as the fundamental is between 20 and 2000 Hz. For fundamentals above about 2000 Hz, the nervous system cannot respond rapidly enough to follow the envelope periodicity, and so for a pitch to be heard in those regions, sound energy in the form of a sine-wave component must be present at the corresponding frequency. A place mechanism mediates pitch perception in those higher frequency regions.

In the case of the missing fundamental, just two adjacent harmonics are often sufficient to give the sensation of pitch. This is most likely where low harmonic numbers are used, as in the case of the organ quints discussed above, which use the second and third harmonics. Whether two or more harmonics are used to produce the pitch of the missing fundamental, the components must be fairly loud to produce the effect. Plomp (1966) measured listeners' thresholds for detection of the missing fundamental and found that for the corresponding pitch to be barely audible, the tones producing the effect have to be around 50 or 60 dB above threshold. (The decibel, dB, measure of intensity is described below.) Musical context helps make the missing fundamental more apparent, however. Houtsma and Goldstein (1972) showed that pairs of components at rather remote harmonic numbers (10 and 11 times the fundamental frequency, for example) can give rise to appropriate pitch sensations when embedded in a minimal musical context, that of two successive pitches forming a recognizable interval. In their experiment, Houtsma and Goldstein asked listeners to recognize the interval, rather than to match the pitches separately. Pitch matching is very difficult when the harmonics producing the missing fundamental are so remote, and interval recognition turns out to be a much easier task. As we show in Chapter 4, people's ability to recognize the musical scale intervals of their culture (as in the NBC television network chime pattern) is remarkably good. Houtsma and Goldstein's experiment takes advantage of that fact. It is also a nice example of the role of context in helping to clarify a difficult or ambiguous perceptual situation. We return to Houtsma and Goldstein's experiment below, as it also raises questions about the adequacy of a simple periodicity model to explain the perception of these pitches.

Amplitude Modulation

One way to produce a complex wave in which the pitch is determined by the periodicity of the waveform is to control that periodicity directly by modulating the amplitude of a pure tone up and down very rapidly. This amplitude modulation, which consists of periodic changes in the amplitude of the sine wave over time, is illustrated in Figure 2.19. There, a carrier frequency, a pure tone at 2000 Hz, has its amplitude varied at a rate of 200 times per second. Notice that for each cycle of the periodic undulation of the waveform envelope, there are 10 cycles of the carrier. In Example 2f, you hear first a 200 Hz tone. Then you hear the 2000-Hz **2f** carrier with the 200-Hz amplitude modulation imposed on it. Last, you

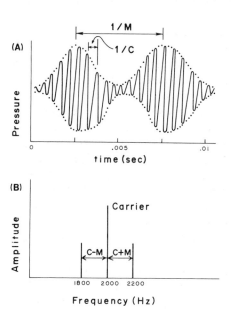

Figure 2.19 Waveform (A) and spectra (B) of a sine-wave carrier of frequency C, amplitude modulated at frequency M.

hear the 2000-Hz tone alone, without modulation. Notice that the pitch of the modulated tone is the same as that of the 200-Hz sine wave: The pitch corresponds to the modulating frequency (M) and not to the frequency of the carrier. As you can see from Figure 2.19, the spectrum of the modulated wave contains no energy at 200 Hz, but only in the region of 2000 Hz, namely, the 2000 Hz carrier (C) plus two sidebands at a separation of 200 Hz from the carrier above and below ($C + M$ and $C - M$). There is a very clear review of the mathematics involved in Stevens and Davis (1938, Appendix 2). In the case illustrated here, C is an integer multiple of M, and so the carrier and sidebands at 1800, 2000, and 2200 Hz constitute three harmonics of a missing fundamental at 200 Hz, the modulating frequency. In cases where C is not an integer multiple of M, the pitch of the complex becomes ambiguous and hard to determine (Ritsma & Engel, 1964). However, when Plomp (1966) brought a pitch shift of the periodicity of upper harmonics into conflict with the pitch shift of an actual fundamental frequency by simultaneously altering them in different directions, the reported direction of pitch shift followed the periodicity of the waveform rather than the fundamental for fundamentals up to about 1400 Hz. In what follows, we concentrate on stimuli in which C is some integer multiple of M, since those stimuli have the clearest pitches and are most useful for demonstrating the importance of the carrier frequency in determining timbre.

In a series of experiments Broadbent and Ladefoged (1957; described very lucidly by Broadbent, 1962) explored the roles of carrier and modulating frequencies in our perception of amplitude-modulated stimuli. They presented vowel-like sounds dichotically, that is, with separate stimuli in the two ears. The vowel-like quality of the stimuli arose from the use of carrier frequencies that were integer multiples of the modulation rates and from modulation rates in the range of the fundamental frequencies of speech (around 200 Hz). In such stimuli, the carrier frequency determines the place of stimulation along the basilar membrane, while the modulation rate determines the periodicity-mediated pitch. When the modulation rate (and; hence, the pitch) was the same in both ears, the dichotic stimuli fused into one perceived vowel sound even if the carrier frequencies were different. When the carrier was the same in both ears but the modulation rates were different, the listener heard separate sounds in the two ears at different pitches. The results showed that (1) the auditory system was fusing sounds from the two ears into one percept on the basis of pitch, (2) that pitch was determined by the periodicity of stimulation and not by place of stimulation, and (3) stimulation of the two ears in analogous places but at different periodicities did not lead to a fused percept. Fusion on the basis of pitch occurred even though the stimuli being fused were coming from opposite spatial directions and had their sound energy (carriers) at different frequencies. This is similar to what happens when several instruments or voices produce the same pitch at the same time—they all blend into one mass of sound in which it is difficult to distinguish the separate voices.

In addition to the blending of dichotic signals on the basis of modulation rate, Broadbent and Ladefoged also confirmed what had been known in a general way since the time of Helmholtz (1877/1954), that frequency of spectral energy in sustained vowel-like tones determines timbre. In their stimuli, the carrier frequency C determined what vowel the stimulus would sound like—*ah, oh, eh,* and so forth. Two tones with the same modulation rate (M) but different carriers would have the same pitch and blend together when presented simultaneously, but when heard separately they would have different timbres; that is, they would resemble different vowels. We return to timbre differences and their physical correlates in Chapter 3. For now, let us summarize the result that for M in the range of about 100–1000 Hz and C in the range of about 1000–5000 Hz, M determines pitch and C determines timbre. These results taken together with the other result just reviewed suggest that for these stimuli, pitch is coded by a periodicity mechanism in the auditory system and timbre by a place mechanism.

Before leaving the comparison of place and periodicity mechanisms in audition, we should note that the theory of pitch perception is still in dispute. For example, Plomp (1976) rejects both place and periodicity mechanisms as viable explanations of all the phenomena. He suggests that some form of complex pattern-recognition model will prove adequate. Such a model would base pitch perception on the analysis of the pattern of stimulation of those harmonics of a complex wave that are spatially separated enough in the cochlea to be distinguishable. One of the reasons for Plomp's rejection of a simple periodicity model is that pitches can be heard even when periodicity has been eliminated. For example, the periodicity of the amplitude-modulated wave in Figure 2.19 arises because the three components are so synchronized as to alternately reinforce and cancel each other—they are in phase. Those phase relationships can be changed so as to eliminate the waxing and waning of the complex wave. If the sidebands are shifted in phase so that their peaks coincide with the instant the carrier is crossing zero going in a positive direction, the periodic undulation of the complex wave will disappear entirely. But Wightman (1973) shows that the pitch corresponding to the separation (M) of carrier and sidebands is not destroyed by that manipulation of phase. Such a pitch must be coming from some mechanism other than place or periodicity mechanisms in their simplest forms.

Just how complex this mechanism must be is suggested by one of the conditions in Houtsma and Goldstein's (1972) experiment described above. In addition to presenting pairs of remote harmonics in the same ear, they presented pairs dichotically; that is, they fed one harmonic to one ear and the other harmonic to the other ear. The surprising result was that listeners were still able to recognize musical intervals corresponding to the missing fundamentals of successive pairs. Therefore, there must be some central mechanism in the auditory system that can take information from the two ears and combine it in determining pitch. It seems reasonable that such a mechanism makes use of the prior pitch processing done by the place and periodicity mechanisms of the peripheral auditory system, but no one yet knows how such a mechanism would work.

At the start of this chapter, we introduced a number of ways of describing sound waves. One of the most important principles of acoustics we used was that simple sine waves can be superimposed on one another to form various kinds of complex waves. We emphasized this principle with examples that you can work out on graph paper. The reason for that emphasis is that it is by no means obvious at first how such superimposition takes place, and it takes working with the idea for awhile until it seems natural. In fact, it took some time in the history of physics before this principle was generally accepted, much less well understood. Feather (1964) provides an entertaining review of the history of acoustics, which notes that even as late as the late 1700s there were competing theories attempting to explain the coexistence of different frequencies of sound in the same room without mutual destruction. Some thought, for example, that sine waves of different frequencies must be transmitted independently by air molecules of different sizes. It was not until the work of Thomas Young (1773–1829) that it began to be generally understood that a complex waveform can be embodied in the motion of a single molecule of air and that that complex motion can be expressed as the addition of simple components, as in Figure 2.7 (see Hunt, 1978). (Students of the history of psychology will notice here that the influence of Young's work on Helmholtz parallels his influence on Helmholtz's theory of color vision.)

LOUDNESS

Just as pitch corresponds in a relatively straightforward way to the frequency of a sine wave, so loudness corresponds to its intensity. In the above discussions we represent intensity in terms of amplitude. At this point, it is useful to introduce another measure of intensity, which is more convenient for both physical and psychological purposes. The measure of intensity we use is the decibel (dB) scale. It is a logarithmic scale of the power in the acoustic waveform. The acoustic power in a sine wave is proportional to the square of its amplitude, and so the decibel scale is expressed terms of the logarithm of the amplitude squared. Logarithms are useful both for the measurement of sound intensity here and for the description of musical scales of pitch in Chapter 4. Therefore, we spend a paragraph developing the concept for the reader who may not have encountered them before.

Logarithms involve a notational convention in arithmetic by which numbers may be represented as exponents of some constant number, called the base. In the following definition of the logarithm, the number b is the logarithm of the number c, using the base a:

$$a^b = c$$

means

$$\log_a c = b.$$

That is, if the bth power of a is c, then b is the logarithm of c using the base a. For the decibel scale, we use the base 10 in the following examples. (In Chapter 4 we use 2 as a base in pitch scales.)

$$10^1 = 10$$
$$10^2 = 100$$
$$10^3 = 1000$$
$$10^4 = 10,000,$$

which are paralleled by the same series expressed logarithmically,

$$\log_{10} 10 = 1$$
$$\log_{10} 100 = 2$$
$$\log_{10} 1000 = 3$$
$$\log_{10} 10,000 = 4.$$

Notice that each time we add 1 to the logarithm, we multiply the number it refers to by 10. A wide range of numbers is collapsed on its upper end by transformation into logarithms. The distance from 1000 to 10,000 is one unit along the scale, just as the distance from 10 to 100 is. Notice also that addition of logarithms corresponds to multiplication of the numbers they represent. For example,

$$\log_{10} 10 + \log_{10} 1000 = \log_{10} 10,000$$

corresponds to

$$10 \times 1000 = 10000.$$

This relies on the logarithmic translation of the rules for operating with exponents, namely if

$$a^b = c \text{ and } a^d = e$$

then

$$a^{(b+d)} = c \times e$$

and

$$\log_a c + \log_a e = \log_a (c \times e).$$

Finally, one consequence of this last rule is that multiplication of logarithms is used to represent powers of numbers, as follows:

$$100^2 = 100 \times 100 = 10,000$$

and

$$\log_{10} 100 + \log_{10} 100 = \log_{10} 10,000$$

and so

$$2 \times \log_{10} 100 = \log_{10} 10,000.$$

Decibels

Now we have all the pieces necessary for the logarithmic conversion of amplitudes into decibels. A decibel is one-tenth of a bel (named after the inventor of the telephone, Alexander Graham Bell). The difference in bels between the power of two sine waves is simply the logarithm of the ratio of the power of one to the power of the other. Since the power is given by squaring the amplitude, intensity (I) can be calculated as follows:

$$I \text{ (in bels)} \times \log_{10} (A_x/A_0)^2.$$

Using the rule developed above that the exponent of a number may be brought outside the logarithm as multiplication, we get

$$I \text{ (in bels)} = 2 \times \log_{10} (A_x/A_0).$$

and since 1 bel = 10 decibels,

$$I \text{ (in decibels)} = 20 \times \log_{10} (A_x/A_0).$$

This is the definition of the decibel scale. The amplitudes may be expressed in any units of pressure such as pounds per square inch—dynes/cm^2 is usual in the metric system. It is customary to express the intensity level of a given sound (with amplitude A_x in the equation) in terms of some very low reference level (A_0 in the equation), for example, 0.0002 dynes/ cm^2. If that reference level is used, the intensity of A_x is called decibels sound pressure level (SPL). Intensity in decibels always represents the *difference* between two sound waves whose amplitudes are entered into the equation. Notice that since $\log_{10} 10 = 1$, a 10 to 1 ratio of amplitudes means a 20 dB difference in intensities and that this is true no matter where along the intensity scale the sounds fall. That is, going from 20 dB SPL to 40 dB SPL entails a tenfold increase in amplitude, as does going from 40 dB SPL to 60 dB SPL. The increase from 20 dB to 60 dB thus involves a hundredfold increase in amplitude.

Under optimal conditions, the human ear is sensitive to intensities ranging from near 0 dB SPL to near 120 dB SPL, encompassing about six 20-dB increments, each consisting of a tenfold increase in amplitude. Thus, the range of amplitudes over which the auditory system must operate is of the order of $10^6/1$ (1,000,000/1). For practical purposes—for example, in recording music—the extremes of this range need not be reproduced. At around 120 dB SPL, sounds begin to become painful. (In fact, too much exposure to excessively intense sounds, as in some rock music, can cause hearing loss; see Rupp, Banachowski, & Kiselewich, 1974.) Normal ambient noises make sounds below about 20 dB SPL difficult to hear. But even the 80 dB range between 20 and 100 dB SPL involves a sizable ratio of amplitudes of $10^4/1$.

Before we proceed, let us reiterate the two main properties of logarithmic scales that are important to remember. First, linear, additive increments along the decibel scale correspond to multiplicative, ratio increments in the amplitudes of the sound waves. Second, since the decibel scale is a scale of amplitude *ratios*, there is no point on it corresponding to zero amplitude. All measurements must be made in terms of some reference amplitude greater than zero. (Remember that zero as the denominator in a ratio is not permissible in arithmetic.)

In addition to the reference level of 0.0002 dyne/cm^2, used for measuring dB SPL, a second reference level is commonly used, namely, the listener's threshold for a pure tone at a particular frequency. (The threshold represents the quietest sound the listener can reliably detect.) Intensity with reference to that threshold is referred to as dB sensation level (SL). Both these reference levels are shown in Figure 2.20. The left-hand ordinate scale is calibrated in amplitudes in dyne/cm^2. The right-hand ordinate is calibrated in corresponding dB SPL. The listener's threshold for pure tones at different frequencies is shown in the lowest curve in the figure. This curve represents the baseline for measuring dB SL—it is by definition the set of points at 0 dB SL. Note that the threshold varies in dB SPL from frequency to frequency—that, in particular, tones in the very

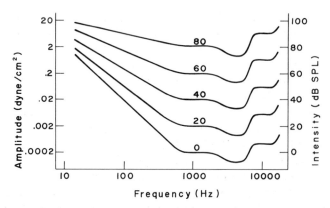

Figure 2.20 The audible frequency spectrum, showing the threshold of hearing and equal-loudness contours at 10-phon intervals for pure-tone stimuli. (After Fletcher & Munson, 1933.)

high and very low registers are much harder to detect than tones in the middle. For example, the listener's threshold for tones at 100 Hz is about 32 dB SPL. A tone 10 db above that threshold—that is, at 10 dB SL—would thus be at 42 dB SPL. The 0-dB SL threshold curve, which is called the listener's audiogram, is one of the measures obtained in a standard hearing test.

The Phon Scale

Now we can turn from physical measures of intensity to psychological measures of loudness. The first loudness scale we look at is based on the decibel scale in a rather direct way. Note that we do not use the decibel scale itself as a loudness scale. It is clear from Figure 2.20 that such an approach would not work, since intensities SPL that are perceptibly loud at 1000 Hz are inaudible at 50 Hz (e.g., a 1000-Hz tone at 40 dB SPL). Sensation level measurements (that is, intensities relative to threshold) are also unsatisfactory measures of loudness because when listeners match the loudness of pure tones at different frequencies, they match tones with different sensation levels (dB SL). A simple solution in constructing a psychophysical scale for loudness is to rely on listeners' judgments of equal loudness for pure tones of different frequency. For this scale, a pure tone of 1000 Hz serves as the (arbitrarily selected) reference tone. The loudness of the 1000-Hz tone in phons (the unit of measurement, pronounced "Fonz") is defined as its sensation level in decibels. Tones at all other frequencies have the same loudness in phons as the 1000 Hz to which they are equally loud. To set up the phon scale, psychol-

ogists had listeners adjust tones at different frequencies to equal the loudness of sample 1000-Hz tones. This procedure generated the set of equal-
loudness contours of Figure 2.20. All the tones across the frequency range
that fall on the same equal-loudness curve were judged to be of the same
loudness, and that loudness in phons is the sensation level (dB SL) of the
1000-Hz tone on the curve. The threshold curve from the audiogram was
taken as zero loudness across all frequencies.

It is clear from Figure 2.20 that loudness in phons does not always
match sensation level. For example, with a 100-Hz tone, a sensation level
of about 6 dB corresponds to a loudness of 10 phons, while at 1000 Hz, a
6-dB SL tone has by definition a loudness of 6 phons. This example
illustrates a general rule apparent in Figure 2.20, namely, that loudness
grows more and more slowly as a function of intensity as frequency
descends below about 500 Hz. This unequal variation of loudness with
intensity at different frequencies is of concern to the audio engineer designing stereo equipment. This variation is especially important since the
low register transmits much of the sound energy produced by the lower
instruments. (500 Hz is in the middle of the treble staff.) Thus, most
stereo systems come equipped with a loudness control, which produces
equalization of loudness across frequencies in the low frequency regions
as the intensity level is adjusted up and down. Consider the case in which
the stereo amplifier is turned up to an intensity level of 80 dB SPL for
tones across the frequency range and the listener hears a good balance
between low and midrange sounds. Then suppose the level is reduced 40
dB SPL across the board. Suddenly, tones in the range below 100 Hz
become all but inaudible, while tones in the 1000-Hz range remain at a
loudness level of 40 phons. What is needed is a level control that reduces
low-frequency intensities more slowly than midrange intensities as it is
turned down, matching the pattern of the equal loudness contours in
Figure 2.20. This is exactly what the loudness setting of a stereo set does.
It is usually added to the operation of the intensity level control by moving the appropriate switch from "normal" to "loudness." Just how much
compensation a loudness function should provide is not entirely clear,
since Green (1976, p. 284) notes that "the behavior of the contour at very
low frequencies, less than 100 Hz, is still a matter of considerable dispute."

While we are on the subject of intensity controls in stereos, we must
mention an anomaly in the history of psychoacoustics that led to the
mildly unfortunate result that many level controls are labeled volume.
Back in the 1930s, some investigators (e.g., Stevens, 1934) thought that in
addition to pitch, loudness, duration, and timbre, it would be useful to
introduce a fifth dimension of sounds, namely, volume. This term seems

to have caught on with manufacturers of radios and hi-fi sets. Though it is true that listeners are able to rate sounds in terms of volume, it is also true (as Ward, 1970, observes) that listeners are able to rate sounds with some moderate consistency on almost any adjective scale one can imagine: *darkness, liquidity,* and even *pear-shapedness.* In order to establish such a psychological dimension as fundamental, we need to show that (1) listeners are able to make precise judgments of the attribute in question, as they can with octave judgments in pitch (see Chapter 4) and with loudness equality, and (2) the attribute is independent of other attributes of sound and hence really needed. Volume fails on both these counts. Judgments are only moderately consistent, and volume judgments can be predicted almost perfectly from the combination of frequency and intensity: Lower and louder tones have greater volume than higher and softer ones; and a low, soft tone might have the same volume as a high, loud one. Therefore, we do not believe that the dimension of volume is necessary for the description of the sensations of tone. Moreover, it is misleading for manufacturers to use the label *volume* for a control that varies only one underlying component of that dimension, namely, intensity. (And with the loudness control switched on, the knob actually *reduces* bass response as volume is increased, contrary to the implication of the label.) We recommend that manufacturers use lables such as intensity or level for the knob that controls intensity level.

The Sone Scale

Now we return to more serious matters. An alternative way to develop a loudness scale is to use the listener's judgments of the relative magnitudes of loudness among sounds at different levels, rather than equal-loudness judgments. This method, developed by Stevens (1936, 1955) and known as *magnitude estimation,* leads to a loudness scale with units called *sones.* As with the phon scale, 1000 Hz is taken as the reference frequency, and a 1000 Hz tone at 40 dB SL is assigned a loudness of 1 sone. Listeners assign numbers to the loudnesses of other sounds in relation to the loudness of the standard, telling how many times louder each new sound is than the standard. If a sample sound is twice as loud as the standard, they assign it a number twice as large. If it seems one-third as loud, they assign it a number one-third as large as the standard. Each listener's ratings of successive presentations of each sample tone are then averaged to give their overall mean rating of that tone, and those ratings are averaged across many listeners to give a generally applicable sone scale for loudness. Figure 2.21 shows such a scale. The advantage of the sone scale is that it is useful in predicting the loudness of various stimuli

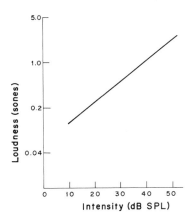

Figure 2.21 Stevens's scale of loudness in sones.

other than pure tones. Loudness in sones is an indicator of how loud a sound is in relation to the standard, regardless of the physical makeup of the sound in question.

There are two more things of which we need to be aware in using these loudness scales—one a caution and the other a theoretical problem. First, the caution. Neither the phon scale nor the sone scale tells us about discrimination. Thus, the fact that equal-loudness contours lie closer together in the lower frequency regions of Figure 2.20 does not mean that discrimination among intensities is better in that region (in fact, it is worse), nor does the steepness of slope of the loudness function in Figure 2.21 tell us anything about discrimination. Second, a theoretical problem remains. The prediction of the loudness of a complex tone from the loudnesses of its sine-wave components has proven especially difficult. An article by Marks (1979) explores the intricacies of predicting the loudness of complex tones quite lucidly, and Green (1976) provides a good outline of rules of thumb currently in use. The problem is complicated by the mutual masking of adjacent components, to which we now turn.

Masking and Loudness

The prediction of the loudness of certain simple kinds of complex tones is reasonably well understood and relies on the fact that when two sine-wave components of the tone are close together, they tend to mask each other out and their combined loudness is diminished. If all the components are of equal intensity and equally spaced in frequency, then the prediction of their loudness is well understood. The overall result is that there is a critical bandwidth of frequencies within which tones will inter-

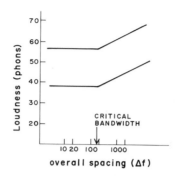

Figure 2.22 The effect of spacing of components of a complex tone on its loudness. (After Zwicker, et al., 1957.)

fere with each other. When pure tones are added to a stimulus within that critical bandwidth (keeping the total energy of the sound constant), they do not add to the loudness of the sound. However, adding tones outside the critical bandwidth increases loudness. Figure 2.22 presents the results of experiment by Zwicker, Flottorp, and Stevens (1957). They presented listeners with complex tones consisting of four components and varied the frequency spacing of the components. When the components were centered around 1000 Hz, they could spread them over a region of about 180 Hz before a noticeable change in loudness would occur. As the tones were spread beyond 180 Hz, the loudness of the complex began to increase. The conclusion they drew from this is that if pure tones are separated enough in frequency, their individual loudnesses will add together in determining the loudness of the combination. However, if the components are close together in frequency, their mutual interference will diminish perceived loudness. The critical bandwidth over which the loudness of complex tones is affected varies with the frequency of the center of the complex, as shown in Figure 2.23. Critical bandwidth is an important determinant of consonance and dissonance, as shown in Chapter 3.

Pitch and Intensity

One question that never fails to interest musicians who begin to explore the psychology of music is whether pitch and intensity interact—whether making a tone louder will change its pitch or whether changing its frequency will change its loudness. If these were true it would be of central importance, since we would then have to specify intensity every time we wanted to predict pitch from frequency. And in musical performance, it would be necessary to specify exact intensity levels if similar pitches were

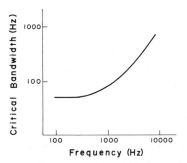

Figure 2.23 Critical bandwidth as a function of center frequency of a complex tone or noise band. (After Zwicker et al., 1957.)

to be produced in successive performances of the same piece—a notoriously difficult procedure in any event, patently impossible in any actual performance setting where different listeners sit in different spatial relationships to the players. Fortunately for simpiflifying the lives of musicians, there is no reason to believe such an effect operates in music. One obvious conclusion from the various studies beginning with that of Mach in the 1860s, reviewed by Ward (1970) and Plomp (1966), is that the phenomenon is elusive, with different listeners experiencing different effects. The closest thing to a generally valid rule is that, for some listeners at very high intensities (of the order of 80 or 90 dB SPL), pitches of pure tones above about 800 Hz are shifted upward and those below 800 Hz downward as intensity increases (Stevens, 1935). The magnitude of the effect can be as great as 0.5 semitone (a quarter step). It is important that these observations were made with monaural (one-ear) presentation of pure tones, a condition that never occurs in music. The effect could conceivably be used in music produced by synthesizer and intended to be listened to via headphones. But even then, the composer would have to realize that different listeners would perceive the effect idiosyncratically. Thinking about the supposed effect in terms of complex tones will lead you to see that it would be unlikely for such a thing to be significant. Each complex tone in music usually has components both above and below 800 Hz, and the effect would be pulling these components in opposite directions. Further, the above discussion of pitch coding in the nervous system concludes that much of our sensation of pitch arises from the periodicity of the complex waveform, and such pitch perception is not affected by changes of intensity. (Intensity does affect place of stimulation, and such an explanation seems viable for the observed changes in the pitch of pure tones; Békésy, 1960.)

Attack Functions and Transients

We have referred to the difficulties of predicting the loudness of complex sound waves from their physical descriptions. Those difficulties are considerable even for steady sounds with an intensity that remains constant over a relatively long period of time. The difficulties are compounded for predicting the loudness of sounds that change rapidly over time—that have transient components. As an example of transients, Figure 2.24 shows onset functions for a violin and a piano playing the same note. As you can see, the two instruments vary radically in their distribution of sound evergy over time. The piano tone starts very strongly and then dies away, while the violin only reaches its stable, steady-state level after 30 or 40 msec. These differences in the pattern of transients produced by various instruments are important cues to timbre, and we return to them in Chapter 3. For now, we wish to note the difficulty of predicting the loudness of such a rapidly varying sound wave from its waveform.

There are two other aspects of attack transients to consider before we leave them. First, as a practical matter, it is very difficult to record abrupt onset transients accurately. Electronic equipment has to be very good to respond to such rapid changes in intensity as shown in the piano onset in Figure 2.24. In the history of sound recording, it is the quality of reproduction of piano sounds that has been the main indicator of technical progress, and that is true because of the difficulty of reproducing strong transients. If you read reviews of new equipment, you will find an indication of how well an amplifier or speaker responds to such transients by looking at its response to square waves—sound waves which, instead of undulating smoothly as sine waves, alternate abruptly between two pressure levels. Abrupt alternations are hard for electronic components to follow without distortion, usually in the form of overshooting or under-

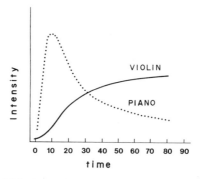

Figure 2.24   Onset functions of violin and piano tones.

shooting the corners. One result involving loudness is that inadequately reproduced piano transients balance differently with more or less accurately reproduced stringed instruments on a recording than if heard live. Hence, the 1930s musician recording chamber music had reason to be dissatisfied not only with the timbre of the recorded sound of the piano, but also with the fact that good balance achieved in performance was systematically misrepresented on the record.

A second complication introduced by transients is that they violate one of the assumptions of the translation of waveforms into spectra via Fourier analysis. The translation illustrated in Figure 2.7 depends on the assumption that the sound wave being analyzed continues in its periodic undulations indefinitely in time. This is not strictly true for any actual sound but is more or less correct for sounds that last a long time relative to the length of their period; for example, a typical vowel sound in speech might last about 150 msec with a period of about 4 msec. When amplitude changes rapidly, tones cannot be analyzed into component frequencies with the same degree of precision. We have already encountered examples of this fuzzing of frequency in tones that die out because of damping (Figures 2.14 and 2.15) and in tones whose amplitude modulates periodically over time (Figure 2.19). Rapid transients, such as those of the piano, create a spread of acoustic energy that is difficult to specify with respect to frequency and difficult to record. In fact, these last two difficulties are just two sides of the same coin: The difficulty of accurately recording the spread of frequencies and the difficulty of recording sudden changes of intensity are the same difficulty viewed from the complementary perspectives of the Fourier spectrum and the waveform.

LOCALIZATION

The trend since the early 1960s in the direction of stereophonic or even quadrophonic home sound systems has made people more aware of localization effects in music than ever before. Since the 1930s, more hours have been spent (at least by nonmusicians) listening to music over the radio or TV or on records than in live concerts. Until the early 1960s, this music was presented monophonically, that is, through one loudspeaker enclosure with all the sounds from the original performance coming from one direction. The illusion of the spaciousness of the original performance hall could be conveyed by reverberation—sounds reflected off distant walls behind the microphone—on the recording. But information as to the actual positions of instruments and voices was largely lost in monophonic presentation. The only cues available to the listener to differentiate the different instruments were their pitches, timbres, and loudnesses (and perhaps the alteration of those cues as with, for example, the offstage trumpet call). With the advent of stereophonic recording, additional cues to localization could be provided.

As you know from listening to complex musical textures with many instruments playing at once, added localization cues make it much easier to focus on the various parts the instruments are playing. This is true whether the complex texture is in classical, rock, or country and western genre. In any of these, a relatively soft solo part by voice, guitar, or violin can be heard much more clearly if we can pinpoint its location in space as well as its pitch and timbre. We can use localization cues to focus our attention on it. This is especially important in the recording of music composed for live presentation from the era before composers had ever imagined stereophonic recording. One critic, reviewing Toscanini's superb monophonic recording of Beethoven's *Missa Solemnis,* observed the recording engineer's creation of an "electronic monster" of a trombone in a passage where it was important that the trombone part be heard distinctly. What the recording engineer did was place a microphone directly in front of the trombonist and mix in a heavy dose of that part into the monophonic recording at the critical moment. Otherwise the part would have been completely masked by the rest of the texture. All the engineer had to work with were loudness cues to help the listener differentiate the part. Had he had localization cues, he could have more nearly approximated Beethoven's intention.

Composers can use spatial arrangements to clarify musical form. An example is the videotaped performance of George Crumb's *Ancient Voices of Children,* presented occasionally on the Public Broadcasting System (available on Nonesuch record 71255). In the third song, "Dance of the Sacred Life-Cycle," each of three sections ends with the phrase, "Let the branches ruffle in the sun / and the fountains leap all around," sung to a characteristic melody and accompanied with a stroke of bells. In the performance, the soprano soloist walks slowly up a long ramp as she sings the verse. As she comes to the end of a section, she stops before one of the sets of bells placed at intervals along the ramp and strikes the bells as she finishes the chorus. Then she walks on, singing the next verse. The dramatic pattern serves to delineate the musical pattern for the audience.

In addition to the subtle effects of localization in clarifying complex musical structures, localization has been used by various cultures to achieve a number of aesthetic ends. One of the main uses is in producing antiphonal patterns. *Antiphony* refers to the practice in which two groups of spatially separated musicians sing or play alternately, for example, the case in which a soloist sings the verse of a song and a choir sings the chorus. Many cultures use this type of song structure, and antiphonal effects were common in medieval European church music. Antiphonal interchanges between celebrant and choir (or celebrant and congregation) still survive in most Christian churches in either sung or spoken form. Some of the most striking uses of antiphonal effects in Western church music were made by Giovanni Gabrieli around 1600. Gabrieli was the resident composer at St. Mark's cathedral in Venice. St. Mark's is cross-shaped and had two organs, one on each side of the church. Gabrieli made use of this design by placing a choir and orchestra with each organ and having them play back and forth antiphonally. He made extensive use of the brass instruments of his time, including the ancestor of the modern trombone. He had no modern trumpet, but rather a cornetto, which had external keys covering holes so that it was somewhat like a soprano saxophone with a cup mouthpiece. In the twentieth century, we are used to this music played on modern instruments with pristine clarity. (e.g., the Columbia album, *The Antiponal Music of Gabrieli,* has the brass sections of three major U.S. orchestras, with a chart indicating which players occupy which stereo locations.) It is interesting to compare such clear performances using instruments of similar timbre with performances closer to those Gabrieli could have produced (e.g., the Vanguard album, *Processional and Ceremonial Music*). In either case, the stunning antiphonal effects that Gabrieli intended remain intact.

In Gabrieli's antiphonal music, consider some of the performance problems that arise because of the spatial separation of the performers. Sound travels at about 345 m/sec. If the two choirs were only 34.5 m apart and Choir 1 played a chord, it would be 0.1 sec before the onset of the sound reached Choir 2. Then if Choir 2 synchronized its attack on the chord with what it heard from Choir 1, Choir 1 would hear Choir 2's attack 0.2 sec after *they* had started playing. Two-tenths of a second is a very long time in terms of people's ability to discriminate time delays—longer than the average speech syllable, for example. Choir 1 would perceive Choir 2 as lagging miserably. The performance solution is to have both choirs start together, led by a conductor in the middle. But then each choir would perceive the other as lagging by 0.1 sec. Each musician would have to resist the impulse to slow down to achieve synchrony with the other group. True synchrony would be perceived only by listeners near the conductor in the middle. The situation is helped by the acoustics of the church. Reverberations off the walls make the onsets of sounds less distinct, blending them into gradual swells without precise beginnings or ends for listeners in all parts of the church.

A second example of antiphony comes from the Mbuti pygmies of the Congo valley (Turnbull, 1961; Turnbull & Chapman, n.d.). Like many African cultures, the Mbuti have antiphonal forms of music, with a chorus of men and a chorus of women singing back and forth to each other. But the most striking use of antiphony is directly involved with the most important Mbuti religious beliefs. The Mbuti live in a very congenial physical enviromment. They are hunter–gatherers, and the forest provides them with what they need. In one of their most important ceremonies, the people of the village, about 20–25 in number, gather to sing antiphonal songs. Two or three young men go out into the forest and get the *molimo*, a long tube designed to be sung into, from its hiding place. The young men run through the forest singing into the *molimo*. The position of the sound is always changing. The song of the *molimo* is continually interspersed with that of the choirs in the village. The sound of the *molimo* never stands still but is always moving and pervades the forest. The antiphonal relationship of the *molimo* and the singing of the village symbolizes the special relationship between the benevolent forest and the people who live there. (Chapter 9 explores this example in more detail.)

Cues to Localization

Stevens and Newman (1936) investigated the cues people use to determine the direction from which sound is coming. Reflections off walls contribute difficult-to-control cues to localization (as in the case of the off-stage trumpet), and so Stevens and Newman carried out their experiment on the top of a building. They did it late at night so as to eliminate traffic noises. They seated their listeners on a sort of barstool situated well above the roof of the building and set up a loudspeaker on an arm pivoted at the base of the barstool so that it could be rotated around the listener. Then they presented pure tones over the loudspeaker and asked the blindfolded listener to point out where the sound was coming from. They found that people could determine the direction of the sounds most precisely in the frequency regions below 1000 Hz and above 3000 Hz. They attributed this result to two factors. In the low frequency region the sound wave reaches the near side of the head perceptibly sooner than it reaches the far side. Sound waves traveling at 345 m/sec take about .44 msec to travel the (roughly) 15 cm from one side of the head to the other, that is, from one ear to the other (0.15 m/(345 m/sec) = 0.00044 sec). For a pure tone in the frequency range up to 1000 Hz, the time delay between the two ears is much smaller than the period of the wave. But as the frequency approaches 2000 Hz, the period approaches 0.5 msec. The first peak of a 2000 Hz wave arrives at the farther ear at about the same time the second peak of the same wave arrives at the nearer ear, causing the auditory system to be confused as to the direction of the sound. Localization based on time delays between ears does not work at all at 2000 Hz and works well only up to about 1000 Hz.

Above 3000 Hz, another effect seems to be operating. Tones below 3000 Hz tend not to be reflected by the head. The size of the thing that reflects a given sound is determined by the wavelength of the sound in the air. If the wavelength is long relative to the size of the object, the sound just flows around the object. Shorter wavelengths are reflected. With sound traveling at 345 m/sec, the wavelength of a 172.5 Hz tone—that is, the distance in the air from one peak of the waveform to the next—is 2 m (Wavelength = Velocity/Frequency). You can see this must be true if you visualize the wave of the sound coming toward you as you stand still. If the waves travel toward you at 345 m/sec, and 172.5 of them are reaching you per second, then they must be 2 m apart. At 690 Hz, the wavelength is 50 cm. At 2300 Hz, the wavelength is 15 cm, the approximate diameter of the head. In the frequency region above 2300 Hz, the greater loudness of the sound on the side from which it comes begins to be an important cue to localization. For lower frequencies, the sounds pass around the head without much interference and are almost as loud on one side as on the other. But above 3000 Hz, the wavelengths are smaller than the diameter of the head, and so the head reflects them quite effectively. The ear farther from the sound source is in a sort of "shadow" and receives less intense stimulation. Thus, above 3000 Hz and below 1000 Hz, localization is better than in the middle of the range, but for different reasons. Below 1000 Hz, localization is based on cues involving time delay between the ears, and above 3000 Hz, it is based on intensity differences.

With the complex sounds of speech and music, the frequencies are usually spread all across the spectrum, and localization judgments are based on both these mechanisms. In recording, however, unless the listener can be assumed to wear headphones, there is no way to control the exact time relationships between sound waves reaching the two ears. With loudspeakers, time delays will change as one moves around the room. And in a large auditorium, sound waves reflected off the walls will confuse the auditory system's analysis of time delays as cues to localization. Therefore, stereo recordings rely almost exclusively on intensity cues for localization. The instruments you hear coming from the right-hand speaker are louder in that speaker than in the left. The balance control on the stereo amplifier simply controls the relative intensity of sound coming from the two speakers. By turning the balance control, you can adjust the apparent direction of the sound source.

When you wear headphones, you cannot turn your head in relation to the direction of the sound. But in a free field, in most everyday listening situations, you can turn your head to orient toward sounds. This is usually functional because it serves to direct your eyes toward the sound and because localization acuity is much better for sounds directly in front or behind than for sounds out to the side. Average localization errors for sounds straight ahead are of the order of 5°, while errors for sounds off to the side are of the order of 10 or 15° (Pollack & Rose, 1967; Stevens & Newman, 1936). One issue that has been investigated is whether localization improves when one can move one's head in relation to the sound source. Pollack and Rose (1967) found that head movement per se did not improve localization. However, if the sound was of great enough duration to allow the listener to turn the head while the sound continued, then localization with free head movements was superior. Localization for sounds directly in front of the listener was about the same whether or not head movements were permitted.

Figure 2.18 shows the combination of two beating tones. When presented simultaneously to the same ear, their successive reinforcement and interference brings about a waxing and waning of the sound. When two beating tones (for example, 500 and 501 Hz) are presented to the two ears dichotically (that is, one tone in each ear), what is heard is one tone whose position is always changing. This is because the phase relationship of the two sound waves is always changing. First, the peaks of one waveform are ahead, and then they fall behind the peaks of the other waveform. You can see this happening in Figure 2.18. The auditory localization system interprets the shift back and forth as a shift in the position of the sound source. The source seems to rotate around the head. If you listen to

2g   Example 2g with headphones you can hear this rotation. In view of the arguments presented above, you would not expect this rotation to be perceived for tones much above 1500 Hz. This expectation was confirmed by Perrott and Nelson (1969). But as Houtsma and Goldstein (1972) showed, dichotic pairs of tones above 1500 Hz with frequency differences of about 200 Hz produce faint sensations of pitch. Perrott and Nelson found that in the 1500-Hz region, dichotic frequency differences of 80 Hz were more noticable than smaller frequency differences. Perhaps similar auditory mechanisms are responsible for binaural beat phenomena and for the puzzling pitch phenomena observed by Houtsma and Goldstein.

One phenomenon that seems to demonstrate the existence of a temporal, periodicity-preserving mechanism linking the two ears is what has been called the masking-level difference (MLD) effect. Suppose a pure tone is fed to the right ear along with a continuous white noise at a level just high enough to mask the tone. The tone is no longer audible. (White noise has a wide range of frequencies randomly present and sounds like the hiss of a radio tuned between stations.) Then suppose the same noise is fed to the left ear. Twice as much noise is being presented as before, but now the tone can again be heard. The same noise in the two ears has waveform peaks at the same times, though (since it is noise) those peaks come at random points in time. The temporal localization mechanism thus localizes the noise in the middle of the sound field. The tone is localized to the right, since that is the only ear in which it occurs, and thus is spatially separated from the noise. As a control condition in the experiment, different random noises are presented to the two ears. Then the release of the pure tone from masking does not occur. That is because the peaks in waveforms of the two noises in the two ears are no longer temporally correlated and so not localized into one apparent source. We use the same mechanism in separating a barely audible single instrument's solo from a noisy background produced by all the other instruments of a large orchestra playing at once.

A related phenomenon, pointed out by Békésy (1967), is that if a continuous noise is directed toward you from a long row of sources, such as the sound of surf along the beach, you will localize the sound as being directly opposite you. This is because the leading peak of each part of the waveform comes to you first from the section of beach nearest you. Your temporal localization mechanism concludes that that is the true direction of the source. Békésy checked this phenomenon in the laboratory by setting up a row of loudspeakers all emitting the same white noise. As the listener walked along the row, he always heard the location of the sound source as directly opposite him: The source seemed to move as he moved.

Another phenomenon that comes under the heading of localization and involves intensity cues could well be called an auditory illusion. Carterette, Friedman, Lindner, and Pierce (1965) investigated the effects of exposing one ear to a very loud sound over a long enough period of time to adapt the response of that ear. Previous investigators had found that after one ear had been adapted to noise for a period of 5 or 10 min, the threshold for sounds in that ear was raised considerably: It took the ear some seconds to recover from adaptation. Carterette et al. decided to use a measure of adaptation that takes advantage of the very precise localization capabilities of humans. After exposure to a loud adapting noise in one ear, they presented listeners with a probe noise in both ears and had the listener adjust the relative intensities of the noises so that the sound image appeared to be centered. Without adaptation, a centered image occurred with equal levels in the two ears. After adaptation, the sound image was localized away from the adapted ear; that is, the probe noise had to be more intense on the adapted side to produce a centered image. After 10 min of an adapting noise at 90 dB SPL, the probe noise had to be 28 dB greater on the adapted side to produce a centered image. But Carterette et al. made a very striking discovery in another condition of their experiment in which they omitted the presentation of the probe noise to the nonadapted ear. Even when no stimulus was presented on the opposite side from the adapted ear, the sound image of a brief, soft probe noise was localized toward that ear and away from the adapted ear. To paraphrase the words of the song, "I hear music when there's no one there," the listener hears a probe noise when there is no sound coming from that direction, as a result of adaptation.

Our final example of phenomena related to localization relies on time delays rather than intensity differences for its effect. Kubovy, Cutting, and McGuire (1974) presented listeners with a cluster of pure tones tuned to the notes of a G-major scale in the frequency range 300–600 Hz. Such a combination sounds like a horrendous discord. In one of their conditions, the same stimulus was presented to both ears, but with one ear leading the other in phase by 1.0 msec. This made the combined dichotic stimulus sound like a noisy discord coming from the direction of the leading ear. After presenting the discord for 1.5 sec, Kubovy et al. then shifted the phase of *one* of the eight tones so that the previously trailing ear now led, just for that tone. That shifted the localization of that tone to the other side, leaving the rest of the discord coming from the same side as before. When the appropriate sequence of notes in the scale were thus shifted, listeners heard the melody "Daisy, Daisy," coming from one side and the noise from the other. This phenomenon is closely related to the MLD effect, discussed above. In a second condition, Kubovy et al. shifted the frequency of one of the components up 5 Hz in one ear and down 5 Hz in the other ear. Were that component presented alone dichotically without the other seven components, it would have produced binaural beats. But with the other components present, binaural beats did not occur. What the listeners heard when a sequence of components was shifted in that way was again a melody corresponding to the sequence of shifted pitches—"Daisy, Daisy"—but this time it was not localized differently from the background noise. In fact, the melody in this second condition seemed, if anything, to be more perceptually prominent than in the first condition. (In neither condition could the melody be heard by listening to just one ear's stimuli monaurally.) The auditory system is apparently able to use phase-based localization cues to disambiguate pitches in a confusing context.

SUMMARY

Underlying the many differing musical traditions of the world is the human auditory system and the fundamental similarity of the sounds which that system processes. In this chapter, we have examined the basic psychological dimensions of pitch and loudness and their relationships to the acoustical dimensions of frequency and intensity. We save the detailed discussion of timbre for Chapter 3 and duration for Chapter 7.

Our discussion of pitch perception involved consideration of the anatomy and physiology of the inner ear, and we found that the phenomena of beats and the missing fundamental raised important questions about the place and periodicity theories of pitch perception. Throughout, we have referred to musical examples and demonstrations of the psychophysical issues under discussion. In our discussion of loudness, we introduced the concept of logarithm (which becomes even more important when we consider musical scales in Chapter 4) and also some alternative ways to psychophysically scale the dimension of loudness. We have considered phenomena demonstrating the interaction of pitch and loudness, and addressed the topic of localization effects in auditory, and, especially, musical, perception.

3

Timbre, Consonance, and Dissonance

We also have sound-houses, where we practise and demon-
strate all sounds and their generation. We have harmonies
which you have not, of quarter sounds and lesser slides of
sounds. Divers instruments of music likewise to you un-
known, some sweeter than any you have. . . . We make div-
ers tremblings and warblings of sounds, which in their origi-
nal are entire. We represent and imitate all articulate sounds
and letters, and the voices and notes of beasts and birds.
. . . We also have divers strange and artificial echoes, reflect-
ing the voice many times, and as it were tossing it; and some
that give back the voice louder than it came, some shriller
and some deeper; yea, some rendering the voice, differing in
the letters or articulate sound from that they receive. We have
also means to convey sounds in trunks and pipes, in strange
lines and distances.

(Francis Bacon, New Atlantis, 1627/1974, p. 244)

INTRODUCTION

If we ever need confirmation that science fiction sometimes anticipates the technological feats of later ages, this paragraph from Bacon should provide it. Here Bacon forsees the mechanical synthesis of speech sounds, transformations of natural timbres, and radio- and telephone-like communication. In the twentieth century, production of sounds by electronic machines has become a reality. Just as Bacon foresaw, these artificially produced sounds not only mimic the human voice and other sounds of nature, but also provide the possibility of creating new sounds never before heard. This chapter begins with an overview of the perception of timbre, or tone-color—those psychological properties of sounds that make them qualitatively distinguishable from each other even if they should have the same pitch and loudness. Following that discussion, we turn to a consideration of the closely related phenomena of consonance and dissonance—psychological properties of sounds arising from their simultaneous combination.

TIMBRE

Timbre has always been the miscellaneous category for describing the psychological attributes of sound, gathering into one bundle whatever was left over after pitch, loudness, and duration had been accounted for. Unlike the psychophysical relationships involved in the latter categories, which are relatively straightforward, the relationships underlying timbre are complex and multidimensional (Plomp, 1976). The psychological attributes clustered under the heading *timbre* fall along more than one psychological dimension; that is, sounds do not simply differ in how much timbre they have. And there are several physical dimensions whose variation causes changes in timbre that interact with each other in complex ways. As a start in breaking down this complexity into manageable units, let us first distinguish between two types of physical correlate of timbre: the steady-state correlates of vowel-like timbre differences and the transient (rapidly changing) correlates of consonant-like timbre differences. *Vowel* and *consonant* are terms borrowed from speech, but we shall see that those categories of physical timbre cue are quite applicable to music perception. The vowel-type cues to timbre differences are what make *ah, oo,* and *ih* different from one another. Consonant-type cues differentiate *pa, ba, ga, ka,* and so on. We start with a description of vowel and consonant perception as it relates to musical timbre perception and then describe some studies specifically directed to the latter. (References for the general statements about speech in the following sections may be found in Denes & Pinson, 1973; Lehiste, 1967.)

Vowels

The vowels of speech, such as *ah, eh, oh,* and *oo,* differ in timbre. A little playing around with the vowel sounds you can make with your own voice will convince you of several important facts about vowels. First, a vowel can be extended indefinitely in time without changing its timbre. That is, you can keep saying *ah* as long as you want, and it will still sound

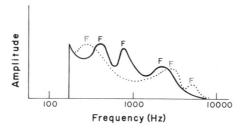

Figure 3.1 Idealized spectra of the English vowels *ah* (solid line) and *eeh* (dotted line)
(phonemes /a/ and /i/). F, formant frequency.

like *ah*. This is what we mean when we say that the physical correlates of
vowels are steady-state cues. Second, you can change the pitch of a
vowel within broad limits without affecting its timbre very much. Sing *ah*
up and down the scale and it still remains *ah*. Third, you can stay on the
same pitch and change the timbre of the vowel, as in changing *ah* gradually to *oo*. Fourth, you can change the loudness without changing the
timbre appreciably. These examples show that vowel timbre is largely
independent of pitch and loudness and that it depends on some steady-
state properties of the speech sound. As Helmholtz (1877/1954) correctly
surmised, those properties of the speech sound that differentiate one
vowel timbre from another involve the shape of the spectrum envelope.
The modern theory of vowel perception and production is primarily due
to Gunnar Fant (1956, reprinted in Lehiste, 1967).

Figure 3.1 shows spectra for two different vowel sounds: *ah* and *eeh*.
Notice that the peaks in the spectrum envelope (called formants) are in
different frequency ranges for the two vowels. You can convince yourself
of the difference in spectral content by finding a piano and shouting at it.
Depress the right-hand pedal (to release the dampers on the strings) and
shout, "Hah!" Then shout, "Hee!" Listen to the difference in the echo
from the piano. Different strings in the piano will resonate at different
frequencies corresponding to the formants in the two vowel sounds.
Those same spectral peaks cause stimulation at different places along the
basilar membrane, and that is what provides the brain with a cue to the
differences among vowels.

One question that musicians have raised ever since Helmholtz's discovery is whether the critical features of formants are their absolute or their
relative frequencies. That is, Is it the absolute frequency of the formant
peaks or the distance in frequency above the fundamental that serves as
the important cue to vowel quality? This question has been answered in a
study by Slawson (1968, Experiment 3) showing that vowel quality is
primarily determined by the absolute frequency of the formants. Slawson

asked listeners to rate the difference in sound quality between pairs of synthesized steady-state sounds. Among his stimuli were pairs like those of Figure 3.2. In the pair of vowels in (A), the formants were shifted, changing the vowel sound (as in Figure 3.1). In the pair in (B), the formants remained constant while the fundamental frequencies shifted by a factor of 1.5, giving a pitch shift of about 7 semitones (a perfect fifth). In the pair in (C), both the fundamental and the formants were shifted. Examples 3a–f correspond to the frequency spectra in Figure 3.2. The **3a–3f** vowels in the a–b pair (Figure 3.2A) sound different from each other, and are, in fact, what people would call different vowels (*ah* and *aw*). Slawson wanted to know in which of the other pairs the sounds would be rated more similar to those of the first pair—pair c–d (Figure 3.2B), in which the formants remained constant through a pitch shift, or pair e–f (Figure 3.2C), in which both fundamental and formants were shifted by the same logarithmic amount.

In general, Slawson found absolute, not relative, formant frequency to be the most important determinant of timbre. That is, the vowels in c–d (Figure 3.2B) sounded much more like the vowels in a–b (Figure 3.2A) than did the vowels in e–f (Figure 3.2C). We will see shortly why such an auditory code for vowel timbre has ecological validity in the process of

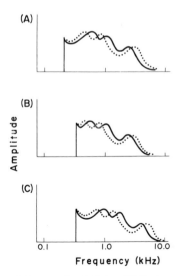

Figure 3.2 (A) Spectra of the vowels *ah* (/a/; solid line), and *aw* (/ɔ/; dotted line). (B) Same spectrum envelopes as (A), but with fundamental frequency raised (pitch changed). (C) Spectra of (A) with the fundamental frequency and spectrum envelope shifted by the same logarithmic distance.

speech production and perception. Before that, however, let us avoid an oversimplification of Slawson's results by noting two slight corrections to the absolute–formant–frequency theory. First, even though constant formant placement produced lower difference ratings than placement in a constant frequency ratio to the fundamental, *some* movement of formants in the direction of a pitch shift produced the lowest difference ratings between pairs of stimuli. Slawson found the optimal formant shift to be about 10% where the pitch had shifted an octave. Second, though listeners showed considerable agreement between their judgments of the musical timbre of sound pairs and judgments of vowel quality, there was one small deviation from that pattern. With timbre judgments, there was a slight tendency toward lower difference judgments associated with *relative* formant constancy for just those stimulus pairs in which both the fundamental and the formants had been shifted by exactly the same logarithmic interval, that is, in which the ratios of formant frequencies to fundamental remained exactly constant. We return to this result below.

VOWEL PRODUCTION

That constant formant frequencies should provide cues to the timbre of vowel sounds in speech is not surprising when we consider how vowels are produced (see Chapter 2). Try saying *ah* and notice where your tongue is in your mouth. Now say *eeh* and feel what happens to your tongue. It goes from down low in your mouth to up high. Figure 3.3 shows a cross-section of the vocal tract for those two vowels. For *ah,* the tongue leaves the vocal tract as open as possible. For *eeh,* the back of tongue divides the vocal tract into two segments. Physically, the open (as for *ah*) vocal tract behaves as a resonating air column stopped at one end, resonating at a frequency having a wavelength four times its length. Since the vocal tract is about 6.6 inches long, a sound wave traveling at 1100 ft/sec takes 0.002 sec to go up and down it four times (that is, 6.6 in × 4 = 26.4 in = 2.2 ft; 2.2 ft/1100 ft/sec = 0.002 sec). A sound wave with a period of 0.002 sec has a frequency of 500 Hz. If the vocal tract were a uniformly cylindrical tube stopped at one end, its resonances would be at 500 Hz and all odd-number multiples of 500 Hz—1500, 2500, 3500, and so on. But because

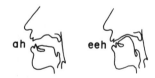

Figure 3.3   Vocal tract configurations for the vowels *ah* (/a/) and *eeh* (/i/). (After Denes & Pinson, 1973)

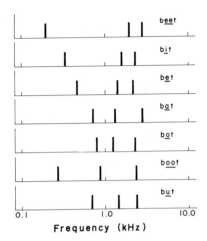

Figure 3.4   Typical formant frequencies for several English vowels.

the vocal tract varies in diameter from place to place, its resonances are shifted somewhat from these ideal values. In the case of *ah,* the frequencies of the first two resonances (formants) are about 700 and 1100 Hz. Moving the tongue to the position that produces "eeh" cuts the vocal tract into at least two pieces. The new pieces have shorter lengths and, hence, higher resonant frequencies. In fact, a resonance now appears around 2300 Hz. You can see the resonances for *ah* and *eeh* in the spectra in Figure 3.1. Figure 3.4 shows typical formant frequencies for several vowels in English.

Since the vocal tract is well designed for producing constant formant frequencies, it makes sense that these should be used as a code for certain speech sounds, namely, the vowels. Vowels are produced with acoustic characteristics that remain stable for time periods of the order of 0.17 sec. In the ear, the formants of the different vowels produce a different pattern of places of stimulation on the basilar membrane, as described in Chapter 2. The experiments of Broadbent and Ladefoged (1957; Broadbent, 1962) showed that important cues to vowel quality do involve regions of stimulation on the basilar membrane.

MUSICAL INSTRUMENTS

Musical instruments vary widely in the intensity patterns of partials (overtones) in their steady-state tones. Figure 3.5 shows steady-state patterns for several different instruments. The instruments shown here all have partials close to integer-multiple harmonics of the fundamental frequencies corresponding to the pitches of the tones. For many instru-

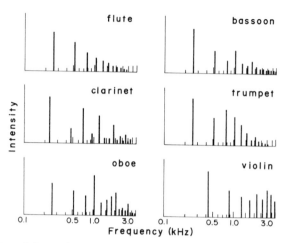

Figure 3.5 Typical steady-state spectra for various instruments.

ments, steady-state timbre seems to be determined to a first approximation by more or less constant formant frequencies, as it is with vowels. This is characteristic of the stringed instruments (e.g., violin), the double-reeds (e.g., oboe, bassoon), and the brass (e.g., trumpet, tuba) (Olson, 1967; Seashore, 1938; Slawson, 1968). We suppose that the perception of steady-state timbres for such instruments is handled by the same auditory mechanisms that mediate vowel timbres. Some types of instrument, however, have spectrum peaks that vary with fundamental frequency. The flute, for example, has a very strong fundamental and a series of harmonics that diminish in intensity with increasing frequency. The clarinet has strong first (fundamental) and third harmonics through much of its range. For these instruments, it seems likely, as R. Erickson (1975) suggests, that listeners acquire a sort of "timbral constancy" as they become familiar with the sounds of those instrumental groups. As noted above, Slawson (1968) found a tendency for listeners to give more similar ratings to stimuli in which the fundamental and formants moved the same logarithmic distance than the constant-formant model predicts.

The steady-state pattern of basilar-membrane stimulation suffices for discrimination of vowel-like timbres, and so the question arises whether steady-state patterns are a sufficient basis for all musical timbre discrimination. Saldanha and Corso (1964) showed that they are not. Saldanha and Corso made tape recordings of 10 different orchestral instruments all playing the same three pitches (middle C at 262 Hz and the F and A above that). College orchestra members found the clarinet, oboe, and flute easiest to identify and had the most difficulty with trombone, violin, cello, and bassoon. Listeners' overall performance with intact recordings of the tones was around 47% correct—well above a chance level of less than 3%. But when Saldanha and Corso chopped off the initial portion of each taped tone (eliminating onset transients but leaving the steady-state part of the musical-instrument tone), performance dropped markedly to 32% correct. The onset of a musical-instrument tone contains very important cues to the identity of the instrument. Musical timbre depends on more than steady-state formant-placement cues. In fact, it depends critically on transient cues produced during the first 20–50 msec following the onset of the tone. Such transient cues correspond to the cues for consonants in speech.

Consonants

Saldanha and Corso (1964) found that onset transient patterns are far more important cues to instrument identification than are transients at the termination of a tone, so we concentrate on those. There are several ways in which the components of a complex tone can vary during onset. First, the overall onset can be rapid or slow; second, the onset may be accompanied by transient noises; and third, the relative intensities of the harmonics can change over time, sometimes constituting a shift in formant frequency (which is typical of consonants in speech). We consider these factors in turn.

ONSET RAPIDITY

The first set of onset characteristics to consider is the overall rate of onset, which can serve as a distinctive cue to instrument timbre (Winckel, 1967). The speech sounds *tah* and *ah* differ in abruptness of onset, as well as in other ways. Among orchestral instruments, the ends of this continuum are well illustrated by the trumpet and violin. The trumpet attack is like the syllable *tah*—in fact, the onsets of both the syllable and the trumpet tone are initiated by the sudden release of air flow by the tongue behind the teeth. The violin attack is much slower and smoother. Figure 3.6 shows typical onset patterns for the five lowest harmonics in trumpet and violin tones. Trumpet onsets are very rapid, reaching a peak intensity within the first 20 msec, while the violin onset is more gradual and takes over 50 msec to reach a peak. The steady-state formant patterns of the trumpet and violin are fairly similar. In fact, Saldanha and Corso found that when onset transients were removed and the tones equalized in overall intensity, the two instruments were often confused.

One byproduct of the difference in attack functions between stringed and wind instruments is difference between their use in orchestration.

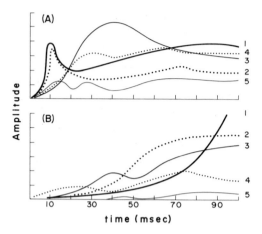

Figure 3.6 Typical onsets of (A) trumpet and (B) violin tones. The intensities of the different harmonics are indicated by curves with different numbers. (After Winckel, 1967)

Because of the gradual onset of their individual tones, it is relatively easy to get a large group of violinists to start a note at what sounds like the same time. Any differences between the intensities of neighboring instruments at a given instant will be quite small. However, it is very difficult to get a large section of trumpets (or French horns or clarinets) to attack a note with sufficient synchrony that the listener cannot notice time differences between individual attacks. The steepness of the attack function makes intensity differences between slightly asynchronous neighbors quite obvious. In Chapter 2, we describe the high degree of precision attained by the auditory system in resolving time delays between impulses arriving at the two ears. This resolving power is brought to bear in discovering minute asynchronies of attack. Thus, Western orchestras have a large number of strings and relatively few woodwinds and brass. They pride themselves on the ability of their brass and winds to play in perfect synchrony and shudder when they do not. The implications for the life of the high school band director, who must train large numbers of young wind players to synchronize their attacks, are obvious.

In considering Figure 3.6, it is important to remember that not all violin attacks are as smooth as the one shown, nor (to a lesser extent) are all trumpet attacks as abrupt. The technique of the instrument provides for variations in abruptness; for example, the violinist can strike the strings forcefully with the bow instead of starting the tone gently. Such variations in attack can produce additional noises as well as changes in the onsets of harmonics, and to those we now turn.

NOISE BURSTS

In addition to the regular pattern of harmonic components, the onsets of musical tones and spoken syllables often contain brief bursts of noise. Figure 3.7 presents schematic sound spectrographs of the syllables *tah* and *dah*. The noise burst at the start of the syllable, produced by the sudden release of air by the tongue, is shown as a brief vertical spread of energy. Such noise bursts are psychologically important attributes in both speech and music. In speech, the presence of the sudden noise burst distinguishes the stop consonants, such as /p/, /t/, and /k/, from other types of consonants such as /s/ and /v/ and /m/. The temporal relationship between the noise burst and the onset of vocal chord vibration that generates the harmonic components of the sound distinguished what are called voiced consonants (/b/, /d/, /g/) from voiceless (/p/, /t/, /k/). The delay between noise burst and harmonics is longer in the voiceless consonants, as can be seen with /t/ versus /d/ in Figure 3.7 (Lehiste, 1967). We note briefly other uses of noise in speech: The consonants /s/, /z/, /f/, and /v/ are characterized by noises of greater duration, and voicing (in the /z/ and /v/) consists of vibrating the vocal chords (and generating harmonics) simultaneously with the noise. Whispering is accomplished by producing noise continually and shaping it into vowel formants by adjusting the resonances of the vocal tract (see Chapter 2).

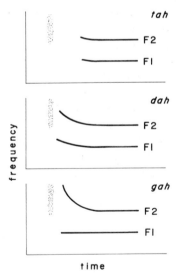

Figure 3.7 Schematic sound spectrogams of the syllables *tah, dah,* and *gah* (/ta/, /da/, /ga/).

Flutes and strings have noisier attacks than other types of instrument, while brass instrument attacks are usually low in noise (Grey & Gordon, 1978). A flute can be played with a "breathy" quality (as by a number of jazz flutists) by continuing noise production through the sustained part of the tone. The noise in the flute attack is caused by the air stream passing by the mouthpiece before the air column within the flute begins to resonate. With the violin, the bow scrapes on the string before resonance begins.

SPECTRAL ENERGY SHIFTS

A third way in which onset transient patterns can differ is in the way the relative intensities of energy in different regions of the spectrum change over time. Some instruments, such as the clarinets and saxophones, generally maintain the same relative intensities of harmonics from the beginning of the tone on through the steady state. With other instruments, the distribution of energy across the spectrum changes in the transition to steady state. This can be seen in Figure 3.6, where the fundamental frequency does not reach its steady-state level until after the first 100 msec of the tone.

With the stop consonants, the shift of spectral energy follows regular patterns and amounts to a shift in formant frequencies. This phenomenon was discovered by acousticians at the Haskins Laboratories (Delattre, Liberman, & Cooper, 1955, reprinted in Lehiste, 1967) and is apparent in the contrast between *dah* and *gah* in Figure 3.7. Formants appear to originate from particular frequency ranges in the spectrum (called loci) and then shift within the first 50 msec of the syllable to their steady-state positions. The locus varies with the particular consonant and appears to be a cue to consonant identity. The locus for the second formant of the consonants /t/ and /d/ is in the region of 1600–1800 Hz; that for /p/ and /b/ in the 700–800 Hz region. The locus for /k/ and /g/ is much higher—in the 3000 Hz region—and operates only if the second formant of the vowel is above about 1200 Hz (as it is for *eeh* but not for *ah,* see Figure 3.2). The frequency region of the locus is related directly to the movements the vocal tract makes in producing the consonant. With /t/ and /d/, the tongue begins the syllable by moving from behind the teeth to its position for the steady-state vowel. As the tongue moves, the resonances of the vocal tract (see Chapter 2) change from those produced with the tongue behind the teeth to those of the vowel. That shift of resonances is reflected in formant transitions that appear to start at the resonance frequencies corresponding to the original position of the tongue—the consonant loci.

Note in connection with the three transient phenomena just discussed—onset rapidity, noise bursts, and energy shifts—that in terms of the discussion in Chapter 2, all three introduce a spread of energy, or *noise,* in the spectrum. Because of such rapid and complex spectral changes, these aspects of sound present the greatest challenge to accurate sound reproduction and electronic synthesis.

PITCH AND DURATION

It is clear from the above considerations of its vowel- and consonant-like aspects that timbre interacts with pitch and duration. When the pitch of a tone is changed by changing the fundamental frequency, the spectral distribution of energy is changed. Within broad limits, this has little effect on timbre—we can sing the vowel *ah* from low in the bass range (50 Hz) to the middle of the soprano range (500 Hz) and produce sounds that are clearly *ah*'s and not *eeh*'s or *oh*'s. However, as the fundamental frequency ascends through the region of first-formant frequencies (see Figure 3.4), steady-state timbre is affected. The highest notes sopranos can sing (above 1000 Hz) begin to cut into the region of second formants, and differences among vowel qualities tend to become lost.

Percussion instruments present some exceptions to a rigid independence of pitch and timbre. Drums, gongs, and bells often have indistinct or ambiguous pitches due to a proliferation of anharmonic partials, and changing the pitch is often indistinguishable from changing the timbre. A more complicated case is that of some types of Chinese gong that produce pitch glides as a musically important part of their sound. The glide can go up or down by as much as 2 or 3 semitones (Rossing & Fletcher, 1983). Such gongs provide an exception to the general rule that pitches are fixed at discrete levels in the musical scale (see Chapter 4). The musically important aspect of these gong tones seems not to be their pitch but rather the whole configuration of sound, including the pitch glide. This is perhaps not surprising in a culture with a tone language, in which the direction of pitch glides changes the meaning of a syllable. These gongs seem to provide a borderline case in which the categories of pitch and timbre merge.

Changes in duration can affect consonant-like aspects of timbre when tones are made so brief that their steady-state portions are truncated severely or eliminated altogether. What is left is the cluster of onset transients with their noises and energy shifts. This often leads to a difference in sound quality between short and sustained tones. Example 3g **3g** presents the same passage from a Bach organ work first played very staccato, with very brief notes and relatively long spaces between them, and then played legato, with longer notes connected together. In the legato version, the steady-state quality of the sound dominates, giving it a smooth, flowing quality. The staccato version has a brilliant sparkling quality arising from the transient components of timbre.

In closing this section on the acoustic cues to timbre differences, we want to say that this account only scratches the surface of a region abounding in complication and subtlety. For example, we have not discussed the timbre of anharmonic sounds, such as those of bells and gongs. We suppose that the auditory system relies on the same sorts of cues for anharmonic sounds as for harmonic, but the area remains to be explored. Many cultures emphasize the aesthetic value of subtleties of anharmonic timbres of bells and gongs. In Java and Bali, the amplitude fluctuations produced by the interaction of anharmonic partials of gong sounds is denoted by a special term, *ombak* (Giles, 1974). The *ombak* of large gongs are frequently refer to well-known mythical characters (for example, Bima laughing). Gongsmiths can apparently control the acoustic properties of gongs so as to produce desired timbral effects, and gongs are judged according to how well they approximate the accepted standards. The acceptability of a gong timbre in this sense is determined both by its individual sound and by how well its *ombak* fits the ensemble for which it is intended. Giles' study is notable for its careful methods, but the timbre of anharmonic clusters is still a largely unexplored area.

Instrumental Timbres

MULTIDIMENSIONAL SCALING

We turn now to specific results of studies of listeners' judgments of the timbres of musical instruments. Here and in several other places, we describe studies that use multidimensional scaling techniques, so for the reader unfamiliar with them we describe them briefly in this section. Multidimensional scaling is aimed at constructing a spatial representation (a "map") of a person's judgments of similarities and differences (or degrees of relatedness) among a set of stimuli. The representation, if successful, should place each stimulus in relation to the others so that the distances among them represent degrees of similarity. That is, highly similar stimuli are represented as close together, and dissimilar stimuli as farther apart. It is an empirical question whether a given group of stimuli can be arranged so that distances on just a few dimensions represent the degree of similarity among them. Consider the case of three stimuli. The lengths of lines in Figure 3.8 represent amount of dissimilarity among the stimuli represented by the points a, b, and c. In (A), all three points fall on one straight line (one dimension) since $ab + bc = ac$. But it could easily have happened that the sum of the dissimilarities ab and bc could have

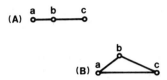

Figure 3.8 Examples of distances among three points in which (A) two of the distances added equal the third, and all three points fall on one dimension; and (B) the sum of any two distances is greater than the third, and two dimensions are required.

been greater than *ac,* giving the triangle in (B) and requiring two dimensions for their representation. The pattern among *any* group of three stimuli can be represented in two dimensions (and the pattern among any *n* stimuli can be represented in *n* − 1 dimensions). So one empirical question is whether the judged similarities permit a representation in fewer dimensions; that is, Are there regularities in the pattern of judgments that can be disclosed by a spatial representation in just a few dimensions?

A second empirical question is whether, given that the stimuli can be represented in a few dimensions, those dimensions make sense? If the grouping of stimuli provided by the multidimensional scaling process converges with the results of other studies using different methods or with analyses of physical or structural properties of the stimulus set, then the multidimensional representation is more useful than if it simply appears to be a haphazard grouping of the stimuli. If the representation makes sense in terms of our other knowledge, then we can ask what it discloses about the psychological dimensions of the stimulus set. In the present case, we can ask what the major dimensions are that govern listeners' judgments of similarity of timbre. Are those dimensions related, for example, to traditional groupings into instrumental families such as strings, woodwinds, and brass?

SCALING STUDIES

Plomp (1976) carried out a multidimensional scaling study using synthesized versions of the steady-state tones of nine different instruments—three strings, three woodwinds, and three brass—all playing F above middle C. Plomp's study extended Slawson's (1968) results concerning formant placement as a determinant of steady-state timbre. Plomp found that timbre judgments were closely related to the pattern of the spectrum envelope, including formant placement. To arrive at this result, Plomp carried out multidimensional scaling on both the pattern of listeners' similarity judgments and the pattern of energy distribution in the tonal spectra (analyzed into 15 bands, each spanning one-third octave, across the range of the stimuli). Three dimensions emerged from both analyses, and when Plomp projected the results from the timbre judgments on the results of the spectrum analysis, he found that the two sets of points matched very closely, with correlation coefficients better than .90. This means that both the timbre judgments and the physical analysis were based on the same information, namely, the distribution of sound energy in the spectrum. Insofar as formant frequencies are an important component of Plomp's spectral analyses, his study corroborates Slawson's (1968) results with vowel sounds. In fact, Plomp (1976) applied similar techniques to the analysis of vowel sounds and obtained results that closely paralleled Slawson's. Thus, formant placement seems to be the dominant component of steady-state timbre for both musical instruments and vowels.

A second aspect of Plomp's results sheds light on the results of Saldanha and Corso (1964). Plomp found that listeners' clusterings of the instruments followed traditional instrumental groupings up to a point, but there were some noteworthy exceptions. The bassoon was closer to the French horn and trombone than was the trumpet, and the stringed instruments did not cluster closely overall. Steady-state timbre judgments seem closely related to spectral content of tones, but steady-state spectral content does not seem as closely related to instrument family. Thus, the confusions Saldanha and Corso observed when onset transients were removed from steady-state tones are not surprising.

Grey and Gordon (1978; Gordon & Grey, 1978; Grey, 1977) carried out a related series of studies applying multidimensional scaling methods to a set of 16 instrument tones that included both transient and steady-state portions. The tones were converted to digital versions (see Chapter 2) for controlled presentation. In the initial study, Grey (1977) used tones (all E-flat above middle C) from the following sources: one flute, four double-reeds (two oboes, an English horn, and a bassoon), five single-reeds (two clarinets and three saxophones), three brass (a trumpet, a French horn, and a muted trombone), and three strings (a cello played three different ways). Grey obtained a scaling solution with three dimensions, shown in Figure 3.9. The first dimension appeared related to spectral energy distribution in the steady-state. It separated the French horn and cello played *sul ponticello* at one extreme (as having narrow bands of low-frequency energy) from the trombone and oboes at the other (which had broader-band and/or higher-frequency energy). The second dimension was related to the onset and offset patterns of the spectral components and separated the single reeds (whose harmonics were synchronized in the attack) from the other instruments (with a more muddled onset of unsynchronized harmonics). The third dimension was related to noisiness of attack, separating instruments with high-frequency noise in the attack (the single

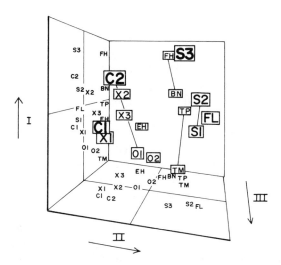

Figure 3.9 Three-dimensional scaling solution in which distances represent judged dissimilarity of Grey's (1977) stimuli. Woodwinds: FL, flute; O1 and O2, oboes; EH, English horn; BN, bassoon; C1, E♭ clarinet; C2, bass clarinet; X1, X2, and X3, saxophones. Brass: TP, trumpet; FH, French horn; TM, trombone. Strings: S1, S2, and S3, cello played different ways. (After Gordon & Grey, 1978, p. 26)

reeds, flute, and oboe) from the other instruments. These dimensions are entirely in keeping with the above outline of important steady-state and transient components contributing to timbre judgments.

The results in Figure 3.9 show clustering to some degree in terms of the traditional categories of instrument families, such as woodwinds, brass, and strings. However, the exceptions to that pattern (notably the flute and bassoon in the case of the woodwinds) show that timbre judgments are based on physical properties of the sound rather than category membership. And the physical differences in the sounds are related directly to the means by which the instrument produces its tone (just as the timbres of different syllables in speech are related to the way the vocal tract produces them). As Grey and Gordon (1978, p. 1499) say, "This may indicate that clustering is based more upon perceived features of tone than to some cognitive recognition or class-membership naming function."

Grey and Gordon (1978; Gordon & Grey, 1978) further demonstrated the importance of spectral patterns by repeating Grey's study but with spectrum envelopes traded among four pairs of tones: trumpet–trombone, French horn–bassoon, normal cello–muted cello, and bass clarinet–oboe. Those pairs are connected with lines in Figure 3.9. Grey and Gordon found that when spectrum envelopes were switched, the positions of the instruments in the scaling solution tended to exchange places, especially along the first dimension. These results suggest that the shape of the spectrum envelope is a feature that can be varied independently of other features such as attack. Grey and Gordon (1978, pp. 1499–1500) remark that "one hears the tones switch to each other's vowel-like color but maintain their original articulatory pattern of attack and decay, . . . [for example,] a bassoon with the highly explosive attack of a brass instrument and a horn with the rounder attack of a reed instrument."

Miller and Carterette (1975) carried out a study very similar to those just described, except that they used synthesized tones. In one study, the stimulus dimensions were fundamental frequency (200, 400, or 800 Hz), shape of spectrum envelope, and attack-decay function (shape of waveform envelope). This provided for sounds that were brass-like (strong attack and sustained tone) and piano-like (strong attack and exponential decay) as well as sounds with trapezoidal attack-decay functions (smooth onset and offset). Miller and Carterette obtained a three-dimensional scaling solution in which all three physical dimensions affected similarity judgments. The strongest dimension was fundamental frequency (pitch). The second dimension separated the piano-like sounds from the others. The third dimension separated sounds with strong attacks from those with trapezoidal onsets and offsets.

In a second study, Miller and Carterette eliminated pitch differences among the stimuli and varied (1) number of harmonics (three, five, or seven, with intensities decreasing across frequency), (2) overall attack envelope, and (3) pattern of relative onset times of the different harmonics. This last was varied by delaying the onset more the higher the harmonic. At one extreme, a cluster of low harmonics came in together, followed by a delayed series of upper harmonics. At the other extreme, the low harmonics came in with relatively long temporal spacing, followed by a cluster of higher harmonics. When they scaled the similarity judgments, Miller and Carterette found that the first two dimensions were related to number of harmonics. The first dimension separated clusters having three, five, and seven harmonics, and the second dimension separated the five-harmonic tones from the other two types. The third dimension was related to overall attack envelope, with the ordering: piano, brass, and smooth. The relative onsets of harmonics appeared to affect similarity in some cases but did not have consistent effects across the other stimulus dimensions. This study confirms the above emphasis on spectral content and attack functions as primary determinants of timbre.

In an additional study with Grey's (1977) 16 instrument tones, Grey and Moorer (1977) compared digitized versions of the tones (as above) with versions that had been analyzed and then synthesized using the time-varying pattern of intensity and frequency parameters given by the analysis. The synthesized tones were thus acoustically simpler than the originals—steadier in their patterns over time—than the originals. Grey and Moorer's main finding was that the synthesized versions of the tones were judged highly similar to the originals. These results mean that certain aspects of musical tones can be treated as more or less irrelevant in the determination of timbre, especially subtle fluctuations of parameters during the steady-state. Grey (1978) showed that this is especially true when the synthesized tones are presented in musical context.

USES OF TIMBRE

The foregoing account describes the principal physical parameters underlying timbre perception and provides some idea of the extensive range of possible sounds that can be created by varying them. It remains to consider the possible musical uses of timbre differences. Of course, exciting timbres and their accurate reproduction can serve as ends in themselves, as certain record jackets for Richard Strauss tone poems or Ravel's *Bolero* will quickly convince readers: "Incomparable recording technique . . . conveying a high fidelity quality they could not have imagined" (Ravel, 1956). And, advertising hyperbole aside, there is no denying the immediate sonic attraction of a luscious violin sound or the voice of a favorite singer. However, timbral differentiation can serve deeper, more serious, musical purposes.

Like localization (Chapter 2), timbre can help delineate musical structure and thereby improve musical communication. In Western music, two major technological developments that came to fruition in the eighteenth century—the baroque organ and the symphony orchestra—put a wider range of timbres at the disposal of composers than ever before. Both the organ and the orchestra developed in the late nineteenth century into musical vehicles capable of overwhelming the listener with glorious sounds. But in the eighteenth century, both organ and orchestra were more modest media, providing a range of tone colors that could give contrasting voice to the different elements in a piece. Certainly, Bach was capable of dramatic use of stunning sound effects, as in the Toccata and Fugue in D Minor. But the great body of the organ works rely on there being timbre *differences* available to the organist. The particular choice of voices is optionally variable within broad limits as the range of choices observable in practice shows. The timbre differences provide, like localization differences, a way of making the thematic interplay of Bach's contrapuntal texture clear.

The use of timbre to delineate structure perhaps becomes more obvious when we contrast it with the resources available in another genre familiar to most of our readers: the nineteenth century piano literature of (for example) Beethoven and Chopin. There, with at best a restricted range of possible timbral contrasts (as by controlling duration or using the *una corda* pedal), the pianist must rely primarily on contrasts of loudness and articulation to clarify musical structure, since the available timbral dimensions are so limited. Generally speaking, fewer simultaneous event sequences can be presented clearly by using loudness than by using timbre to differentiate the parts—as listening to Beethoven and Bach will quickly convince the listener. In fact, Bach's orchestral writing—full of elaborate counterpoint—is plainly the work of an organist, while Beethoven's— more straightforward and dramatic—is the work of a pianist.

Timbre is used in Java to differentiate musical events as well. Hoffman (1978) describes the use of timbre in this Indonesian musical system both to differentiate melodic lines (as in the Bach fugue) and to clarify cyclic temporal patterns (see Chapter 7). Hoffman notes a historical trend since the late 1800s toward greater reliance on timbre (as opposed to pitch patterns) to indicate temporal cycles, thus providing for freer, less constrained melodic development.

One of the most exciting contemporary uses of timbre is being developed by Wessel (1979) and his colleagues at the Institute de Recherche et Coordination, Acoustique—Musique (IRCAM) in Paris. By using mulidimensional scaling, the researchers at IRCAM can create a personal timbre space that reflects a composer's own judgments about tonal similarities. Then elaborate sound synthesizing computers make available the whole range of sounds in the timbre space, with all their gradations and nuances. The ideal arrangement would be to provide all of this flexibility to the composer creating musical structures.

CONSONANCE AND DISSONANCE

> *All Nature is but art, unknown to thee;*
> *All chance, direction, which thou canst not see;*
> *All discord, harmony not understood;*
> *All partial evil, universal good:*
> *And, spite of pride, in erring reason's spite,*
> *One truth is clear: whatever IS, is RIGHT.*
>
> (Alexander Pope, *An Essay on Man*, 1733/1911, p. 24)

Consonance and *dissonance* refer to properties of simultaneous sounds of different pitches. There are two aspects of these phenomena we discuss in this section. First is the relationship between sensations of consonance and physical properties of stimuli presented in isolation—what Plomp

(1976) calls "tonal consonance." This is well understood for pairs of pure tones, and (at least to a first approximation) the dissonance of combinations of complex tones can be predicted directly from the dissonance of their pure-tone components. Second is the question of how tone combinations, judged consonant or dissonant in isolation, are used in musical context. There it is important to remember the cultural relativism of Pope's (1733) *Essay*—that broadening the context can make that which was discordant, harmonious.

Tonal Consonance

PURE TONES

Helmholtz (1877/1954) correctly surmised that the dissonance of a pair of complex tones was produced by interference among their pure-tone components. This reduced the problem to the question of what produced dissonance between pure tones. Helmholtz believed that dissonance was due directly to speeded up beats between the tones (see Chapter 2) producing a sensation of roughness. This is very close to the right answer. Dissonance is in fact due to interference between adjacent pure tones, but the interference is more complicated than that due to just beats. The interference is associated with the general pattern of interaction of pure tones in the auditory system described by the critical bandwidth. Recall from Chapter 2 that the critical bandwidth is the frequency region over which stimuli interact in producing sensations of loudness. Plomp and Levelt (1965) discovered that the interaction of tones in producing dissonance is also well described by the critical bandwidth.

Example 3h presents two pure tones. One tone is at a steady frequency **3h** of 524 Hz. The other starts at 524 Hz and ascends until it reaches 1048 Hz, an octave above. At the start of the example, the two tones cannot be heard as separate pitches. As the two tones diverge, notice that the beats between them speed up and then become so rapid that single beats cannot be heard individually. Separate pitches are not yet heard. Then the sound becomes rougher and definitely dissonant. Dissonance reaches a peak at a separation of about 30 Hz (about 1 semitone) and then recedes. As the tones emerge from the highly dissonant region, the two pitches become more and more distinct. Dissonance decreases (consonance increases) steadily up to a separation of about 100 Hz (3 or 4 semitones) and then remains generally constant up to the octave. Plomp and Levelt (1965) obtained consonance ratings of pairs of tones differing in frequency separation and centered on five frequencies at octave intervals between 125 and 2000 Hz. Figure 3.10 shows an example of their data from pairs centered on 500 Hz. Notice that just as in Example 3h, the tone pairs start

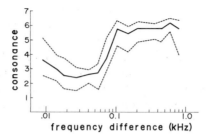

Figure 3.10 The judged consonance of pairs of pure tones centered on 500 Hz. Solid line, the median judgment; dashed lines, the upper and lower quartiles. (After Plomp & Levelt, 1965, p. 553.)

out relatively consonant, and then consonance decreases as the tones diverge, reaching a minimum around 30 Hz. Then consonance increases to a plateau of maximal consonance beginning around 100 Hz. Plomp and Levelt found that when they plotted the frequency separation giving maximal dissonance against the center frequencies of the tone pairs, the curve matched the curve describing the critical bandwidth (Figure 2.23) very closely. Thus, the various patterns obtained at different frequencies could be summarized conveniently in a schematic curve relating consonance to frequency separation in proportion to the critical bandwidth (Figure 3.11). The most dissonant interval is at about one-quarter of a critical bandwidth, and the plateau of maximal consonance is reached at about one critical bandwidth.

Notice from Figure 2.23 that the size of the critical bandwidth grows as a function of frequency across most of the auditory range but that below about 500 Hz, it begins to level off and in the range of 100–200 Hz, is

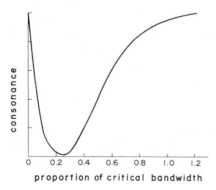

Figure 3.11 Curve summarizing consonance judgments as a function of frequency separation proportional to the critical bandwidth. (After Plomp & Levelt, 1965, p. 556.)

essentially constant. If the rapid-beats hypothesis of dissonance production had been correct, the frequency separation required for maximal dissonance would have remained constant across the entire range. That is not the case. Further, it is quite plausible that dissonance should be predicted so well by the critical bandwidth function, since dissonance, like loudness summation, is a phenomenon directly related to the interaction of auditory stimuli adjacent in frequency.

One important musical consequence of the relationship shown in Figures 2.23 and 3.11 between frequency separation and dissonance should be noted here. From 500 Hz up, the critical bandwidth is reasonably close to a constant frequency ratio between tones, averaging 2 or 3 semitones. Thus, the most dissonant intervals in that region lie around a quarter of that value—a quarter step (0.5 semitone) to somewhat less than a semitone. However, in the lower octaves, especially below middle C, the curve levels off to a constant frequency *difference* rather than a proportion. As frequency descends, this constant difference (about 20—25 Hz for the most dissonant interval) becomes a greater and greater proportion of the center frequency of the interval. Around middle C, the most dissonant interval is at a frequency separation of 8 or 9%, or 1.5 semitones. An octave lower, the most dissonant interval is around 16—18%, or about 3 semitones (a minor third). At the C below the bass staff (65 Hz), the separation is around 35%, or somewhat more than 5 semitones (a perfect fourth). Musical thirds and fourths are quite dissonant in the midrange of the tuba and string bass—a fact immediately noticed when four-part Bach chorales are transcribed for tuba quartet. Composers take account of this in avoiding intervals of less than a fifth in the lower ranges, as we discuss below.

COMPLEX TONES

As Plomp and Levelt (1965) supposed, the consonance of harmonic complex tones can be predicted quite well by supposing that the harmonic components interact pairwise in the manner shown in Figure 3.11. The dissonance produced by the interaction of pairs of adjacent tones adds up to the total dissonance of the pair of complex tones. This was demonstrated by Kameoka and Kuriyagawa (1969a, 1969b), whose results are shown in Figure 3.12. Notice that there are peaks of consonance whenever the fundamental frequencies of the complex tones stand in a simple integer ratio. This is because at integer ratios, the harmonics tend to coincide, contributing no dissonance to the mixture. Those harmonics that do not coincide produce dissonant interactions with their neighbors according to the pattern in Figure 3.11. The nearly related fourths, fifths,

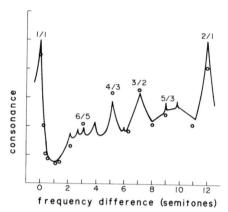

Figure 3.12 Consonance of pairs of harmonic complex tones. The curve represents theoretical calculations and the points data. (After Kameoka & Kuriyagawa, 1969b, p. 1465.)

and octaves (ratios of 4:3, 3:2, and 2:1) produce the highest peaks, since complex tones at those intervals share the greatest number of harmonics. Thirds (5:4, 6:5) share fewer harmonics and so produce lower peaks. As Plomp (1976) notes, this means that the "mistuning" of thirds in equal-tempered tuning is less noticeable than that of fourths and fifths.

If Plomp and Levelt's theory is true, then dissonance due to separation of adjacent partials should predict the dissonance of pairs of complex tones whether the complex tones are harmonic or not. This is, in fact, the case, as Geary (1980) demonstrated. Geary used complex tones in which upper partials were spaced at multiples of the square root of 2 times the funamental frequency (rather than at integer multiples of the fundamental). Geary (1980, p. 1785) concludes: "The sound pairs with matching frequency components were chosen [as more consonant] more often than those with near misses."

MUSICAL PRACTICE

Plomp and Levelt (1965) demonstrated that Western composers as different in style as J. S. Bach and Anton Dvořák take implicit cognizance of the consonance relationships illustrated in Figures 3.11 and 3.12. They plotted the intervals produced between adjacent harmonics for the simultaneous tonal combinations in movements from Bach's Third Organ Sonata and Dvořák's Tenth String Quartet. Figure 3.13 shows representative data from this study. The interquartile range of intervals fell between 0.25 and 1.0 critical bandwidths, suggesting that the composers were aiming for a variety of consonance levels approaching moderate degrees of dissonance.

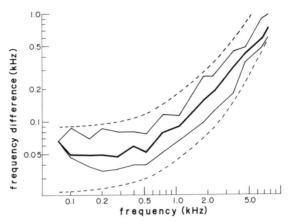

Figure 3.13 The distribution of simultaneous intervals in a Dvořák String Quartet in relation to the critical bandwidth and one-fourth of the critical bandwidth (dotted lines). Solid lines indicate the median and quartiles of the interval distribution in each octave range. (After Plomp & Levelt, 1965, p. 559.)

Figure 3.13 accounts simply for the dissonance of individual chords treated in isolation. It says nothing about the way chords are used in musical context. Western music does not consist of sequences of chords of all about the same level of dissonance. Composers use chords dynamically to achieve patterns of tension and release in ways that complicate the relatively simple picture of tonal consonance just presented. To those complications we now turn.

Musical Consonance

The psychoacoustic approach to understanding audition achieves its successes by presenting stimuli in isolation and measuring the psychological correlates of changing one or two stimulus dimensions at a time. For such complex events as musical stimuli, psychoacoustics can serve to lay a groundwork and to describe in broad outline the limits of possible musical sounds that must pass through the auditory system. However, the simplicity by which psychoacoustic approaches succeed becomes, itself, an impediment to the exploration of complex stimuli whose perception is dependent on both context and experience. We explore such complications concerning pitch in Chapter 4 and concerning duration in Chapter 7. Here we explore contextual complications regarding consonance and dissonance.

The studies described above regarding tonal consonance provide a psychoacoustic foundation for consonance as perceived in musical contexts.

A function such as that in Figure 3.11 tells us several useful things about the conditions and limits of musical context. For every interval of pure tones, it assigns a dissonance value. The dissonance values decrease up to a certain interval and then level off. According to this model, adding a harmonic at the octave to a pure tone cannot enhance the consonance of its combination with other tones, but it *can* increase dissonance. The dissonance values from Figure 3.11 can be used to order all combinations of pure tones according to their dissonance. And since the dissonance of combinations of complex tones is based on the sum of the dissonances contributed by the interaction of their pure-tone components, we can derive functions, such as that in Figure 3.12, from which we can obtain orderings of various sorts of complex tones along the dimension of consonant to dissonant. In what follows, we assume that musicians more or less agree on this underlying psychoacoustic ordering of tonal combinations according to tonal consonance. Where listeners and performers and composers differ among themselves is in their expectations and stylistic usages regarding that ordering in musical contexts.

There are a variety of ways in which the underlying ordering of tones according to tonal consonance can be put to use in the context of a musical style. First, the range of consonances in use can vary from very narrow to very wide. Second, the mean level of consonance in a style can be set at the consonant or the dissonant end of the scale, or somewhere in between. Third, dissonance can provide a dynamic function in the temporal organization of music—a dissonance is that which requires resolution to a consonance. Thus, tonal combinations that require resolution, regardless of where they fall on a scale of *tonal* consonance, can be heard as *musically* dissonant. Fourth, consistent usages in certain contexts can even reverse the sense of the scale, so that what would ordinarily be heard as tonally consonant requires resolution to what would ordinarily be heard as tonally dissonant. We discuss the first two of these issues together and after that, return to the second two.

The history of Western music since 1600 provides a good example of a shift in both the average level of dissonance and in the range of dissonances used (Grout, 1960). Figure 3.14 shows this shift schematically. In the sixteenth century, pieces typically ended with intervals of fourths and fifths (5 or 7 semitones). A hundred years later, pieces ended with thirds in their chords (3 or 4 semitones). Since the sixteenth century, tonal combinations previously thought dissonant have come into more and more common use, and the range of contexts in which tonal dissonances can function dynamically has broadened considerably. Listeners in 1800 were startled by Beethoven's opening his First Symphony with a "dissonant" chord, and in 1805, by his use of two diferent chords simulta-

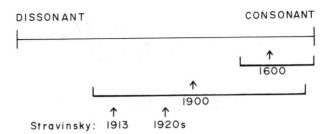

Figure 3.14 The continuum of tonal consonance showing the mean level and range of dissonance used during various periods in Western music.

neously in the Third—passages we now consider tame. Along with the shift in mean level of dissonance, the range of dissonances used has broadened in that the consonant end of the scale has remained in use.

This shift fits well with Helson's (1964) conceptualization of adaptation level. Along any sensory continuum the adaptation level is the level we are used to. The shift toward greater tonal dissonance brings about a shift in the listener's adaptation level. Further, Helson shows that what we prefer is just a little different from our current adaptation level—we like moderate changes. For example, people prefer bath water that is just a little different from their body temperature of 38°C. There is a narrow range on either side of the current adaptation level that will be preferred in a novel stimulus. As listeners adapt to greater amounts of tonal dissonance, there is a gradual shift along the continuum. Helson's model also explains why a shift toward greater consonance is sometimes attractive— for example, Stravinsky's backing away in the 1920s from the dissonances of *Rite of Spring*. We return to questions of preference in Chapter 8.

The foregoing could be true even of the use of tonal combinations in isolation. However, in music, tones are always used in a dynamic context—the present set of tones grows out of the preceding set and leads to the following set. In this dynamic sense, the musically dissonant chord is one that requires resolution. Psychologically, such "requiredness" (Köhler, 1938) depends upon the listener's knowledge of the style and the expectancies that knowledge generates. We return to those aspects in Chapter 6. Here the important point is that dynamic temporal relationships among tones can lead a tonally consonant stimulus to be heard as musically dissonant, that is, to have an unsettling effect that requires resolution. Cazden (1972) provides a number of examples of such effects. The most extreme case is of a single note, a low C on the piano, in Beethoven's *Appassionata* Sonata 26 measures before the end of the first movement (see Figure 3.15a). Cazden points out that the lone low C has just as much need as the C with dominant harmonies at the end of the

Figure 3.15 Musical examples (A) from Beethoven's Sonata op. 57, and (B) in which the sense of the tonal consonance continuum is reversed.

example to resolve to an F and hence, is musically dissonant though tonally consonant.

In Beethoven, though there are occasional violations of parallel ordering between tonal and musical consonance, generally the tonal framework preserves that ordering. However, it is possible to establish general tonal frameworks in which tonally dissonant chords are heard as a home base from which one departs into the tonally consonant—in which the usual scale of consonance and dissonance is reversed. The composer Robert Rodriguez (who suggested the quote from Pope at the start of this section), in discussions of the history of the use of dissonance, called our attention to some examples of this. One example is the middle movement of Bartók's Second Piano Concerto, which opens and closes with a series of chords built out of fifths stacked on top of one another (for example, C–G–D–A–E . . .). Bartók is successful in establishing this tonally dissonant complex as a reference point in the movement. The return to this dissonant reference at the end of the movement is heard as a satisfying conclusion rather than as something requiring further resolution.

3i   In a more modest way, the contrived ostinato in Example 3i (Figure 3.15B) demonstrates the same phenomenon. The initial chord (A–D–G) is built of stacked fourths, which are tonally dissonant. The movement to the second chord (A^b–E^b–A^b) is heard as a departure requiring resolution, even though the latter is tonally consonant. That resolution is provided by a return to the first chord. Then the low D enters, which according to nineteenth-century notions should be heard as the root of a D–F–A chord, forcing the G to resolve downward to F. However, the low D resolves upward to E, adding yet another fourth to the stack; and that is heard as a satisfying resolution. Here the usual ordering of consonance and dissonance is reversed by a simple musical context.

From the above discussion, we can see that both the psychoacoustic foundations and the musical elaborations are required for an understanding of consonance and dissonance. Musical usage introduces complications of the underlying relationships, yet those alterations are never completely arbitary but occur within the limitations of the auditory system.

SUMMARY

   This chapter has dealt with two aspects of the quality of sounds: timbre, referring to the ways in which single sounds of the same pitch and loudness can differ in tone quality, and consonance (vs. dissonance), referring to sound qualities arising from the interaction of two or more perceptually distinct, simultaneous sounds. We divided the discussion of timbre into two categories labeled vowel and consonant, drawing the analogy to the sources of acoustic cues to the timbres of speech sounds. Vowel-quality, or steady-state, timbre arises from the intensity pattern of upper partials or overtones in the acoustic spectrum. Consonant-quality, or transient timbre, arises from changes in the spectral pattern over time, most importantly during the first 50 msec after the onset of a sound. Demonstrations were provided showing that both aspects of timbre are important in music.

   In the discussion of consonance and dissonance, we showed how sensations of dissonance arise from the interaction of pure tones falling within a quarter of a critical bandwidth of one another. (*Critical bandwidth* refers to a frequency range over which acoustic energy is integrated in the ear.) The critical bandwidth is proportionally large in the lower frequency range used in music, with the result that musical intervals that sound consonant in the midrange become more dissonant when transposed downward. The dissonance of combinations of complex tones arises from the pairwise interaction of adjacent components, with the result that harmonic complex tones are most consonant when their fundamental frequencies stand in small integer ratios to each other. We distinguished between tonal consonance as an immediately apparent feature of tonal combinations in isolation and musical consonance as a quality of relative stability and rest (vs. instability and restlessness) tone combinations might display in musical contexts. We suggested that the history of the use of tonal consonance and dissonance is music may be affected by listeners' need for moderate novelty—for tonal combinations slightly different from ones their psychological adaptation level leads them to expect.

4

Musical Scales

The individual parts of a melody reach the ear in succession. We cannot perceive them all at once. We cannot perceive backwards and forwards at pleasure. Hence for a clear and sure measurement of the change of pitch, no means was left but progression by determinate degrees. This series of degrees is laid down in the musical scale.

(Helmholtz, 1877/1954, p. 252)

INTRODUCTION

Of the perceptual dimensions used in music, pitch is unique in having a scale dividing it fairly rigidly into discrete steps. Steps of loudness are designated in musical scores with labels such as *p, mp, mf,* and so forth, but these are relative indicators whose meaning changes with context. The temporal continuum is divided into discrete beats, but the duration of the beat changes with tempo. Timbre is multidimensional, and all its dimensions admit of more or less continuous variation. Pitch alone is organized into discrete steps. This is true in almost all the cultures of the world. We say almost all because there are some cultures that often use chants on two pitch levels for which it is difficult to define a scale. For example, the Hawaiian *oli* chant (described by Roberts, 1967) is primarily monotonic, with wide latitude in the pitch separation of a lower secondary tone. Like the Hawaiian, several cultures in widely separated parts of the world use two-pitch chants, and it seems a matter of semantics whether we call the two pitches with their single discrete step a scale or not. Further, there is some evidence that as such a chant becomes more intense and excited, the single melodic interval becomes expanded, perhaps in continuous fashion (Sachs, 1965). Nevertheless, most of the world's music is based on scales having stable, discrete steps. The sizes of the steps vary from culture to culture, though virtually all use the octave as a basic interval.

In our discussion, we first consider a set of cognitive constraints on scale construction that seem to operate through much of the world. We show how the application of those constraints in various combinations leads the various possible forms of scale in different cultures. Following that, we turn to a discussion of alternative ways psychologists and musicians have looked at pitch scales, leading to a discussion of contemporary multidimensional-scaling approaches. We conclude the chapter with an overview of the use of scales in a variety of cultures.

It is a puzzle for psychology why the music of the world uses discrete steps from pitch to pitch rather than the continuous series of all possible pitches. In his discussion of this problem, Helmholtz (1877/1954, pp. 250ff.) suggests that a scale of discrete pitch levels provides a psychological standard by which the listener can measure melodic motion. If melodies consisted of continuous changes of pitch like the wailing of a siren, the listener would still have to learn a scale in order to comprehend the amount of those changes. In that case, the listener would have a very difficult time learning the scale, since the actual notes of the scale would seldom occur (and seldom be marked) in the perceived music. The cognitive tasks of musician and listener are immensely simplified by restricting the set of pitches to the graduated degrees of a scale. Knowing a musical scale gives the listener an immediate basis for comparing the sizes of pitch intervals and judging the extent of melodic motion. (Helmholtz's argument is a special case of a general argument concerning cognitive frameworks made by Kant, 1787/1933, pp. B xxxix f., footnote.)

Beyond providing a measure of melodic motion, the scale provides a cognitive framework that facilitates the remembering of the pitches of a melody. This is especially important in nonliterate cultures where the human memory is the only vehicle by which melodies are preserved. Without culturally established scales, the reproduction of tunes and their transmission from generation to generation is a haphazard affair. We present evidence below that people's memory for familiar tunes using familiar scales is indeed very good. Some researchers go so far as to argue that because the scale is a mutually shared category system among performers and listeners, the listener "hears one and the same music, in different rooms, played on various instruments or sung, transposed, recorded with various equipment with such and such distortion, etc." (Francès, 1958, pp. 34–35).

The pitch categories of a musical scale serve the same kind of psychological function as do discrete categories used in the recoding of many types of messages communicated across noisy channels. Languages use this kind of discrete categorization. There is a certain range of physical sounds which, in English, are heard as *p* (Lane, 1965; Liberman, Harris, Kinney, & Lane, 1961). Certain physical parameters can be changed along a continuum, and up to a point, the sound will remain *p*. However, at a certain point the sound will become a *b* for the listener. Speakers are given considerable latitude in the way they produce *p*'s. They can generate physical sounds anywhere along that part of the continuum mutually recognized as belonging to the *p* category and their listeners will understand them. Further, the listeners will be able to economize what they must store in memory in order to remember the message. Rather than remember all the acoustic parameters of the waveform the speaker actually produced, all the listener must remember is the perceptual category into which those sounds fall. As in language, the categorization of both stimuli and responses afforded by musical scales reduces ambiguity and memory load in hearing, remembering, and producing music. As in most human communication systems, some indeterminacy within categories (intonation error) is allowed in order to achieve greater stability and clarity at the broader level of category identification.

WESTERN SCALES AND EQUAL TEMPERAMENT

Constraints on Scale Construction

The structure of scales in Western music provides a convenient starting place to begin the description of musical scales of pitch. After describing Western scales, we go on to describe certain features of the scale systems of other cultures. Figure 4.1 shows a typical Western tonal scale (C major) along with the fundamental frequencies of the notes. There are several psychological constraints on tonal scale construction found all over the world. First, the pitches of a scale must be discriminable from one another when played in succession. In Western music, the smallest pitch interval between notes, called a semitone, represents a frequency difference of about 5.9%. Such an interval can be found between E and F and between B and C in Figure 4.1. Since humans are capable of discriminat-

Figure 4.1 Standard fundamental frequencies of the Western C-major scale.

ing frequency differences of the order of 1.0% in this frequency range (Shower & Biddulph, 1931), intervals of a semitone would seem to be safely discriminable. The composer Harry Partch (1974), a long-time proponent of microtonal scales, which have intervals smaller than the semitone, notes that the principal limitations on the smallness of intervals are not given by their psychophysical discriminability but by the cognitive systems of the listener—a set of constraints to which we return below.

A second constraint is that tones whose fundamental frequencies stand in a 2:1 ratio (or nearly so; we discuss complications below) are treated as very similar to each other. The interval between frequencies in a 2:1 ratio is called an octave. The two notes labeled C in Figure 4.1 are an octave apart. Tones an octave apart are perceived as similar not only by humans but also by white rats (Blackwell & Schlosberg, 1943). In cultures having labels for the pitches of the scale, tones an octave apart are given the same name. In Western music, for example, tones with fundamental frequencies of 32.75, 65.5, 131, 262, 524, 1048, 2096, and 4192 Hz are all called C. Further, in cultures with functional harmony like the western European tones of the same name have the same harmonic functions when combined simultaneously with other tones. The overwhelming majority of cultures in the world make use of the equivalence of tones an octave apart. The only exceptions we have found are certain groups of Australian aborigines. In their cultures, melodic imitations at roughly octave intervals do not always use the same logarithmic scale intervals, and when men and women sing together, they do so in unison and not in octaves (Ellis, 1965).

A third constraint is that when the octave is filled in with the intervals of the scale, there should only be a moderate number of different pitches, say five or seven. This constraint arises from the cognitive limitation on the number of different values along a psychological dimension people can handle without confusion. Miller (1956) argues that across various sensory modalities, the number of stimuli along a given dimension people can categorize consistently is typically 7 ± 2. With more than seven or so different pitches, people begin to hear two or more pitches as falling in the same category and so defeat the purpose Helmholtz saw for the scale. Most cultures in the world use five to seven pitches in their tonal scales.

A fourth constraint that operates in a few cultures of the world, among them the Western and the Chinese, is that the octave should be divided into a series of minimal intervals, all equal in size, which are added together to construct all the intervals used in melodic scales. Western tuning divides the octave into 12 semitones (a chromatic scale). One advantage of such a system is that a given melody can be transposed so as to start on any note of the tuning system and be reproduced without

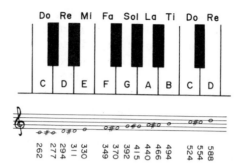

Figure 4.2 The frequencies of the chromatic scale on the piano keyboard.

distortion. Each pitch interval in the transposition will contain the same number of semitones as the corresponding interval in the original. Figure 4.2 shows the octave, beginning on middle C, divided into semitones, with the frequencies of the notes and their arrangement on the piano keyboard. Note that the major scale made up of the white keys (the C-major scale of Figure 4.1) has intervals between successive notes of either 1 or 2 semitones. You could construct a major scale beginning on any one of the keys in Figure 4.2 simply by preserving the same sequence of intervals as in the white-key scale—that is, 1-semitone intervals between the third and fourth and between the seventh and eighth notes of the scale and 2-semitone intervals elsewhere. And each melody with which you are familiar will remain the same melody whichever scale you use. In fact, unless you have absolute pitch, every time you sing "Happy Birthday" you are likely to sing it with a different set of pitches than the time before (that is, in a different key) without noticing the difference. You automatically reproduce the same intervals (measured in semitones) as the time before.

The system of tuning in which all intervals are constructed by adding semitones is called equal temperament. It is important to realize that the notion that all scale intervals should be derivable by the combination of some minimal modular interval (the semitone) arose as a rationalization of the structure of tonal scales already in use. Melodies had been sung using the major scale for centuries (if not millennia) before people thought of the possibility of expressing its intervals in semitones of equal size. While practical approximations to equal temperament were developed over a long period of time both in China and in the West (Kuttner, 1975; McClain, 1979), the exact mathematics of the system were derived in China around 1580 by the scholar Chu Tsai-Yü (Needham, 1962). This discovery made its way to Europe by 1630, and over the next century, came into more and more common use. Bach wrote his *Well-Tempered Clavier* in the 1720s and 1730s as a tour de force demonstration of its usefulness, systematically using major and minor scales beginning on all the 12 possible notes. In what follows, we describe how the frequencies of the semitone intervals are derived.

There is one more constraint that applies in conjunction with the fourth constraint, though it is usually just implicitly assumed. That is that when we apply the various constraints on scale construction that we have just discussed, then the scales we construct should consist of the intervals of scales and melodies already traditionally in use.

Before proceeding to the algebraic derivation of the frequencies of the equal-tempered chromatic scale, let us pause for a brief overview of the musical and psychological requirements such a scale is designed to satisfy:

1. discriminability of intervals,
2. octave equivalence,
3. a moderate number of pitches within the octave (usually about seven), and
4. the use of a uniform modular pitch interval (the semitone) with which to construct approximations of all the intervals of scales traditionally in use.

Equal Temperament

In deriving the equal-tempered chromatic scale of pitches, we rely mainly on the requirements that all octaves (2:1 frequency ratios) are of psychologically equal size and that each octave is divided into 12 equal pitch intervals. One consequence of taking tones separated by equal frequency ratios (e.g., 2:1) and placing them at psychologically equal intervals along the pitch scale (e.g., at octave intervals) is that the resulting psychophysical scale relating pitch to frequency will be logarithmic. Remember from Chapter 2 the definition of logarithm—if

$$a^b = c$$

then

$$\log_a c = b.$$

That is, the logarithm (b) of a number (c) is the power to which one must raise some base (a) to get that number. In Chapter 2, we used 10 as the base. Here we use 2, because of the 2:1 ratio of the octave. Consider the following series of frequencies of pitches we call C:

$$1 \times 32.75 \text{ Hz} = 32.75 \text{ Hz}$$
$$2 \times 32.75 \text{ Hz} = 65.5 \text{ Hz}$$
$$4 \times 32.75 \text{ Hz} = 131 \text{ Hz}$$
$$8 \times 32.75 \text{ Hz} = 262 \text{ Hz}$$
$$16 \times 32.75 \text{ Hz} = 524 \text{ Hz}$$
$$\vdots$$

The series of numbers 1, 2, 4, 8, 16, and so on are all powers of 2:

$$2^0 = 1$$
$$2^1 = 2$$
$$2^2 = 4$$
$$2^3 = 8$$
$$\vdots$$

Note that the exponent gives the number of octaves a given C lies above the lowest C at 32.75 Hz. These exponents can be written as logarithms using 2 as a base:

$$\log_2 1 = 0$$
$$\log_2 2 = 1$$
$$\log_2 4 = 2$$
$$\vdots$$

Hence,

$$\log_2 (32.75/32.75) = \log_2 1 = 0$$
$$\log_2 (65.5/32.75) = \log_2 2 = 1$$
$$\log_2 (131/32.75) = \log_2 4 = 2$$
$$\vdots$$

In general, the number of octaves between two pitches is given by the binary logarithm (that is, the logarithm with base 2) of the ratio of their frequencies. The pitch interval P in octaves between two frequencies f_1 and f_2 is given by

$$P = \log_2(f_2/f_1).$$

Many graphs use a logarithmic coordinates for frequency, so that equal distances on the graph correspond to equal frequency *ratios* (or equal numbers of octaves) rather than equal frequency *differences*. Figure 4.3 presents pitch in octaves as a function of frequency, first with a linear frequency coordinate (A) and then a logarithmic frequency coordinate (B). The piano keyboard resembles (B)—equal distances along the keyboard represent equal frequency ratios, no matter where along the keyboard one is.

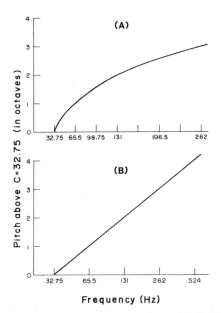

Figure 4.3 The pitch scale on linear (A) and logarithmic (B) coordinates.

Since all the octaves represent equal ratios of frequency, then all the semitones must represent equal ratios as well. This is because each octave contains 12 equal semitones. If we start with an octave C–C′ and move up 1 semitone to the octave C♯–C♯′, we still must have a 2:1 frequency ratio. Here we added a semitone at the top of the octave. In order to preserve the 2:1 ratio of the C♯–C♯′ octave, the semitone we added must have twice as large a frequency difference as the one we took away, as can be seen in Figure 4.2. Both semitones represent a constant 5.9% increase in frequency—to increase pitch by 1 semitone we multiply frequency by 1.059. The number 1.059 arises because it is the twelfth root of 2:

$$2^{\frac{1}{12}} = 1.0594631 \ldots$$

If we start on any pitch and go up to 12 semitones, we reach a pitch one octave higher, a 2:1 frequency ratio. This comes out even if for each semitone increase, we multiply the frequency by $2^{\frac{1}{12}}$, since $(2^{\frac{1}{12}})^{12}$ is just 2. For example, start with middle C (262 Hz) and multiply by $2^{\frac{1}{12}}$ to get C♯:

$$f_C = 262 \text{ Hz} \times 2^{\frac{1}{12}} = 277 \text{ Hz}.$$

To get D, multiply the frequency of C by $2^{\frac{1}{12}}$:

$$f_D = f_{C♯} \times 2^{\frac{1}{12}} = 262 \text{ Hz} \times 2^{\frac{1}{12}} \times 2^{\frac{1}{12}} = 262 \text{ Hz} \times (2^{\frac{1}{12}})^2 = 294 \text{ Hz},$$

and so on. We reach C′ after doing this twelve times, so

$$f_{C'} = 262 \text{ Hz} \times (2^{\frac{1}{12}})^{12} = 262 \text{ Hz} \times 2 = 524 \text{ Hz}.$$

You can work all this out on your handy pocket calculator, and we recommend playing with the calculation of various frequencies of pitches and intervals to familiarize yourself with the scale patterns involved.

Most of the cultures of the world do not use equal-tempered tuning as a basis of their tonal scale systems; that is, they do not use the fourth constraint. They do, however, base their scales on the octave, and that is sufficient to produce a logarithmic scale of frequency. In the above argument concerning the overlapping octaves C–C′ and C♯–C♯′, we could replace C with any arbitrarily chosen pitch X between C and C′ and get the same result. That is, the frequency ratio $f_{X'}/f_{C'}$ has to equal the ratio f_X/f_C. This follows since the X's being one octave apart, fall in a 2:1 frequency ratio. Thus, on a logarithmic scale of frequency, the interval $X–X'$ will equal the interval C–C′, and the interval C–X will equal the interval C′–X'. In most cultures, the note X will be at some interval to C that cannot be expressed as a whole number of semitones.

There are further constraints that often operate on the selection of pitches in tonal scales whether the constraint of equal temperament is operating or not. (In what follows, we use the term *scale* to refer to the sort of tonal scale used in melodies, as distinct from the chromatic scale of all semitones, for example.) First, we might want a scale to contain a variety of intervals. Scales with only one logarithmic interval size between successive pitches do not afford as much possibility for melodic variation as do scales with more different interval sizes. This is apparent in even a simple tune like "Three Blind Mice" (Figure 4.4). Note that the second pair of phrases repeats the contour of the first pair, but with a subtle change of logarithmic interval size (Figure 4.4a). If we were to make all the intervals of uniform size, it would destroy some of the interest of the tune (Figure 4.4b). In Western music, the scale in which all intervals are 2 semitones is called the *whole-tone* scale. Some composers

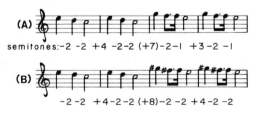

Figure 4.4 "Three Blind Mice" with contour and semitone intervals: (A) familiar version; (B) version using whole tone scale, in which all intervals are equal to 2 semitones.

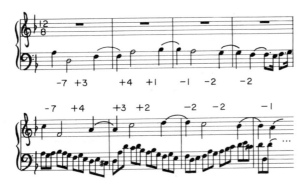

Figure 4.5 The opening of J. S. Bach's *Contrapunctus XIV* from *The Art of the Fugue.*

(e.g., Debussy in the 1890s) have experimented with its use, but the consensus among musicians is that it fails to offer enough intervallic variety to qualify as anything more than a novelty.

The use of the variety of intervals that arise when a thematic contour is moved up and down the scale is particularly apparent in the relationship of a tonal answer to the initial subject in a fugue. The start of a fugue is constructed like the start of a canon or "round" (e.g., "Frère Jacques"), with one part starting out alone with the subject and then continuing with an accompanying line while a second part enters with the subject. Sometimes this second part presents a literal transposition of the subject to a new key, preserving all its logarithmic interval sizes. But in other fugues, the second presentation of the subject is translated along the tonal scale in the same key as the initial presentation, preserving its contour but resulting in a change of its logarithmic interval sizes. Figure 4.5 shows the beginning of "Contrapunctus XIV" from Bach's *The Art of Fugue,* in which the second appearance of the subject varies from the first in its intervallic detail, providing a certain amount of melodic interest. (In fact, the answer changes the mode from minor to major, a contrast Bach plays upon throughout the rest of the fugue.)

Another aspect of the requirement of variety—one that appears only in an equal-tempered tuning system—is what we might call intervallic completeness. Consider the pentatonic scale shown in Figure 4.6. (The interval pattern is the same as that of the black notes on the piano, and it is very similar to the scales used in Chinese, Tibetan, American Indian, and Celtic folksongs.) Under the scale, the possible intervals are diagrammed. Note that only 8 interval sizes (measured in semitones) smaller than an octave occur, out of the 11 intervals that are possible when all the pitches of the chromatic scale are used. There are intervals available in the tem-

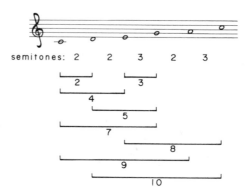

Figure 4.6   A pentatonic scale, with instances of its possible interval sizes within the octave.

pered tuning system of semitones that the pentatonic scale does not use (namely, intervals of 1, 6, and 11 semitones). Thus the pentatonic scale, though it provides considerable variety of intervals, does not provide the greatest variety possible in the semitone system. Balzano (1980) has shown that the smallest number of pitches that provide all of the possible intervals is seven. Figure 4.7 shows that, in fact, the major scale of seven pitches contains all the intervals.

One possibly desirable property of a melodic scale that applies to all systems, equal-tempered or not, is what Balzano (1980) calls coherence. Note that for both the pentatonic and the major scale, all intervals of two scale steps (as measured in semitones) are larger than any interval of one scale step, all three-step intervals are larger than any two-step interval, and so on. Such scales are called coherent. In scales not based on semi-

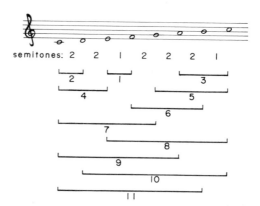

Figure 4.7   The C-major scale, with instances of its possible interval sizes.

"semitones": 3   I   I

Figure 4.8   The ancient Greek chromatic mode.

tone intervals, coherence requires that logarithmic interval size increase with scale-step interval size with no reversals (namely, small logarithmic intervals containing more scale steps than larger logarithmic intervals). Most of the scales in the world exhibit coherence in this sense. Exceptions occur in lyre tunings from ancient Greece (Boring, 1929; Grout, 1960). Figure 4.8 shows the chromatic tuning system described by Aristoxenus (a pupil of Aristotle in the fourth century B.C.). Note that the scale is not coherent in that there is a 3-semitone interval containing one scale step, and a 2-semitone interval containing two scale steps. Coherence seems to be desirable in terms of Helmholtz's "mental measurement of pitch changes" approach, but it is clearly not so essential as to be universally present.

At this point, we can add two more optional constraints to our list of requirements that often figure in the determination of scale structure:

5. maximizing intervallic variety (completeness), and
6. preserving coherence of large and small interval sizes.

CROSS-CULTURAL EVIDENCE

The account given above of the relationship of the psychological dimension of pitch to the physical dimension of frequency is the one that, after weighing the evidence, we prefer to the various alternatives. The main reason for preferring this logarithmic system is its basis in the octave. People are very precise at making octave judgments of successive tones. Further, both musicians and nonmusicians can transpose logarithmic intervals along the scale without distortion, so long as the intervals are part of a familiar tune such as the NBC chimes (Attneave and Olson, 1971). This precision in using octaves and other logarithmic intervals seems nearly universal to all the cultures of the world, even to the extent of agreement on particular kinds of deviation from exact 2:1 frequency ratios for the octave. The evidence comes from both laboratory experiments and instrument tunings.

When adjusting successive tones to a subjective octave, listeners produce a "stretch" in the size of the octave, amounting to about 0.15 semitone in the midrange, or a ratio of about 2.009:1. The amount of stretching increases markedly in the higher registers. In Ward's (1954) study, although listeners differed somewhat among themselves, each individual was quite self-consistent, and Ward was able to develop a coherent (and essentially logarithmic) pitch scale based on their stretched octaves. (All we need to do is to use a semitone based on the twelfth root of 2.009). Figure 4.9 combines data from Ward (1954) and Walliser (1969) to show cumulative deviations of octaves from a 2:1 ratio over a four-octave range. The best confirmation Ward got for this stretched-octave scale was from one of his listeners who had absolute pitch. That listener's scale, based on her octave matches, agreed almost perfectly with her scale based on adjustments of isolated tones to match her internalized scale of note names.

Pianos are tuned with stretched octaves, but the stretch is only about half that found for subjective tuning of successive pitches. The stretch in piano tunings is due to the fact that piano strings, being somewhat stiff and not ideally flexible, have upper partials that are sharp (high in frequency) in comparison with integer-ratio harmonics. As would be expected from the discussion of tonal consonance in Chapter 3, simultaneous tone combinations on the piano sound best when the fundamentals of upper notes are tuned to coincide with the slightly sharp partials of

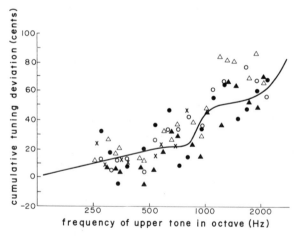

Figure 4.9 Data from octave judgments of Western listeners (solid line: from Ward, 1954, & Walliser, 1969) plotted with tuning measurements from non-Western instruments. X, Burmese harp (Williamson, 1968); circles, *gamelan sléndro*, triangles, *gamelan pélog;* open symbols from Surjodiningrat, Sudarjana, and Susanto, 1969; filled symbols from Hood, 1966. The abscissa represents deviations in cents (hundredths of a semitone) from octaves with 2:1 frequency ratios. (After Dowling, 1978.)

lower notes. This stretch is most pronounced where the relative stiffness of the strings is greatest, due to relative large ratios of diameter to length, namely, in the highest and lowest octaves (Martin & Ward, 1961; Young, 1952). That Western musicians adhere to the larger stretch of the subjective octave described above, rather than gravitate toward the smaller stretch of the familiar piano, strongly supports the argument for the inherent nature of the stretched octave for successive tones.

The adjustment of successive tones to stretched octaves has been replicated with non-Western listeners (Burns, 1974) and is reflected in numerous non-Western patterns of musical instrument tuning. Figure 4.9 shows data from all the precise measurements of tunings of instruments in actual use that we could find. The data definitely cluster around Ward's (1954) octave-judgment curve rather than the baseline. (The baseline represents octaves tuned to an exact 2:1 ratio.) It is essential that data like these be drawn from instruments in current use. Much of the literature on non-Western tunings derives from measurements on museum instruments long out of use. It is obvious that the tunings of stringed instruments would deteriorate rapidly over time. What is not so obvious is that seemingly more robust instruments such as the marimba- and xylophone-like instruments of the Indonesian *gamelan* also lose their tuning over time. Bronze keys need continual tuning adjustment (by filing) as the molecular structure of the metal gradually changes. Wooden keys can be tuned by filing or adding lumps of clay (adding and subtracting mass; see Chapter 2), with the obvious difficulty that the clay might fall off and disrupt the tuning. The resonator tubes of marimba-type (*gender*) instruments are tuned by changing the diameter of the hole in the top of the tube and by filling them with pebbles or sand to the appropriate length, an adjustment that is lost if the instrument is upended.

Most of the data in Figure 4.9 are from Indonesian *gamelan* tunings. It should not be supposed that the variability around Ward's curve represents a more or less ineffectual attempt by the Indonesian musician to match the stretched-octave pitch scale. The variability around the curve is intentional and results from the unique tunings of the various sets of instruments involving the stretching and compression of certain intervals in certain octaves, an effect we discuss below. It is clear from the account of vibrato-producing beats in the paired tunings of Balinese *gamelans* that the instrument makers are capable of achieving considerable precision in tuning. What is clear from Figure 4.9 is that, whatever tuning deviations are introduced, they occur as deviations from a stretched-octave curve and not from 2:1 octaves. (These deviations are small relative to the intervals between pitches in the tonal scales and so do not violate the principle of repetition of scale pattern within each octave.)

Another difficulty with the literature on instrument tunings is a bias on the part of many early investigators to find octaves with 2:1 frequency ratios. This, coupled with the imprecision of measuring instruments, led to more reports of 2:1 octaves than we would expect just from the normal variability of tuning and measurement. Ellis' appendixes to his English translation of Helmholtz (1877/1954) are full of such observations. This bias is very similar to the bias we are about to discuss concerning the establishment of tuning systems on patterns of small-integer frequency ratios.

ALTERNATIVE ACCOUNTS

Along with our preferred logarithmic scale, we need to present two common alternative accounts of pitch scaling and our reasons for rejecting them. One of these accounts comes from the psychophysical scaling tradition of psychology and claims that pitch is related to frequency, not by a logarithmic, but by a power function. The second comes from a numerological tradition in musicology and claims that all the intervals of a tonal scale are (or should be) derivable from small-integer ratios.

Psychophysical Scales

We are claiming that the relationship between pitch and frequency is logarithmic. The most serious alternative relationship, proposed by Stevens (Stevens & Volkmann, 1940), is that of a power function. While the logarithmic function describes correspondences between *additive* pitch increments (semitones and octaves) and frequency *ratios* (Figure 4.3), the power function describes correspondences between pitch *ratios* and frequency *ratios*. In constructing his pitch scale, Stevens used scaling methods similar to those described in Chapter 2 for the sone scale of loudness. For example, he had listeners perform magnitude estimation tasks in which they judged pitch by estimating how many times higher one note sounded than another. (That is, a pitch twice as high should receive a number twice as large.) Stevens calls his unit of pitch the mel, and his mel scale is shown in Figure 4.10, in which both pitch and frequency coordinates are logarithmic. If a power function were really appropriate, then Figure 4.10 would show a straight line relating pitch ratios to frequency ratios. The function is more or less straight in the midrange but breaks down especially in the high register. But the fact that the mel scale is not a power function should not bother us unduly. It might have been a useful function even if it curved (as it does). However, there are more serious

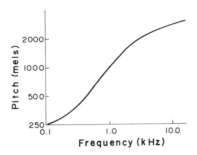

Figure 4.10 Stevens' mel scale for pitch.

reasons for rejecting the mel scale in favor of the octave scale as a psychophysical scale for pitch.

The main reason we prefer the logarithmic octave scale is that people are very precise at making octave judgments and very imprecise at the kinds of judgments required by magnitude estimation. As Ward (1970, p. 412) comments, "Measuring pitch in mels . . . is analogous to pacing off a room for wall to wall carpeting when a steel measuring tape is handy." Both musicians and nonmusicians are precise in making octave judgments for tones presented successively. Further, even with methods very similar to those used by Stevens, results emerge that support the logarithmic pitch scale, at least below 2000 Hz. Null (1974) used both the method of bisection (in which listeners adjust a comparison tone so that it falls midway in pitch between two standards) and a modified magnitude-estimation task. With both methods and both for musicians and for nonmusicians, the logarithmic scale gave a good fit to the data. (But for a dissenting view, see Schneider, Parker, & Upenieks, 1982).

Integer Ratios

A second source of doubts about the logarithmic pitch scale presented here is the musicologist who believes that the intervals of the scale derive from ratios of small whole numbers. For example, Bernstein (1976), in an otherwise admirable book, carries this approach to extremes. We reject this view for several reasons. First, musicians' intonation in practice is best described as an approximation of the tempered tuning system we have been describing (Ward, 1970). The exception to this rule is when small groups play or sing slow passages and have the opportunity to adjust their intonation to small-integer ratios, producing the effects of consonance discussed in Chapter 3. But that practice arose (in the West, at least) only after the development of polyphony and, hence, long after the development of the scale systems. Further, expectations of melodic direction can override the requirements of integer-ratio tuning, as in the case of a sharpened leading tone (seventh scale degree) resolving to a tonic. Insisting on integer ratios (just intonation) that run counter to such dynamic tendencies can be musically disastrous. Rosen (1972, p. 28) notes: "I once heard a quartet play [a certain passage] in just intonation with horrible effect. This is not to say that string players play, or should play, in strict equal temperament: pitch is always subtly altered, but for expressive reasons which have little to do with just intonation."

A second reason to reject integer ratios as a basis of melodic scales is that the supposedly simplest ratio, the octave, does not occur in its pure 2:1 ratio in listeners' adjustments of successive tones. People all over the world stretch the octave by about the same amount, suggesting that the stretched, and not the 2:1, octave is what is built into the human auditory system. Third, it is clear from the history of Western music since 1600 that musicians have found that the advantages for musical practice afforded by tempered tuning far outweigh the disadvantages. This would not be true if integer-ratio tuning had the overriding importance sometimes claimed for it.

It is important to realize that the approaches of both equal-temperament and small-integer ratios arise from attempts to rationalize existing traditional melodic scales. Small-integer systems were the earlier of the two to arise, and equal temperament arose in turn as an answer to musical problems raised by small-integer systems. The importance of small-integer ratios was realized more than 2000 years ago in both China and Greece (Boring, 1929; McClain, 1979), but, of course, the ratios that were measured were not ratios of frequencies (since the ancients did not know about frequency) but rather ratios of the lengths of vibrating bodies: strings (in Greece) or air columns (in China). Musicians in those cultures noticed the practical value of tuning the pitches of the scale so that certain simultaneous combinations of them sounded especially consonant, as discussed in Chapter 3. They noticed also that these consonant intervals arose from strings and pitch pipes having small-integer ratios of length (e.g., the fifth produced by a 3:2 ratio). They then tried to extend the system to derive the pitches of other keys than the one they started with. Such a project was important in second century B.C. China, for example, since each of the 12 keys had come to be associated with a month of the year (Nakaseko, 1957).

Here the early acousticians ran into a problem. A pure 3:2 ratio for the fifth and a pure 2:1 ratio for the octave cannot exist in the same scale. If we generate a cycle of fifths using 3:2 ratios, we use all 12 pitches without repeating: C–G–D–A–E–B–F♯–C♯–G♯–D♯–A♯–E♯(close to F). If we carry that one step further, we should arrive on a C seven octaves above the one we started with. But unfortunately, the twelfth power of $3:2$ is larger than the seventh power of 2, and so the C arrived at by the cycle of fifths will have a different pitch from the C obtained by a cycle of octaves. The difference becomes gradually more pronounced as we progress around the cycle of fifths, so that intonation differences between instruments tuned to play in one key and those tuned to play in another become more noticeable. (Imagine an instrument with a scale based on the A$\sharp$ in the above cycle of fifths playing a C simultaneously with an instrument tuned to the original C.) The compromise represented by equal temperament can be seen as an agreement to hold firmly to the $2:1$ ratio for the octave, making the frequency ratio for the fifth somewhat smaller than $3:2$, namely, $2^{\frac{7}{12}}$.

In summary, the tempered logarithmic tuning system used in Western music is the result of compromises among a variety of constraints arising from the human auditory system, people's cognitive capabilities, and the requirements of musical interest. We turn now to elaborations of the system that reflect further features of human cognition.

MULTIDIMENSIONAL APPROACHES

So far we have been considering the construction of a psychophysical scale for pitch in terms of the two dimensions of pitch and frequency. But there is good reason to believe that pitch is not well represented by just one subjective dimension. Miller's (1956) argument to which we alluded above under the third constraint suggests that along any psychological dimension, the greatest number of categories we can use reliably is about seven. But a musician working within a tonal framework can use many more pitch categories than that. The musician can label the notes of the tonal scale (do, re, mi, etc.) and also tell which octave they came from. Across five octaves, that amounts to using about 36 categories consistently. Thus, if Miller's magic number of 7 ± 2 holds for pitch, there must be more than one cognitive dimension involved.

The intuitions of musicians also suggest that there are at least two dimensions to musical pitch. Pitches can be similar in two principle ways: They can be near each other in pitch, falling in the same general frequency range, and they can be similar in occupying the same place in their respective octaves. Two tones an octave apart (two C's, for example) are similar and are said to have the same chroma. A C and a D may lie next to each other in frequency and may be said to have similar *pitch height*. Figure 4.11 represents these two kinds of similarity by means of a spiral. Tones

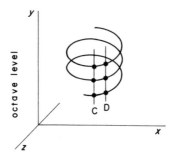

Figure 4.11 Helical model of the pitch scale.

of similar chroma are arranged in the same vertical column, and each turn of the spiral represents an increase in pitch of one octave. Tones similar in pitch height are adjacent to each other along the spiral and project onto adjacent points on the spiral's axis.

The independence of chroma and pitch height can be readily demonstrated with a piano. Start by playing the four highest C's on the piano. Then move down almost an octave and play four D's. Continue dropping by sevenths, playing the notes of an ascending C-major scale. You can hear both the descending series of pitch heights and the ascending series of chromas. Shepard (1964) constructed a more formal demonstration of this independence by creating a pattern in which chroma continuously changes while pitch height remains the same. Shepard's pattern (Figure 4.12 and Example 4a) consists of 10 sine-wave components spaced at octave intervals. The components in the middle of the frequency range are more intense than those on the ends—the top and bottom components would be barely audible if presented alone. Following presentation of 10

4a

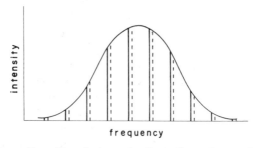

Figure 4.12 Shepard's auditory barber pole, illustrating a change of chroma without a change of tone height. Dashed lines indicate an upward shift in frequency of all components. (After Shepard, 1964.)

C's, the pattern shifts to 10 C#'s (dotted lines in the figure). As the components shift up, those below the middle of the frequency range increase in intensity and those above the middle decrease, leaving the overall intensity envelope centered on the same frequency. The pattern sounds as though it has shifted up in pitch, though only the chromas have changed. The distribution of intensities across the frequency range has not changed. A succession of such changes sounds like a continuously rising pitch, which can be continued indefinitely—a sort of auditory barber pole. The listener can follow the rising pitch only so far, of course, after which it jumps down before starting up again. Burns (1981) has shown that this demonstration works even when the components are spaced at intervals somewhat larger or smaller than the octave. Burns's finding does not necessarily mean that tones an octave apart are not equivalent, however, but only that in such cases, pitch height is the overriding dimension.

In his opera *Wozzeck* (act 3, scene 4), Alban Berg used an effect similar to Shepard's—a continuously rising scale orchestrated so that as the upper instruments reached the top of their compass and dropped out, lower instruments entered at the bottom with the rising pattern. This creates an eery effect appropriate to the nightmare quality of the scene—Wozzeck searching the dark pond for the murder weapon. Berg's effect is not simply tacked on, but grows organically out of the musical structure of the scene. Ascending scales play an important thematic role in this part of the opera, leading to their striking use at the end of the scene.

The spiral in Figure 4.11 represents two aspects that are important in people's understanding of pitch: the close relationship of tones adjacent in the scale and the similarity of tones an octave apart. In accomplishing that representation, we have allowed the physical dimension of frequency to sink into the background. In fact, we could eliminate the frequency dimension entirely, and Figure 4.11 would still be a good representation of the psychological relationships among pitches. It would no longer be a psycho*physical* representation, but rather a multidimensional representation of mental structure. It could represent, for example, the pattern of judgments that listeners produce when judging the similarity of pairs of tones. The similarity judgments could be used to generate a model of the listener's cognitive structure of pitch relationships by means of multidimensional scaling techniques (discussed in Chapter 3). A computer program would take the similarity judgments and try to find a spatial arrangement of the pitches such that more similar pitches would lie closer together and less similar pitches farther apart. The program follows a trial-and-error procedure to search for a pattern that does the least violence to the similarity judgments in the data. The theoretical question is, Will the results of multidimensional scaling correspond to our intuitions concerning the mental structure as shown in Figure 4.11?

Krumhansl (1979) presents some evidence bearing on this issue. Krumhansl played listeners a major triad, establishing the framework of a tonality. Then she played them a pair of notes, and they judged the similarity of the two notes within the tonal framework. The pattern of similarity judgments led to a multidimensional scaling solution in which the pitches were grouped in three more or less concentric rings. The two inner rings contained the pitches of the major scale arranged in order of chroma around a half circle, and the outer ring contained the pitches not included in the major scale arranged so each was closest to its nearest neighbor in the scale. Similarity judgments thus lend partial support to the notion that one component of a multidimensional representation of pitch might be the ordered set of tone chromas arranged around a circle.

Krumhansl and Shepard (1979) collected data of a somewhat different sort. They presented listeners with a major scale minus its last note—the tonic at either the bottom or top. Instead of the tonic, they ended the scale with another pitch in the octave beyond the end of the scale. The listener was asked to judge how good that pitch was as a completion of the scale. This data, too, could be analyzed by multidimensional scaling techniques. Listeners differed in the degree to which chroma (vs. tone height) influenced their judgments, with musically more experienced persons basing their judgments more on chroma. In this study, too, the circle of pitch chromas compatible with the helix of Figure 4.11 appeared. Shepard (1982b) derived a multidimensional scaling solution from this data in which (viewed from one direction) the pitches are arranged chromatically around a circle and in which the tone-height difference between the top and bottom notes is represented by a gap where the circle fails to close. The same solution viewed from another direction shows the pitches arranged as a circle of fifths (C, G, D, A, E, B, F♯, C♯, G♯, D♯, A♯, F, C′) with the C's an octave apart occupying the same position. The circle of fifths represents some important structural properties in the organization of musical pitch. One reason for its importance arises from the central importance of the interval of the fifth itself within the scale, approximating as it does a 3:2 frequency ratio. Another feature of the circle of fifths is that by slicing it through with a straight line, one can separate the seven pitches of a given major scale from the other five pitches. Thus it can be used to represent the close relationship of the pitches of a scale versus the extraneous pitches.

Shepard (1982a, 1982b) took such considerations as the foregoing into account in constructing an idealized model of the psychological structure of musical pitch incorporating two intertwined spirals. This double helix model is shown in Figure 4.13A. In the double helix, each link along the curve of a spiral represents a whole step (2 semitones). Each link across

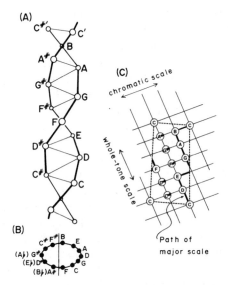

Figure 4.13 (A) Shepard's double helix representation of the cognitive structure of musical pitch. Note that the pattern projects downward onto the circle of fifths (B). (C) The double helix unwrapped onto a plane. (After Shepard, 1982.)

the model from one spiral to the other represents a half step (1 semitone). The vertical dimension in the model is simply tone height, and one could climb an ascending chromatic scale by tracing the sequence of links back and forth between the spirals. Imagine that the model is standing on its end (just as shown) in the middle of the floor and we dropped a ribbon from each node to the floor, with the label of the node at the bottom. Each ribbon extended upward to the ceiling would pass through a series of tones having the same label and lying at octave intervals from each other. The pattern of node labels on the floor is the circle of fifths (Figure 4.13B). Just as noted above, we could draw a line through the circle of fifths dividing the seven notes of a major scale from the others. In Figure 4.13C this has been done for the C-major scale. And the plane rising vertically from that line into the double helix (among the ribbons) would then slice off the notes of that scale. Such a plane also would separate out the pitches of the commonest sort of pentatonic scale as well.

The circle of fifths is important for another reason that we explore more fully in Chapter 5: It expresses the psychological difference between musical keys, or key distance. If we take the plane that divides the notes of a given scale from the other notes and rotate it around the vertical axis by one notch (adding one note and deleting one note), we get a scale in a new key that is very similar to the one we started with. That is, the new key shares all but one of its pitches with the old key. However, if we rotate the plane several notches around the circle of fifths, we get a key that shares fewer notes with the first. Such a key is said to be distant from the first key. Krumhansl, Bharucha, and Castellano (1982) have demonstrated the psychological reality of key distance using listeners' judgments of chordal patterns. In Chapter 5, we present evidence that key distance is a very important factor in judgments of melodic similarity.

Now imagine that the double helix is one of those cookie rollers that imprints a repeating pattern on a flat surface of cookie dough. As we roll it across the surface, the pattern of pitches is "unwrapped" onto the plane as shown in Figure 4.13b. Now the major scale that we sliced off with the vertical plane becomes a zig-zag path. The chromatic scale of half steps is a straight line, as is the whole-tone scale. In addition to capturing the significance of the octave, the circle of fifths, and the major scale, Shepard's model also captures the fact that in context, the different-sized intervals of the major scale are heard as psychologically equal. This is represented by equal distances for both half and whole steps, with the contextual difference represented by difference of direction. The beauty of Shepard's double helix lies in its success in capturing succinctly several important facts of pitch perception in one coherent structure.

We want to emphasize that the structure in Figure 4.13 is a model designed to express certain relationships that listeners perceive among pitches. This does not mean the structure need literally be stored in the brain but only that the relationships it expresses have analogs in brain structure. Note also that a structure like this has no intrinsic implications for psychological processes such as perceiving, judging, and remembering. Different aspects of the structure will become dominant, depending on the task we give the listener in an experiment. We return in Chapter 5 to the effect of task on the listener's perception and behavior.

Before we leave the multidimensional scaling of pitch, we quote Krumhansl and Shepard (1979) in a statement that expresses some significant truths concerning research with musical phenomena. They suggest that multidimensional scaling approaches can be used to disclose individual differences among listeners as well as differences due to the auditory context in which judgments are made.

> To the extent that tones differing in frequency are not interpreted as musical stimuli—because they are presented in isolation from a musical context, because the tones themselves are stripped of harmonic content, or because they are played to musically unsophisticated listeners—the most potent factor governing their perceived relations is simply their separation along a one-dimensional continuum of pitch–height. To the extent that tones are interpreted musically—because they are embedded in a musical context, because they are rich in overtones, and because

they are played to musically sophisticated listeners—simple physical separation in log frequency gives way to structurally more complex factors, including octave equivalence or its psychological counterpart, tone chroma, and a hierarchy of tonal functions specific to the tonality induced by the context. (p. 529)

SCALES IN OTHER CULTURES

The set of pitches in Shepard's model we have just discussed is specific to Western music. We cannot expect the details of its double helix to apply directly to non-Western scale systems. For example, the circle of fifths, a very strong structural element in Western music and a central component of the model, does not play nearly so great a role in non-Western musical systems. However, the more basic structural properties that went into the construction of the logarithmic psychophysical scale for pitch (Figure 4.3) and the single helix expressing octave equivalence (Figure 4.11) seem to us to be quite generally applicable to most of the musical systems throughout the world. This is because nearly all cultures use logarithmic pitch scales in which octave equivalence plays a central role. Those cultures that cannot be said to use such a model do not use an alternative model, but rather use such restricted melodic patterns that the form of their scales beyond the range of one octave is moot. Thus, for nearly all the cultures of the world, the helix of Figure 4.11 represents the underlying psychophysical organization of pitch material. Pitches an octave apart are treated as functionally equivalent in melodies, though each culture fills in the pattern of pitches within the octave in its own way. (In what follows, we discuss scale structure in terms of sets of pitches. For many purposes, the equivalent description in terms of intervals would be more appropriate, since in most cases the anchoring of a pitch label to a specific frequency (as in A = 440 Hz) is irrelevant to both the psychological structure and the culture being discussed. We simply use the pitch-set description for convenience.)

There are certain regularities in the way a culture fills in the octave and in the way it uses pitches in melodies that are best disclosed by considering melodic scales to be constructed out of the underlying tonal material through a process involving several levels of psychological analysis (Dowling, 1978b, 1982c). These levels, shown in Figure 4.14, are (1) the underlying *psychophysical pitch function* that assigns pitches to frequencies, (2) the *tonal material* consisting of all the possible pitches that could be used in melodies, (3) the *tuning system* consisting of a subset of the pitches in the tonal material that could be used as the basis of a variety of modal scales, and (4) the *modal scale* in which the pitches of a tuning

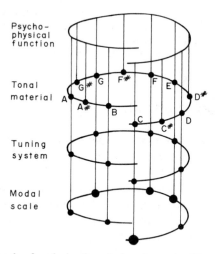

Figure 4.14 Levels of analysis of musical scales, using Western pitch labels.

system are hierarchically organized with a tonal center (tonic) and are used in actual melodies. (Hood, 1971, presents a similar approach that differs from this one in some details.)

Each of these four levels of analysis is formed by making a selection of pitches out of the next higher level or by imposing some constraint on them. The levels progress from the highly abstract psychophysical scale, containing all possible pitches, to the very concrete modal scale, in which the pitches are the actual pitches of melodies. There is good evidence for the psychological reality of these levels, both from the analyses of music theorists in a number of cultures and from laboratory experiments in our own culture. We review these laboratory experiments in Chapter 5. Here we present the theoretical bases of this outline.

Figure 4.14 is constructed in terms of the Western scale system, since that is the most familiar for us and is likely to be familiar to our readers. In it the tonal material consists of all the notes on the piano—the chromatic scale of 12 steps to the octave. The tuning system consists of a selection of 7 out of those 12 pitches—the white notes on the piano that can form the basis of various modal scales. The tuning system is more abstract than any of the modal scales formed from it in that it contains a cyclic pattern of intervals without any specified point of origin. Selecting a point of origin in the tuning system amounts to choosing a specific modal scale (C major in Figure 4.14). In some cultures, the construction of a modal scale out of the tuning system involves the omission of certain pitches as well. Modal scales are the most concrete level in the scheme and involve not only the selection of the pitches of melodies, but also the imposition of a tonal hierarchy that shapes the listener's expectations.

Tonal Material

In many cultures, the number of pitches that are potentially available in all melodies exceeds the number that might actually appear in a single melody. This larger set we call tonal material. Tonal material is the level at which the undifferentiated continuum of the psychophysical scale is divided into discrete categories. In Western music the tonal material consists of the pitches of the chromatic scale, as discussed above. North Indian music provides a good illustration of the use of a level for tonal material. The North Indian octave can be divided into 12 more or less equal steps, and the tonal material divides into a set of two pitches a perfect fifth apart that function as the first and fifth degrees of every modal scale, plus a set of five pitches each of which can appear in either a higher or a lower variant (Jairazbhoy, 1971). The pitches of the tonal material are shown in quasi-Western notation in Figure 4.15. C is used as a point of origin here, but that should not be taken as fixing the pitch level; nor should the Western pitches be taken as anything more than rough approximations of the actual pitches used.

Tuning System

In Western music, we use basically one tuning system corresponding to the interval pattern of the white notes on the piano (see Figure 4.2). This tuning system should not be thought of as having a fixed pitch, however, but rather as capable of sliding up and down. That is, we could recreate the same interval pattern by starting with any pitch on the piano. And we could also create it by singing the same interval pattern beginning with any pitch whatsoever, whether on the piano or not. The interval pattern between successive notes is, in semitones, 2, 2, 1, 2, 2, 2, 1 (see Figure 4.7).

In North Indian music, too, we should conceive of the tuning system as an interval set rather than as a series of fixed pitches. The five varying

Figure 4.15 The tonal material of North Indian music. *Sa, Re, Ga* . . . corresponds to do, re, mi. . . . Brackets denote pairs of pitches of which only one member typically appears in a scale.

Figure 4.16 Three North Indian tuning systems generated by making different selections from the tonal material.

pitch categories from the tonal material (*re, ga, ma, dha, ni*), each of which can take one of two values, generate $2^5 = 32$ *possible* scale frameworks or tuning systems. In addition, there are three patterns in which the F—*ma*—can appear in both natural and sharp forms, giving a total of 35 possible tuning systems. Of these 35, 10 are in common use, and about 10 more are used occasionally. Figure 4.16 gives some examples of tuning system scales (Sanskrit *that*, "framework," pronounced "taht") generated from the tonal material of Figure 4.15. The level of tuning system is especially useful here, since the pitch series of a *that* does not typically appear intact as a modal scale.

Modal Scales

A modal scale is created from a tuning system by imposing a structural hierarchy on the set of pitches. In its simplest form, this structure designates some tones as more important than others (some may drop out entirely) and establishes dynamic patterns of expectation concerning where pitches might not lead in a melodic sequence. At present, Western music relies primarily on two modal scales: major and minor. These are generated from the intervals of the tuning system by taking different starting points in the cycle of intervals (Figure 4.17). Any of the 12 pitches in the tonal material can be taken as a starting point for either mode, giving 24 major and minor keys.

A complication arises in the case of the minor mode as it has been used since the seventeenth century. Melodies in the minor often use a different set of pitches for ascending and descending (Figure 4.18). The descending series is the same as in Figure 4.17, but the ascending series is more like the major mode starting on the same pitch in that the sixth and seventh degrees of the scale are raised. An intermediate form, in which only the seventh degree is raised both ascending and descending, also occurs. In

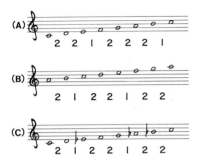

Figure 4.17 Major (A) and minor (B) modal scales in Western music, with intervals shown in semitones. (C) illustrates the generation of the minor mode starting on the pitch C using the interval sequence of (C). The flat (♭) lowers the pitch by 1 semitone.

terms of the conceptual scheme of Figure 4.14, it seems most convenient to introduce these alternate pitches by dipping directly into the tonal material, that is, not by including them in the tuning system.

In Western music through the early 1600s, there were four additional modes available besides the major and minor: those beginning on the second, third, fourth, and fifth steps of the white-note pattern (Figure 4.19). Of these modes, the Dorian and Phrygian are most likely to be encountered today. A common version of the tune "Greensleeves" (Figure 4.20A) is largely in the Dorian, though this tune is often assimilated to the modern minor mode by lowering the sixth degree of the scale (B♭ for B in Figure 4.20A). Phrygian tunes are rarer. One of the more familiar is the old hymn "Oh Haupt voll Blut und Wunden," which appeared as a popular song in the 1960s. Bach used this tune extensively, but by the early eighteenth century, the Phrygian was a very old-fashioned mode. Of five harmonizations by Bach given in Riemenschneider (1941), only one takes the Phrygian tonic (E in Figure 4.20B) as the tonic for the harmonization. Three take the sixth degree (C) as the tonic, letting the melody end on the third degree of the final chord. The remaining harmonization is a hybrid of those two approaches.

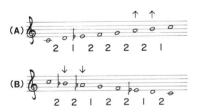

Figure 4.18 Ascending (A) and descending (B) forms of the melodic minor mode. Arrows indicate chromatic alterations.

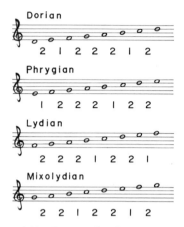

Figure 4.19 Four medieval Western modes.

In turning to a consideration of modal scales in North Indian music, we encounter several complications that are not unusual in non-Western music. First, a mode (Sanskrit *rāg*) includes more than just the pitch series of a modal scale. A *rāg* is associated with a particular aesthetic–affective quality (*rasa*), includes particular melodic phrases and expectations (especially cadence formulas), and is customarily performed at a particular time of day. Second, not only does the modal scale impose a structural hierarchy on the pitches, but modal scales are often "gapped," using only five or six of the pitches available in the *that* tuning system. Further, the

Figure 4.20 Melodies in the keys of (A) D Dorian ("Greensleeves") and (B) E Phrygian ("O Haupt voll Blut und Wuden").

Figure 4.21 Two North Indian scale patterns, based on Figure 4.16A and B, respectively.

type of pattern used in the Western minor mode, where ascending and descending melodic lines use different sets of pitches, is common in North Indian music. In such cases, the descending line is usually taken as a more basic, being involved as it is in cadence patterns at the ends of phrases. Figure 4.21 gives two examples of modal scales, with characteristic directional patterns of melodic lines in the *rāgs* indicated in a sort of shorthand notation, more important notes being given longer time values. *Rāg Des* (Figure 4.21A) is based on *that* of Figure 4.16A. Note that the descending pattern uses seven pitches and contains irregularities in which the first and fourth steps are approached by skips. The ascending pattern is pentatonic (gapped), and the seventh degree is raised. More elaborate examples of chromatic alteration can be seen in *Rāg Ramkali* (Figure 4.21b), based on Figure 4.16b. The ascent is six-toned, while the descent has elaborate turns of phrase involving chromatic alteration of the fourth and seventh degrees.

Indonesian music illustrates some of the same principles as Indian music in the relationship of tuning system and mode, though it possesses unique characteristics. Classical Javanese music has two tuning systems: *pélog* (heptatonic) and *sléndro* (pentatonic). Different sets of instruments in the same *gamelan* are tuned to the two systems, which typically share only one pitch. (The common pitch is useful in occasional modulations from one system to the other in contemporary performances.) Modes in the *pélog* system are created by selecting gapped pentatonic scales from the seven pitches in the system. The term closest to mode is *pathet,* but like the Indian *rāg,* the Javanese *pathet* is as much characterized by particular melodic phrases as by the pitches of its scale (Becker, 1977). In fact, of the three *pathet* in the *pélog* system, two share the same modal scale. All three *pathet* of the *sléndro* system simply use the pentatonic scale of the tuning system pitches. In those cases, characteristic melodic contours are the main distinguishing features of the modes. Unlike the Indian *rāg,* a *pathet* is not associated with a specific *rasa* (affective tone)—there are not enough *pathet* for them to serve that function.

Rather, the classification of *pathet* (at least for the *sléndro* modes) seems to have arisen from the association of particular songs with particular phases of dramatic performances they accompany, in turn associated with particular time periods in the course of an all night performance.

Not only are the two tuning systems of a *gamelan* different from each other, but (as we mentioned in connection with Figure 4.10) each *gamelan* uses different tuning systems from the next, and even within the same *gamelan,* the interval patterns of successive octaves differ in detail. These tuning variations are associated with specific aesthetic qualities. For example, when the interval between the first and second degrees of the tuning system is especially large, the effect is characterized as bright and cheerful, whereas if it is small, the effect is thought to be soft and gentle (Becker, 1977). A particular *gamelan* might thus be thought more apt for playing certain *pathet* than others. Many *gamelans* have proper names that emphasize these affinities. for example, the *gamelan* at the University of Michigan is called Khyai Telaga Madu (Venerable Lake of Honey) because of its "sweet" tuning.

Ornament Tones

There is one remaining class of pitches from the level of tonal material that we have not yet mentioned. Members of this class are what we might call ornament tones. In the music of India especially, there are clusters of small intervals around the notes of the modal scale that can be used to ornament the principle scale pitches with trills and grace notes. The use of these tones, illustrated in Example 4b, has led some to think of Indian music as using microtonal intervals in musical scales. However, as we have seen, the North Indian system of modal scales uses at most seven pitches to the octave, and the additional pitches (15 more in some analyses) appear in a strictly subsidiary role.

Ornament tones also appear in the music of Indonesia. Most instruments of the *gamelan* have a fixed set of five or six or seven pitches to the octave. Vocal soloists, however, are not so restricted. The vocalist can use, as passing tones, pitches from the tuning system omitted from a gapped pentatonic scale by the instruments, as well as introduce microtonal intervals by way of ornament (*surupan*). Players of the bowed two-string spike-fiddle (*rebab*) also follow this practice.

The above outline of levels, going from the abstract and general level of the psychophysical relationship of pitch and frequency to the very specific and concrete level of the selection of actual pitches that occur in actual melodies is found in enough musical cultures to justify according it a certain amount of psychological reality. Additional evidence bearing on this issue appears in Chapter 5. But before leaving pitch scales, we must attend to one more topic.

ABSOLUTE PITCH

No chapter on pitch perception in music would be complete without mention of the phenomenon of absolute pitch—the ability of some individuals to identify the notes of the chromatic scale by name when presented in isolation from other pitches. This ability is a relatively recent development, specific to Western culture, since it is only in the last few hundred years that anything like standard pitches (such as an A of 440 Hz) have come into general use. Ellis (Helmholtz, 1877/1954, Appendix 20, Section H) presents evidence for a fairly wide range of pitch standards in Europe even in the nineteenth century. (Of course pitch standards were in use throughout the history of ancient China, but the standards were customarily changed with the ascent of each new emperor (Needham, 1962). The phenomena associated with absolute pitch cast additional light on some of the main themes of discussion in this chapter: the importance of the octave, the importance of an internalized framework of the scale, and the hierarchical nature of that framework.

The phenomena of absolute pitch have been the focus of heated debate over whether the ability is innate or acquired through musical experience. As Cuddy (1968) points out, the tendency to put the question in all-or-nothing nature–nurture terms gravitates toward the scientifically meaningless, since no matter what experiences a person has, it is impossible to prove that the emergence of absolute pitch was not due to maturation in favorable circumstances rather than to more ordinary processes of learning. In any case, "one can always choose to define absolute pitch so as to exclude all cases where some kind of formal training can be detected" (Cuddy, 1968, p. 1069). It is clear that some factors involved in pitch judgment, both absolute and relative, are very likely innate. (*Relative* pitch involves proficiency at *interval* recognition and production.) The evidence on the importance and pervasiveness of octave generalization suggests such innateness for the primacy of octaves in pitch scales. However, some aspects of absolute pitch abilities cannot be innate, for example, the pairing of note names with frequencies. Although it is clear from the excellent reviews of the subject that are available that absolute pitch is more easily acquired at an early age (Shuter-Dyson & Gabriel, 1981; Ward, 1963), evidence has been accumulating on adults' success in acquiring the ability. This evidence also bears on the question of the psychological structure of pitch scales.

It seems unlikely to us that the ability for absolute pitch is bimodally distributed in the population, that is, that some have it and others do not. It seems more consonant with our experience that people possess the ability in varying degrees and that whether the ability shows up depends on the particular task demands the person faces. Certainly, some of the component abilities necessary to the naming of pitches are present in greater or lesser degree throughout the population (Hurni-Schlegel & Lang, 1978). Terhardt and Ward (1982) found that musicians could discriminate alterations in key of 5-sec excerpts from Bach's *Well-Tempered Clavier*. Their listeners performed well above chance in telling whether each excerpt had been transposed up or down from the original key shown in a score printed on the answer sheet. And nearly everyone possesses a temporally local absolute pitch. That is, after the age of 5 or 6 people are generally able to sing familiar tunes maintaining the same tonic reference pitch throughout; and when the pitch shifts, it is generally to a new consistent frame of reference (Dowling, 1982b). Choir members learn to remember the pitch they just finished singing through all sorts of confusing context in order to enter on that pitch again 20 or 30 sec later. And persons possessing long-term absolute pitch differ in their labeling accuracy, the frequency range over which they can succeed in the labeling task, and the variety of musical instruments for which they can identify pitches. Individuals with good absolute pitch seem to have "stored a limited number of points along the frequency continuum in long-term memory and . . . use this information for classifying current pitch inputs" (Siegel, 1972, p. 86).

It has been clear for many years that training can improve note-naming performance (Ward, 1963), and since the 1960s, more dramatic results have been obtained in adults' acquisition of absolute pitch. Brady (1970) reports his experience teaching himself absolute pitch at the age of 32. He programmed his laboratory computer to produce tapes consisting of a succession of sine waves tuned to different pitches in the chromatic scale. The earlier tapes in the sequence contained high proportions of the pitch C, providing a stable reference point. Brady practiced naming the notes on the tape a half hour a day for two months, receiving feedback after each trial. He avoided trying to solve the task by figuring the relative pitch intervals between successive notes. His conscious task throughout was to retain just the one pitch, the C. After two months, Brady's error rate was negligible and his experience was that "the 'chroma' dimension so overwhelmingly overrode the high–low dimension that most of the tasks, with practice, became very easy" (Brady, 1970, p. 884). Sounds in the environment began to take on codable pitch qualities—the B refrigerator, the child's pull-toy in A. This is not to say that absolute pitch is not easier to learn in infancy, just that it *can* be acquired by some adults.

In his learning of absolute pitch, Brady took advantage of a method explored by Cuddy (1968, 1970, 1971) in a series of experiments. Cuddy found that training methods that emphasized the acquisition of a framework of reference tones among all the notes of the scale led to better pitch identification than training methods in which all the scale notes received equal attention. This was true even when persons of moderate musical experience were learning to label pitch sets defined by intervals of equal numbers of mels rather than by equal musical intervals (Cuddy, 1970). And when the framework for which labels are learned is already a familiar pattern—for example, the F-major triad in the case of music students— performance was especially good (Cuddy, 1971). All of this gives further support to the notion that the scale schemata that are internalized are well characterized as frameworks with definite focal points, hierarchically arranged. This is a theme we return to in Chapter 5.

SUMMARY

Musical pitch is uniquely represented by scales with discrete steps, which function as perceptual categories for hearing, remembering, and producing music. These musical scales appear to be governed by a few major constraints: (1) discriminability of intervals, (2) octave equivalence, and (3) a moderate number of pitches within the octave. This psychological structuring of the pitch dimension is related to the physical dimension of frequency logarithmically, and we have presented theoretical and experimental evidence to support this view. We have also argued that the tempered logarithmic tuning system used in Western music is a product of compromises of these constraints and of performance practice.

We described recent studies that indicate that pitch is more than a unidimensional subjective experience. Pitch adjacency and pitch height (or chroma) can be represented by an idealized model incorporating a double helix, suggesting important relationships for musical cognitive processing. An examination of the Western tempered tuning and scale systems from other cultures supports the hypothesis that people construct scales through several levels of processing: (1) the underlying psychophysical pitch function, (2) the tonal material, (3) the tuning system, and (4) the modal scale. The psychological reality of this anslysis draws face validity from the many traditions of musical pitch systems it describes and is the basis for the study of melodic organization processes in the next chapter.

5

Melody: Attention and Memory

Music is a kind of kaleidoscope. . . . . It brings forth a profu-
sion of beautiful tints and forms, now sharply contrasted and
now almost imperceptibly graduated; all logically connected
with each other, yet all novel in their effect; forming . . . a
complete and self-subsistent whole.

(Hanslick, 1854/1957, p. 48)

Just as the eye completes the lines of a drawing which the
painter has knowingly left incomplete, just so the ear may be
called upon to complete a chord and cooperate in its resolu-
tion, which has not actually been realized in the work.

(Stravinsky, 1956, p. 36)

INTRODUCTION

When we listen to music, our attention fluctuates, focusing first on one aspect and then another in the kaleidoscope. What we remember of a piece depends greatly on what we have attended to in listening. Sometimes our attention is "grabbed" by a salient feature in the stream of sound—a trumpet solo louder and more brilliant than the surrounding texture, for example. We can also direct our attention to features that are cognitively important even though they may not be salient in the stimulus, as when we follow the progress through a complex texture of an inner line that carries important musical information. In such cases, our attention is guided by knowledge structures developed in our experience of the world, called schemata (F. C. Bartlett, 1932; Neisser, 1976). A schema may embody general knowledge of stimulus properties common to many pieces of music, as in the case of our knowledge of tonal scales described in Chapter 4. A more specific type of schema may also embody knowledge of tonal relationships within a particular melody, like a melodic contour. Schemata guide our expectations of what will happen next, and, hence, what we attend to and remember. Schemata and the expectations they generate are always more general than the sounds that are actually heard. That is, expectations are rarely so specific and so dominant as to lead us into perceptual errors. Nevertheless, it is true that two people with two different sets of expectations can listen to the same stimulus and perceive different things.

An example will serve to clarify several of these points. Figure 5.1A shows the notes of the familiar "Frère Jacques" temporally interleaved with the notes of "Twinkle, Twinkle." The two melodies are in different pitch ranges. When the whole pattern is presented rapidly as in Example 5a (7.5 notes/sec), each melody can be heard clearly. The pitch difference   **5a** between the melodies is a salient stimulus feature that we can use to focus our attention on either the upper line or the lower. You can listen at will to one melody or the other, but not to both at once. Virtually any dimension of the stimulus pattern could serve as a basis for focusing attention (Dowling, 1973a). In Example 5b (Figure 5.1B), the pitch ranges of the two   **5b** melodies overlap, but the timbres of the two melodies have been changed (indicated in the figure by filled and open notes). You can still hear either melody quite clearly. The same is true of Example 5c, in which the two   **5c** melodies are distinguished only by loudness. Notice that you can attend to the softer melody almost as well as to the louder. Spatial separation can also differentiate the two melodies, as discussed in Chapter 2. In Example 5d, the melodies are fed through separate stereophonic channels, and it is   **5d** easy to focus on one or the other.

Each of the foregoing examples provides the opportunity for selective attention on the basis of some stimulus dimension: pitch, timbre, loudness, or location. In music not constrained by the one-note-at-a-time restriction of these interleaved melodies, temporal dimensions such as rhythm and meter can be used to distinguish musical lines that the com-

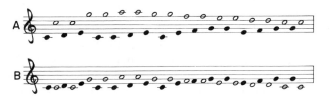

Figure 5.1 The notes of "Frère Jacques" (filled notes) interleaved with those of "Twinkle, Twinkle" (open notes) (A) in different pitch ranges, and (B) in the same pitch range.

Figure 5.2   Transcription of an excerpt from Mozart's finale to Act I of *Don Giovanni,* in which three groups of musicians play different dances simultaneously in different parts of the stage.

poser wants to clarify. Composers often make different lines proceed at different rates. Examples abound, including the running figure versus the hymn tune in Bach's chorale prelude "Jesu, Joy of Man's Desiring," as well as the rapid-fire staccato of Maddalena's griping versus the soaring sublimation of Gilda's resignation in Verdi's Quartet from *Rigoletto.* Differences of rhythm and rate of presentation are especially useful in polyphonic music, where the composer wants to give the listener a choice from among a variety of important musical lines, and in opera, where the composer may desire the simultaneous presentation of several points of view. Mozart, in the finale to Act I of *Don Giovanni,* provides a tour de force of temporal differentiation when he puts two bands on the stage in addition to the orchestra in the pit and has them all play different dances in different meters. Figure 5.2 conveys some of the complexity of Mozart's score. Spatial location, pace (the rate at which the notes go by), and metric organization all provide the listener with the means of focusing on one of the dances and ignoring the others.

Now let us return to the example of the interleaved melodies and demonstrate what happens when two familiar melodies are interleaved but without any simple stimulus feature to distinguish them. The pattern would be like that of Figure 5.1B, but with all the notes the same color. Example 5e presents in just that way a new pair of melodies we think are familiar to you. We expect that the example sounds like a meaningless jumble of notes. Now listen again to "Frère Jacques" and "Twinkle,

Twinkle,'' but this time interleaved in the same pitch range without any physical difference in features (Example 5f). We trust you hear either **5f** melody, depending on which one you attend to. As the example is repeated, try shifting your attention back and forth from one melody to the other. You can hear the melodies clearly in Example 5f but not in Example 5e, yet the only difference between them is that you know which melodies to listen for in 5f. With 5f, you have a pattern of expectancies, a schema, that you can match against the stimulus to check for the presence of the expected melody. With 5e, you do not know which schemata to use and so cannot discern the tunes. Dowling (1973a) verified this phenomenon in an experiment by presenting listeners with pairs of interleaved melodies such as those in Examples 5e and 5f, preceding each pair with a true or a false label. (In 5f the true label is "Twinkle, Twinkle" and a false label might be "On Top of Old Smoky." Is one of the tunes in 5e "Happy Birthday"?) With true labels listeners almost always reported hearing the target tune. With false labels listeners almost never reported hearing the labeled tune even after 20 repetitions, nor did they correctly recognize either actual melody. We suppose that when listeners did recognize a mislabeled melody it was because they guessed correctly which schema to try matching to the stimulus. (We will tell you later what the tunes in 5e are.)

Neisser (1979; Bahrick, Walker, & Neisser, 1981) describes a visual analog of the interleaved-tunes phenomenon. If videotapes of two different games are superimposed on one screen, viewers find it easy to follow one series of events (e.g., a game of catch) and ignore another (e.g., handclapping). When viewers are asked to press a button each time the ball is thrown, for example, their accuracy is affected very little by the presence of the other game on the same screen. This is true even when the ignored game is another game of ball. As with the interleaved melodies, a schema of expectancies provides the person with the means of focusing attention on one series of events and ignoring other series of events even though the two are thoroughly intermingled in the stimulus display. As Bahrick et al. (1981) put it:

> Perception takes place when appropriate schemata are actively and continuously tuned to the temporally extended information that specifies an individual event. Irrelevant events present information, too, but remain unperceived simply because no such active tuning occurs with respect to it. (p. 378)

The Nature of a Melody Schema

Both with interleaved tunes and with superimposed ball games, perceivers can follow the target events, provided they know which schema to use. With interleaved tunes, the critical events are so thoroughly embedded in the context that a rather specific schema (of a particular melody) is required to sort them out. (Incidentally, the tunes in Example 5e are "Mary Had a Little Lamb" and "Three Blind Mice.") This raises the issue of what such a melody schema is like. Several considerations lead us to suppose that it is not likely to be a literal mental copy of the melody. An exact copy would have to be translated—expanded, contracted, and shifted both in time and in pitch—to fit any actual instance of the melody that might be perceived. That is, a familiar melody can be presented at any arbitrarily selected pitch level and at any tempo (within broad limits), and we can still recognize it. Therefore, it seems likely that a melody schema should represent more general higher-order information than specific pitches at specific temporal intervals. Dowling (1978c) suggests that the pitch information in melodies might be stored in a schema consisting of the contour—the pattern of ups and downs—of the melody, plus an indication of where that contour should be hung on a tonal scale. Evidence is equivocal on this issue, but our present guess is that the schema of a familiar tune is somewhat more specific than a contour. If such a schema is more specific than contour, two possibilities occur. One possibility is that the abstract representation of pitches in a melody is the sequence of (logarithmic) pitch intervals. The second possibility is that pitches are stored as a sequence of abstracted chromas (i.e., do–re–mi labels in a movable-do system). We review the evidence, which we believe at this writing favors the second interpretation.

Some of this evidence is based on a type of stimulus that is in a way complementary to the interleaved melodies you have just been hearing. In those, perceptual confusion is produced by mixing two melodies in one pitch region. In our next group of stimuli, confusion is produced by scattering the pitches of one melody across several octaves while preserving their chromas. This is illustrated in Figure 5.3A and Example 5g. The wide leaps of pitch make the melodic line hard to follow. Deutsch (1972) found that such octave-scrambled melodies are very difficult to recognize. Dowling (1978b) found that giving listeners true and false labels for such melodies produced results similar to those described above for interleaved melodies, though displaying lower accuracy. Correct labels produced 80% correct recognition, while incorrect labels misled listeners 25% of the time, giving an overall rate of 77% correct. Leaving the contour intact in the octave-scrambled version is some help to listeners if they are informed of the presence of the contour (Dowling & Hollombe, 1977; Idson & Massaro, 1978). Dowling and Hollombe found performance in that case of about 65% correct. We suppose that both the label and the contour can serve to retrieve a particular melodic schema from among the

Figure 5.3 Melodies in which successive notes have been assigned to different octaves (A) preserving chroma, and (B) with chroma distorted.

many stored in long-term memory. Before positive recognition is reported, however, the schema is checked for chroma matches in the stimulus. If the chromas of the stimulus do not match those of the schema, the proposed schema is rejected. Kallman and Massaro (1979) found that when they preserved the contours of octave-scrambled melodies but altered the chromas by 1 or 2 semitones, correct recognition fell from about 65% (with both contour and chroma) to about 10% (with contour but not chroma). Example 5h presents a chroma-altered version of "Yankee Doodle," shown in Figure 5.3B. This suggests that chroma information is an integral part of the long-term memory representation (schema) for a familiar tune. The fact that recognition is much better than chance when chroma is preserved in these octave-scrambled melodies indicates that some abstraction of chroma, rather than interval sizes, is important, since intervals have been destroyed by the scrambling. And the fact that contour alone is not sufficient for recognition suggests that chromas are included in the schema and not just optionally accessible when needed (as, for example, via a separate scale schema as in Dowling's, 1978b, model).

   In the following, we present evidence supporting the notion that schematic representations of familiar tunes in long-term memory consist of (rhythmically organized) sets of relative pitch chromas and that such representations can be accessed by means of labels and such global melodic features as contour. We also present evidence that the higher-order tonal-scale schema *does* function independently of particular melodies, as Dowling (1978b) proposed. And we look at short-term (episodic) memory, long-term (semantic) memory, and cognitive development with respect to the roles played by pitch, intervals, contour, and tonal scales. Figure 5.4a shows the tune "Pop Goes the Weasel" (A) with various comparisons (B–E) that illustrate the effects of preserving or altering those features of the original. (Example 5i). In (B), the pitches have all been changed by trans-

Figure 5.4 (A) The beginning of "Pop Goes the Weasel" with various comparisons that (B) transpose the same intervals to a new key, (C) imitate the same contour with intervals changed, (D) depart from a tonal scale, and (E) alter the contour.

posing the tune to a different key, but the contour and intervals are the
5j   same as in the original (Example 5j). In (C), some of the intervals have
been altered, and the tune no longer sounds exactly like "Pop Goes the
5k   Weasel" (Example 5k). (C) is still within a tonal scale, but (D) uses
pitches outside any one tonal scale and is atonal while still preserving the
5l   original contour (Example 5l). In (E) the contour is changed, and the tune
5m   sounds very different (Example 5m). We begin our review of the evidence
by considering how pitch is perceived and remembered in a melodic context.

MEMORY FOR MELODIC FEATURES

Pitch

Though even novel, atonal melodies are easily recognized when repeated at the same pitch level (the A–B comparison in Figure 5.4), memory for single pitches is affected markedly by putting them into musical
context. Krumhansl (1979, Experiment 3) found that pitches from a tonal
scale were remembered well when followed by a context of pitches drawn
from the same key, while a context of atonal pitches led to poorer memory for the target pitch. On each trial of the experiment, Krumhansl
presented the listeners with a standard tone (for example, a G) lasting 0.5
sec. The standard was followed immediately by seven interference tones
at a rate of two per second. The interference tones were either from the
same tonal scale as the standard (e.g., C–E–A–F–D–B–C) or were an
atonal sequence not in any key (e.g., C♯–E–A–F–D♯–B–C♯). Following
the interference tones was a 1.5 sec pause and then a comparison tone

that was either the same pitch as the standard or differed from it by 1 semitone. Listeners performed better than 95% correct when the interference tones were from the same key as the standard, while performance fell to about 80% correct with atonal interference. The opposite pattern occurred when the listener was trying to remember a standard tone *outside* the tonal scale of tonal interference tones (e.g., a G#). In that case, tonal interference disrupted memory for the standard outside the key, driving performance below 80%. Atonal interference was not nearly so disruptive, leaving performance at about 90% correct.

What seems to be happening here is not that atonal contexts are disruptive per se, but rather that if the listener is trying to remember a standard pitch as a chroma in a particular key, the atonal context hurts performance. If the listener is trying to remember a pitch foreign to a key, then a context drawn from that key is disruptive and the atonal context is not. The tonal context appears to cause a shift in the listener's internal frame of reference when the interpolated tones are drawn from a different set than the one that incorporates the standard tone. This interpretation was explored further in work done by Kirk Blackburn in Dowling's laboratory. Blackburn used two types of tonal context rather than tonal and atonal and made the listener's task more difficult than Krumhansl's by asking listeners to *imagine* the standard tone. In other respects, the procedure was very similar to Krumhansl's. To aid the listener's imagination, Blackburn played part of a major scale leading up or down to the tonic (e.g., G–A–B or F–E–D), leaving it to the listener to imagine its completion (in this case, C). Five interference tones followed, either from the same key as the target (e.g., G–A–D–E–F) or from a distant key (B or F# major, e.g., F#–G#–A#–D#–F#). The comparison tone was either the imagined target (C) or a semitone removed from it (B or C#). When the interpolated tones were in the same key as the imagined tonic and its scale, performance was around 75% correct. When the interpolated tones suggested a different key, performance was worse than chance—around 40%.

The interpretation that distant-key interference caused a shift in the listener's schematic frame of reference is supported by the pattern of errors when the comparison tone differed from the imagined tonic C. The B could have come from either C major or the distant key (B major or F# major). The C#, however, could have come only from the distant key. False-positive recognitions of the B were about equal for the two types of interference, while false positives for the C# were primarily the result of distant-key interference. The C# sounded very natural when it followed a series of tones with which it could combine in a major scale, whereas it sounded strange and was easy to reject when it followed the C-major scale to which it was foreign.

Memory for a pitch can be altered by contextual shifts other than those involved in the tonal structure. Pitch shifts of notes in brief atonal melodies affect memory for the pitch of neighboring notes. Guilford and Hilton (1933) used pairs of melodies from Seashore's (1919) test of melodic memory. The pitch of one note of the melody was changed upon repetition. Listeners reported hearing changes not only in the actually altered tones, but also shifts (in the same direction) of neighboring tones that had not been altered. In a second study, Guilford and Nelson (1936) repeated melodies without altering any pitches, and listeners still reported hearing pitch shifts. (The atonality of the melodies probably contributed to the difficulty of accurate pitch judgment.) Guilford and Nelson (1937) simplified the task by using three-note melodies containing pairs of identical or adjacent pitches, plus another note separated in pitch from the pair. The three notes could occur in any order, and the listener's task was to say whether the second note of the similar pair was the same as, or higher or lower than, the first. Guilford and Nelson found that the second note of the pair tended to be shifted away from the note that was different in pitch. For example, in the sequence C♯–G–C♯ (with the G higher) the second C♯ was judged lower in pitch than the first. It is as though the listener's internal standard for the pitch C♯ had been shifted upward by the occurrence of the G, and the second (actual) C♯ judged flat by comparison.

Dewar, Cuddy, and Mewhort (1977) provide further evidence of the importance of a tonal scale schema in memory for pitch. They presented listeners with seven-note sequences that were either tonal or atonal. Then they presented a pair of tones, one of which had occurred in the original sequence, and asked the listeners to tell which tone they had heard before. Performance was better with tonal sequences than with atonal (81% vs. 77%). Dewar et al. also included a condition in which the comparison stimuli consisted of the whole seven-note sequences, either intact or with one note changed. Listeners found this task much easier, achieving 99% correct with tonal sequences and 91% with atonal. We can conclude two things from this: (1) The additional information in the whole sequence was useful in judging the accuracy of the single pitch, and (2) this information was especially useful with tonal sequences.

In an extension of this line of work Cuddy, Cohen, and Miller (1979) tested memory for tonal three-note fragments. Listeners were supposed to notice a change in one note of a fragment when it was presented and tested in isolation, or with the addition of a context of two preceding and two following notes. The altered note either remained within the tonal scale of the other notes or departed from it. In comparison to detection of note changes in the fragment alone, addition of a strongly tonal context led to significantly better detection of alterations that departed from the tonal scale. Addition of an atonal context led to worse performance in the detection of alterations whether within the tonal scale or not. The effects of context depend on the degree to which context invokes the listener's scale schemata, a point to which we return below.

In summary, we have seen that the context in which a pitch is heard affects memory for that pitch, and in particular, that tonal scale context can aid in memory for context-compatible pitches and aid in the detection of incompatible ones. Contexts that include pitches outside the scale schema of an inferred tonal scale can interfere with accurate memory and cause systematic errors of judgment. A practical application of this principle is found in choral singing. When a section of a chorus has several measures rest, reentry on the correct pitch is often facilitated by the reentry pitch's being the same as the last pitch sung. As long as the piece stays in the same key during the rest, choristers remember the pitch well. However, if the piece modulates to a new key the entrance is more difficult, even though the pitch is the same.

In the broader scheme of remembering music, remembering a melody involves more than just remembering a series of unrelated pitches. Melodies have global features that pertain to the whole pattern, and one of these is contour. We now turn to a discussion of memory for melodic contour.

Contour

Contour refers to the pattern of ups and downs of pitch from note to note in a melody. The importance of contour in recognition is disclosed in experiments in which comparison melodies sharing the same contour as the original (such as those in Figure 5.4C, D, and E) are easily distinguished from those that do not (as in Figure 5.4F). The relative importance of contour in comparison to other features of melodies is shown by the degree to which the (C–D–E) versus (F) discrimination is strong and the discriminations among melodies like (C), (D), and (E) (that differ among themselves in other features such as pitch intervals and tonality) are weak. Contour is an especially important feature of melodies in immediate recognition where the exact relationship between a melody and the scale schema has not been thoroughly established, as well as with atonal melodies in which there is no scale schema to relate the melody to.

The dominance of contour in the immediate recognition of atonal melodies is illustrated in a study by Dowling and Fujitani (1971, Experiment 1). They presented listeners with pairs of five-note atonal melodies like those shown in Figure 5.5. The comparison melody was either an exact transpo-

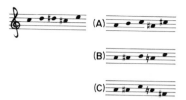

Figure 5.5 Atonal melodies like those used by Dowling and Fujitani (1971, Experiment 1): (A) exact transposition, (B) same-contour imitation, and (C) different-contour comparison.

sition of the original to a new pitch level (Figure 5.5A), an imitation of the original that preserved contour but not interval sizes (Figure 5.5B), or a comparison with a different contour (Figure 5.5C). Listeners found it relatively easy to distinguish between either transpositions (A) or contour-preserving imitations (B) and the different-contour melodies (C), achieving between 85% and 90% correct. Listeners found it almost impossible to distinguish between transpositions (A) and same-contour imitations (B), however, performing at around the chance level of 50%. It appears that these listeners, who had at most only moderate amounts of musical training, based their judgments almost entirely on contour similarity and were unable to detect changes in interval sizes in these atonal melodies.

In a similar experiment Francès (1958, Experiment 9) asked listeners to distinguish transpositions of brief melodies from same-contour imitations. Listeners found the task much harder with atonal than with tonal melodies, suggesting that they did not succeed in remembering the intervals between the notes in the atonal melodies and were confused by imitations that had similar intervals. In that case, contour was the dominant feature. Francès' study had the virtue of using more natural sounding melodies than most studies in this area—melodies having interesting rhythmic patterns. Though Francès' study had the limitation of using only four different melodies over and over again, the fact that its results converge closely with other findings leads us to have confidence in them. We return below to the role of tonal scale schemata in melodic memory. For the present, it seems clear that contour is an especially important feature in the recognition of atonal melodies.

Contour is also important in the immediate recognition of novel melodies in cases where the tonal scale framework remains constant. Dowling (1978b) replicated Dowling and Fujitani's (1971) experiment, but this time used tonal melodies. Figure 5.6 illustrates the types of comparison melodies in this study. Note that the tonal imitation (C) remains in the tonal key of the original; that is, it is constructed from notes of the same tonal

Table 5.1

Area under the Memory Operating Characteristic, as Estimated
Percentage Correct

| | Transposition compared to: | | |
| | Tonal imitation | Atonal imitation | Different contour |
Group			
Dowling (1978b)			
Inexperienced	49	59	81
Experienced	48	79	84
Dowling and Fujitani (1971)	—	53	89

scale. Comparison (C) preserves the same *diatonic* intervals (measured along the tonal scale) as (A) while altering the *chromatic* intervals. Listeners were unable to distinguish between (A)–(B) pairs and (A)–(C) pairs in this experiment, showing that contour is the dominant feature in those comparisons. Example 5n presents first an (A)–(B) pair and then an (A)– (C) pair so that you can hear how similar the (A)–(C) melodies sound. The data are shown in Table 5.1 along with the corresponding condition of Dowling and Fujitani's experiment. Discrimination between transpositions and same-contour tonal imitations is around the chance level of 50%, while discrimination between transpositions and different-contour melodies is better than 80%. Notice that while Dowling and Fujitani's listeners could not distinguish transpositions from imitations where both were atonal, Dowling's (1978b) listeners could do so at better than chance levels where the transposition is tonal and the imitation atonal. Tonality itself can be used as a cue, and naturally enough, the more experienced listeners were better at using it (79% vs. 59%). We return to this study in our discussion of tonality, but for present purposes, it is clear that listen-

5n

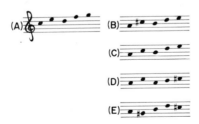

Figure 5.6 Tonal melodies used by Dowling (1978b): (A) initial melody of trial, (B) exact transposition, (C) tonal imitation with different intervals, (D) atonal imitation with different intervals and pitches outside tonal scale, and (E) different-contour melody.

ers have difficulty discriminating tonal imitations in the same key from transpositions and that this leaves contour the dominant melodic feature in determining the listeners' responses.

Contour is an important feature in the recognition of familiar melodies. White (1960) and Dowling and Fujitani (1971, Experiment 2) demonstrated that listeners can recognize distorted versions of familiar tunes in which the pitch intervals between notes are changed while the contours are preserved. Dowling and Fujitani used a set of tunes of which the first two phrases could be regularized into the same rhythm, thus eliminating rhythmic pattern as a cue. Undistorted versions of these tunes were recognized almost perfectly, while distortions in which contour had been destroyed were recognized only 30% of the time (a little better than chance). When the distortion preserved contour information, performance rose to about 60% correct. Performance improved somewhat more if *relative* interval size information was included with the contour, that is, if larger intervals remained larger after distortion and smaller ones remained smaller.

Key Distance

The relative importance of contour information in melody recognition varies with tonal scale context. The ease with which listeners can distinguish between transpositions of a melody and same-contour different-interval imitations depends upon the relationship between the key of the test melody and the key of the original. In Chapter 4, we introduced the notion of distance between keys and reviewed evidence from mulitdimensional scaling that key-distance has psychological reality. Here we discuss the effects of key-distance on melody recognition. Distance between keys is measured in music theory by the number of different pitches in the tonal scales of the two keys. This can range from one out of seven scale pitches at the near end to six out of seven at the far end. This is illustrated in Figure 5.7 in which three major scales are shown as selections of pitches from the chromatic scale of 12 semitones in the octave. The C-major and the D-major scales are relatively close, sharing all but two of their pitches, while the C-major and B-major scales are distant, having only two pitches in common.

In a series of experiments, J. C. Bartlett and Dowling (1980) manipulated the key relationships between the initial melody and the comparison melody in a pair, using an immediate recognition paradigm very similar to those described above. Comparison melodies were of the types shown in Figure 5.6 but in a variety of keys. For example, on a *tonal imitation* trial, the first melody of a pair might be in C major starting on the first degree of

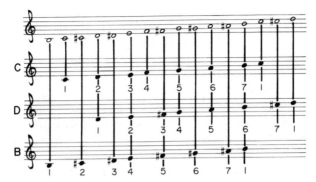

Figure 5.7 Closely and distantly related keys seen as selections of pitches from the tonal material. Closely related keys (e.g., C and D) share more pitches than distantly related keys (e.g., C and B).

the scale, and the second melody might be in D major and shifted to begin on the third degree of the scale (F♯). That would be a *near-key tonal imitation*. A *far-key tonal imitation* might be an imitation in B major, starting on the third degree of the scale (D♯). In this sense, the tonal imitations used by Dowling (1978b), illustrated in Figure 5.6C, are *same-key tonal imitations*. Bartlett and Dowling (1980, Experiment 1) replicated Dowling's (1978b) study and obtained very similar results, with performance on recognizing transpositions and rejecting same-key imitations, atonal imitations, and different contour stimuli all falling within five percentage points of the results shown in Table 5.1. The additional result that Bartlett and Dowling found was that as key distance of imitations was increased from same to near to far, listeners were less confused by them and found them easier to reject. In subsequent experiments Bartlett and Dowling (1980) found that this key-distance effect was mainly due to listeners' better rejection of far-key imitations, rather than to better recognition of far-key transpositions.

   This result suggests that listeners use schematic scale information in solving certain aspects of the transposition-recognition task. Since the exact pitch intervals between the notes of a novel melody are difficult to remember, the listener uses melodic contour in conjunction with the chroma set of the scale. Where the key of the comparison melody is very similar to the key of the original, imitations are hard to reject because they share the contour and chroma set of the original. When comparison melodies are shifted to a far key, the chroma set is different and no longer misleading. The interval information available in the listener's memory, though meager, is sufficient to reject imitations with greater than chance accuracy. (Note that it takes only one mismatched interval to reject an imitation, and the imitations used in these experiments each had several interval changes.) Key distance had little effect on recognition of transpositions. The reasons for this are probably complex. We consider below possible explanations for different effects of key distance on recognition of transpositions and imitations. But first we describe some additional effects of tonal context and key distance.

In the study described above, Cuddy, Cohen, and Miller (1979) tested whether listeners could detect alterations in three-note tonal sequences. The sequences were either presented alone or embedded in contexts that varied in tonal strength from atonal to strongly tonal. On each trial of the experiment, the listener heard a standard melody followed by a transposition *and* a transposition with one of its pitches altered. Each trial was presented five times, and each time the order of the two transpositions was randomized. The listener's task was to say which comparison melody was the accurate transposition. The transpositions were either to near or to far keys, and the altered notes either remained inside the new key or departed from it. As we would expect, the altered notes that went outside the key were especially easy to notice when there was a strong tonal context. What is at first sight surprising in the results of Cuddy et al. is a key-distance effect running in the opposite direction from that obtained by Bartlett and Dowling (1980). With alterations remaining inside the key of transposition, listeners were better at distinguishing between exact and altered transpositions in near keys than in far keys. (This was true with strong tonal context and without context, but not with atonal or weak tonal context.) We believe the difference in results between these two studies to be attributable to a difference in method. The method that Bartlett and Dowling used presents the original melody and the comparison just once, and it is likely that the listener is not able to shift effectively to the schema of the comparison. In that case, the listener is confused by near-key imitations because of failure to shift to a new key. Far-key imitations are not so confusing, because obvious violations prevent their interpretation in the original key. In contrast, the method of Cuddy et al., with its repetition of each trial, provides ample opportunity for the listener to shift to the key of the comparison. This is more effectively accomplished to near keys than to far, and so the listener performs better with the near keys. Both studies illustrate the importance of the tonal scale schema and key distance, but in different ways.

Intervals and Chromas

Though contour is useful in the recognition of familiar tunes stored in long-term memory, it is clear that intervals (patterns of chromas) are much more important there than in the immediate recognition of novel melodies in the studies discussed above. Recall that in the study by Attneave and Olson (1971) discussed in Chapter 4, even nonmusicians could recreate the interval pattern of the NBC chimes quite precisely at arbitrarily chosen pitch levels. Accuracy in noticing distortions of intervals of familiar tunes is a common finding. Bartlett and Dowling (1980, Experiment 2), in their series of experiments on key-distance, tested immediate recognition of melodic phrases drawn from either familiar folk songs or unfamiliar pseudo–folk songs. In the difficult task of distinguishing transpositions from same-contour imitations, performance was much better with familiar than with unfamiliar melodies. The imitations of unfamiliar melodies were not so confusing as those used by Dowling (1978c), probably because they were rhythmically more interesting. Performance with unfamiliar melodies was around 70% (with chance at 50%). But with familiar melodies, performance leapt to about 90%, indicating very good recognition of intervals. This provides documentation of the ease with which listeners are able to reject interval-distorted versions of familiar tunes such as those you heard in Example 5k.

The recognition of a familiar tune is an example of the use of long-term (semantic) memory. Psychologists contrast long-term and short-term (episodic) memory (Lindsay & Norman, 1977). The use of short-term memory is illustrated by the recognition of a novel melody first presented immediately before the comparison. Generally speaking, short-term memory is thought to be limited in capacity to about seven items at a time and to hold information for periods of up to about 30 sec. That information needs to be written into long-term memory if it is to be remembered for a longer period. Long-term memory is viewed as virtually unlimited in capacity and as able to store items for indefinite periods of time. The difficulties with recognition of items in long-term memory arise largely from the problem of retrieval, that is, of finding the relevant memory record from among the immense number of records stored there. The question of *which* item one is searching for looms very large. In shortterm memory, the question of which item one wants is usually not crucial. The items are already available to be tested for a match. These differences in memory processes lead to differences in the importance of the various features of a melody to be recognized, depending on whether long-or short-term is involved. For example, it seems likely that relatively specific information (such as chromas or interval sizes) is more important in long-term memory processes, where a melody has to be differentiated from a large number of similar alternatives, than in short-term memory where the few alternatives are already available. This is what Dowling and Bartlett (1981) found.

This result—the importance of chroma or interval information in long-term memory—at first surprised Dowling and Bartlett. They were sure of the importance of contour information in short-term memory and expected that contour would also dominate in long-term memory. They were also thinking of the way composers use contour similarity to give unity to a piece. The first movement of Beethoven's Fifth Symphony is a prime example of this type of writing. Beethoven's familiar four-note theme is first presented with an interval of 4 semitones between the last two notes and then repeated immediately with an interval of 3 semitones. During the next 30 sec, the theme is repeated over and over with intervals of 1, 3, 4, 5, and 7 semitones. The same contour recurs through all of these repetitions, and it seems unlikely that any listener could escape having it firmly engrossed on his or her memory by the end of the 8-min movement. Beethoven was relying on the listener's memory for contour to provide structure for his piece. Since those memories need to last over periods of minutes within the piece, and, in fact, last for years afterwards, they would seem to involve long-term memory processes.

Dowling and Bartlett (1981) set out to explore these possibilities with an experiment requiring memory for excerpts from Beethoven's String Quartets. They collected pairs of presentations of themes related in the same way as the first two presentations of the first theme in Beethoven's Fifth, that is, pairs in which the second presentation imitated the first with the same contour but different intervals and chromas. Listeners heard a series of 18 excerpts including one member of each pair. Then after a 5-min pause, the listeners were tested with a series that included exact repetitions of what they had heard before, imitations (the other members of the pairs), and completely different excerpts not heard before. Listeners were told to try to recognize the imitations, giving positive responses both to them and to the exact repetitions. Listeners succeeded at recognizing exact repetitions, distinguishing them from completely different excerpts with 75% accuracy. But listeners were unable to distinguish the same-contour imitations from different items, performing at chance level (50%). This was surprising in view of the great similarity of repetitions and imitations, which not only shared the same contour but were almost always drawn from consecutive passages in the same piece (as with the Beethoven's Fifth example) and thus had similar tempo, instrumental color, and loudness. Listeners failed to recognize imitations even when instructed to do so and when the relationship of imitations and repetitions was explained and illustrated. It seems that these moderately experienced listeners could use their long-term memories in recognizing the pattern of interval sizes (or chromas) in novel pieces of music but could not recognize contours. For contour to be effective in retrieval from long-term

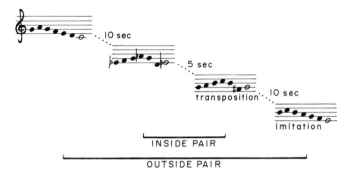

Figure 5.8 Structure of a trial in Dowling and Bartlett's (1981) inside–outside procedure. Listeners responded following the third and fourth stimuli in each trial.

memory, it seems that the melody must be very well learned and familiar (Dowling & Fujitani, 1971, Experiment 2). It seems likely that a crucial feature of Beethoven's Fifth is that the theme is presented several times (not just once) within a span of time during which earlier presentations are still in short-term memory.

Dowling and Bartlett (1981, Experiment 4) explored the phenomenon of accuracy of interval information in long-term (vs. short-term) memory using a method that directly contrasted the two processes. Figure 5.8 shows the structure of a trial in this experiment. On each trial, the listener hears two pairs of melodies: an outside pair and an inside pair. The first member of the outside pair must be held in long-term memory while the listener evaluates the inside pair using short-term memory. Comparison melodies in both pairs included transpositions, tonal imitations, and different-contour items. Listeners were instructed to try to distinguish between transpositions and imitations, as well as between transpositions and different items. With the inside pairs, listeners distinguished transpositions and imitations from different items (75% and 72%, respectively) but not from each other. This is essentially the same pattern as found in the earlier short-term memory results shown in Table 5.1. With the outside pairs, performance was, of course, generally worse. But the relative difference between transposition and imitation recognition tended to widen. Recognition of transpositions was at 65%, but recognition of imitations was at 57% (as compared to different items). That is, recognition of transpositions fell 10% going from short-term to long-term memory, while recognition of imitations fell 15%. This suggests that the accuracy of interval or chroma information that listeners have for familiar melodies begins to develop during the first few times those melodies are entered into long-term memory. As Dowling and Bartlett (1981, p. 30) say, "While interval information is difficult to encode, it is apparently retained with high efficiency in long-term memory.''

We believe that the ease of recognizing undistorted familiar tunes, as well as the relative importance of interval information in long-term memory, is based on listeners having stored in memory a sequence of relative pitch chromas (pitch levels in a tonal scale) rather than a set of intervals between tones. This is because when the intervals are distorted but the chromas are left intact, recognition is still possible, as in the experiment by Kallman and Massaro (1979), discussed above. When the chromas as well as the intervals are destroyed, then the melody becomes virtually unrecognizable. With unfamiliar tonal melodies, the chroma set of the scale becomes more important than the particular chromas of the melody itself, and confusions arise when the melody shifts in pitch but the scale does not. As long as the comparison melody preserves the contour of the original and uses the chromas of the same scale, the two will be confused. However, the degree to which chromas are represented in the listeners memory may depend upon individual differences in training in the use of tonal scale systems, as the following experiment suggests.

In this experiment, Dowling (1982a) transposed the interval patterns of melodies, in some cases leaving the pattern of chromas intact and in other cases changing it. Chroma is based on the place of a pitch in a tonal scale and so can be manipulated by changing tonal context. A melody using the first, second, and third degrees of the scale (do, re, mi) can have the same intervals as one using the fifth, sixth, and seventh degrees (sol, la, ti), though its chromas will be different. As long as a melody avoids the seventh and fourth degrees of the scale, it can be shifted from the do–re–mi position to the sol–la–ti position without any distortion of intervals. The shift of position can be determined by a chordal context pausing on the tonic and the dominant chord, respectively. (The tonic chord is based on the first scale position, do, and the dominant chord is based on the fifth scale position, sol.) This is illustrated in Figure 5.9. The original melody (in black notes in line A) begins and ends on C (do) in the key of C major, and that assignment of chroma values is established by the chordal context that precedes it. The comparison melodies are both transpositions of the same interval pattern to start and end on D. In (B) the chordal context establishes that D as first degree (tonic) of D major, and so (B) retains all but one of the same chromas as (A). In (C) the context makes D the fifth degree (dominant) of G major, and so the chromas are changed from do–re–mi (1–2–3) to sol–la–ti (4–5–6). The stimuli in Figure 5.9 can be heard in Example 5o. This experiment was conducted as a continuous running memory task, in which the listener heard a succession of stimuli like those in Figure 5.9, and responded to each according to whether or not it had

5o

Figure 5.9 Examples of stimuli in which chroma is varied while interval pattern remains constant: (A) an initial melody of a pair; (B) a near-transposition with most of the same chromas and intervals, with one chroma changed; (C) an exact transposition with different chromas and same intervals (Dowling, 1982a).

occurred before in the series. Some of the stimuli were first members of pairs and had not been heard before, while others were second members of pairs that were transpositions or imitations of earlier items. In this case, imitations had the same contours as originals but had one pitch changed as in Figure 5.9B. Listeners were asked to respond positively only to exact transpositions. Since the lag between the presentation of an item and its mate was a little more than a minute and filled with responses to other items, this procedure presumably tapped long-term memory processes. Thus, it was not surprising from the evidence reviewed above that performance in distinguishing transpositions from imitations was relatively good. Musically inexperienced listeners performed in the 60–65% range on that task, both with chromas the same and chromas altered on test. However, moderately experienced subjects succeeded in that distinction only when chromas remained the same, performing around 65% correct. When chromas in the test stimulus were changed, experienced listeners fell to chance (50%) in distinguishing transpositions from imitations. (Experienced listeners were better overall at contour recognition—distinguishing transpositions *and* imitations from different stimuli—but worse overall at interval recognition.) This leads us to conclude that both inexperienced and experienced listeners store accurate interval information in long-term memory upon first hearing a novel melody. Inexperienced listeners store this information simply *as intervals,* perhaps using the type of automatic interval processing system suggested by Deutsch (1969, 1982). More experienced listeners make use of the tonal scale schema they have learned to store interval patterns as chroma patterns. This strategy works well so long as chroma remains constant when memory for intervals is tested. It breaks down when chroma changes. With recognition memory, we encounter the same types of individual differences in the use of scale schemata found by Krumhansl and Shepard (1979) with multidimensional scaling methods (discussed in Chapter 4). According to this explanation of Dowling's (1982a) results, inexperienced listeners should not perform appreciably worse than experienced ones in discriminating *atonal* transpositions from imitations, and, in fact, Dowling and Fujitani (1971, Experiment 1) found a correlation of only .23 between years of musical training and such performance.

From the above review, we can see that the features of contour, interval size (or chroma), and tonal scale system all play a role in the adult's perception and memory for melodies. Next we turn to the child's development of auditory cognition, and there, too, we find the same features important. But before leaving adult cognition, there are two points we wish to reinforce. (1) Different features of melodies can have different importance depending on task demands. Thus, contour is an important feature in short-term memory tasks, but not so in long-term memory, where many stored melodies share the same contour and interval sizes become important in differentiating among them. (2) Individual differences among people with different developmental backgrounds are important to consider in constructing a theoretical model of music cognition. This is especially true of behaviors that involve the use of elaborate schemata (like the tonal scale) that depend upon training.

DEVELOPMENT

The same kinds of features that are important in adult information processing are also important in tracing the development of melody perception and memory. Different features become important in the child's behavioral repertoire at different ages, and this lends further support to the assertion that the various sets of features are psychologically distinct. In the remaining section of this chapter, we review evidence that melodic contour is already distinguishable early in infancy and that young infants can match the pitches of single tones. The child's ability to reproduce more than a phrase or two of a melody does not typically develop until sometime after the age of 2 years, and even then, the pitch of an extended melody generally wanders. Around the age of 5 years, the child becomes aware of changes of key and tonal center, and the melodies sung at that age wander less in pitch. It is not until a few years later, however, that the child is able to notice small changes of intervals or chromas in familiar melodies, a task at which the adult is very adept.

It is useful to think of the features involved in the processing of melodies as organized into the sorts of schemata we have been talking about, in fact, perceptuomotor schemata in Piaget's sense (Piaget & Inhelder, 1969). These schemata govern perception, memory, and production in both the child and the adult. We discuss numerous examples of the operation of these schemata in adult behavior in Chapter 4 as well as in this chapter. Tonal scale schemata are among the last to form in development; among the earliest are schemata for melodic contours. As we will see, young children deal with melodies in terms of contour. They notice changes in the contours of heard melodies, and when they sing, it is contour they control.

Infancy

When an infant observes a new bloom or buzz in William James' (1890) blooming, buzzing confusion, it becomes startled. A number of researchers have used this startle reaction to distinguish the types of stimulus change that babies notice from those they do not. Specifically, the researchers observe the baby's heart rate. A sudden slowing of heart rate indicates startle. In a typical study, an auditory pattern is repeated over and over. On the first presentation, the baby is startled and exhibits heart-rate deceleration. Then as the baby gets used to the pattern, heart rate returns to normal—it adapts. After the baby adapts to the first pattern, the pattern is changed to a new one. The question is, What types of change in the pattern cause a new startle? The use of this paradigm requires babies who have sufficiently strong shifts in heart rate to indicate both startle and adaptation and who do not become too fussy or distracted in the experimental situation. Usually about half the 5-month-olds tested provide usable data.

Chang and Trehub (1977a) got 5-month-old infants to adapt to six-note melodies. The melodies had a tempo of 2.5 notes/sec and were atonal with rather large intervals between the notes. The first melody was repeated 30 times over a 5.5 min period while the infant adapted. Then Chang and Trehub shifted to a new pattern. The new melody was either a transposition of the first melody (up or down 3 semitones) or a permutation of the order of the notes of the transposition. The first of these new melodies preserved the contour of the original, while the second did not. In both cases, the shift in overall pitch level was the same, and new melodies contained exactly the same pitches. Chang and Trehub found that the babies reacted to the melody with the changed contour but not to the transposition. (The principal features of these results have since been replicated with more sophisticated methods by Trehub, Bull, & Thorpe,

1984.) It makes sense that contour should be a salient feature of tonal patterns for young infants just embarking on learning language. Nine-month-olds have been observed to babble using the sentence intonation contours of adult English. And in tone languages (spoken mostly in Africa and Southeast Asia), the pitch contour of a syllable is phonemic; that is, it makes a difference in meaning.

Though an infant of 6 months cannot sing a melody after an adult model, babies of that age can match the pitches of single notes quite accurately. Kessen, Levine, and Wendrich (1979) conducted a study in which an adult got the infant's attention and then sang a pitch (a note of the D–F–A triad well within the infant's vocal range). To the researchers' (initial) surprise, the infant attempted to sing the pitch back. After some practice at this task, which the infants apparently enjoyed, the babies became quite accurate. They matched the correct note of the triad two-thirds of the time, and when they produced a successful match, it was usually quite well in tune. There is also evidence that 3-month-old infants notice changes in pitch chroma, in the sense of responding similarly to pitches an octave apart. Demany and Armand (1984) used a method much like Chang and Trehub's. They found that after habituation to a brief sine-wave melody, infants were not startled by substitution of pitches an octave away from corresponding notes in the original but were startled by changes to pitches somewhat more or less than an octave away.

During the first 2 years of life, the child produces a number of behaviors that later become integrated into an overall pattern of musical behavior. Matching pitches, (noted above), recognizing specific tunes, singing single phrases from tunes, inventing phrases and spontaneous songs, and beating regular rhythmic patterns usually appear during this time. Our own experience as well as various reviews of observed onset times for these behaviors (Ostwald, 1973; Révész, 1954; Shuter-Dyson & Gabriel, 1981) convinces us that the ages at which children first do these things vary widely. Continued experience performing the various behaviors is perhaps more important to the child's development than age of onset. Regarding pitch matching, Kessen (1981) notes that it tends to disappear in subsequent development unless it continues to be practiced. We agree with Kessen that it is often helpful to the child's musical development to have a somewhat older sibling modeling these behaviors and providing stylistically accessible music in his or her own practicing. The sophisticated adult music the parents listen to or perform is generally far beyond the infant's comprehension. An older sibling provides a steady input of oft-repeated simple songs. As an illustration, one of us (WJD) has two daughters 2 years apart. The elder first labeled a tune (in the sense of consistently making a specific response to a specific tune) at 18 months. When the younger was 9 months old, the older child developed a passion for "Old Macdonald Had a Farm," with its repeated chorus "ee-ai-ee-ai-oh." She sang it alone or with others several times a day for a month, and then the frequency tapered off to several times a week. At around 11 months, the younger daughter began to respond with some variant of "ee-ai-ee-ai-oh" whenever she heard the first phrase of "Old Macdonald." Tested systematically at 12 months, she rarely generalized to the openings of other familiar tunes. Intensive exposure to a tune she could comprehend seems to be a major factor in her use of tune labeling 6 months earlier than her sister. It is also important that the experience with the tune occurred in a socially meaningful setting. That is, when she heard the tune, it was from members of her family, usually inviting her participation by glances and nods. Her family was obviously having a good time with the tune, and so she approached it as a fun game to learn, just as the babies did in the Kessen et al. (1979) pitch-matching study.

Childhood

As children progress through the second year of life, they sing more and more coherently. Infants in their first year typically do a good deal of vocal play, exploring the pitch and dynamic ranges of their voices and the various timbres that are possible. During the second year, they do not leave off vocal play, but they also begin to produce patterns that an adult would recognize as coherently organized songs. These songs consist of short phrases, often just one phrase repeated over and over at different pitch levels. The pitch wanders without regard for any stable key but almost always moves by discrete steps from one focal pitch to the next. Some of the pitch intervals seem to follow adult models, but others do not. In the songs we have observed (Dowling, 1982b, 1984), no one interval seems to predominate. Some observers have been impressed with a tendency to descending minor thirds (3 semitones; e.g., Moog, 1976), even trying to see a cross-cultural universal there. In our opinion, the evidence is weak. If a mean of all descending interval sizes were taken from a large sample of 2-year-olds' songs, we would not be surprised if that mean were somewhere close to a minor third. The variance in the samples we have observed, however, is large enough to argue strongly against children of that age having a stable interval of a minor third or any other size.

Example 5p was produced by a girl just turning 2 years. It is typical of her songs between the ages of 18 and 30 months. It is elaborate relative to most of her songs, having two phrase contours that alternate, rather than just one repeated contour. The words, her own invention, repeat. (Not all her songs had definite words—some went "la, la, la," and others had

5p

vocalizations of the "ee-ai-ee-ai-oh" sort.) This song is a member of a family of spontaneous songs produced around this age. The simplest member of the family consisted of a descending phrase with the words "Duck on my house," repeated at different pitch levels. Pitch is controlled via melodic contours, but there seems to be no overall pitch organization such as we expect in adult songs. The song does not stay in one key, nor does it modulate coherently. Rhythm is relatively well controlled and regular. (It is interesting to compare these songs with the organization of the opening of Beethoven's Fifth—the formal idea is the same in that a contour is repeated over and over, but Beethoven exerts tight control over numerous other parameters.)

When we attempt to teach a child of 2 or 3 a simple song, they usually succeed in reproducing only a phrase or two. Davidson, McKernon, and Gardner (1981) taught a simple song to children spanning the preschool years in age. Children of 2 and 3 were able to reproduce the contour and rhythm of single phrases, but with varying interval size and wandering pitch. As children got older, they were able to combine more phrases into closer and closer approximations of the model. The interval relationships of the adult major scale began to emerge, but only locally within phrases. Four-year-olds could maintain stable pitch and intervals for a phrase or two but then slid to a new key in the next phrase. Their reproductions of the whole song pattern from beginning to end were fairly good.

The progress of the child from 2 to 4 in song learning is strikingly parallel to progress in learning stories. At the earlier age, the child tends to focus on an isolated incident from the story, for example, "Bad wolf chase pig." This is repeated, just as one phrase of a song is repeated. Later, more and more incidents are integrated into a meaningful sequence with the beginnings of a coherent plot. At the later ages, the child integrates several different phrases into a coherent song, both with spontaneous songs (Dowling, 1984) and familiar nursery songs. The child of 3 can sing songs as elaborate as the "Alphabet Song" ("A, B, C, D, . . . " to the tune of "Twinkle, Twinkle") through from top to bottom, getting the correct order of words with the correct melodic contours, but of course with wandering pitch. (Example 5q).

5q

Around the age of 5 or 6, the child acquires the sense of a stable key. Two converging lines of evidence lead us to this conclusion. First, Davidson et al. (1981) found that 5-year-olds could reproduce their little song reasonably well, staying within a single key throughout the whole song or through large sections of it. When the key changed, it was generally a sudden shift to a new key that was then stably maintained, rather than by gradual wandering. Second, Bartlett and Dowling (1980, Experiment 4) found that children of 5 or 6 noticed changes of key when the change was

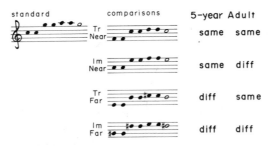

Figure 5.10 Schematization of results of Bartlett and Dowling (1980, Experiment 4). Tr, Transposition; Im, Imitation.

to a distant key (i.e., one that introduced several changes in pitches of notes in the scale) but not when the change was to a nearly related key (that introduced few such changes). This result, obtained with short-term recognition of familiar melodies like "Twinkle, Twinkle," was an instance of the key-distance effect discussed above. But the 5-year-old has only one component of the adult behavior pattern, namely, the ability to notice a change of key. The child at this age is still unlikely to notice small changes in the pitch intervals of familiar melodies that are obvious to the adult. Figure 5.10 gives a qualitative outline of this result. The 5-year-old responds on the basis of key but not interval size. Bartlett and Dowling found that by 8 years, the child had generally developed the adult pattern, responding to changes of both key and intervals.

The child's development of the ability to notice changes in the key of a melody is closely related to other aspects of melodic information processing. It is around this age that the child becomes able to utilize the fact that a tone sequence is tonal (rather than atonal) in order to detect changes in its intervals. (Here we refer to more noticeable changes than those in Bartlett and Dowling, 1980.) Zenatti (1969) gave children the rather difficult task of saying *which* note of a three-note melody had been altered in pitch. Five-year-olds could not perform this task any better than chance, but by 6 or 7, performance was better than chance, with performance on tonal sequences markedly better than performance on atonal ones. The 6-year-old can use an internalized schema of the tonal scale in performing the task. Another related phenomenon is Imberty's (1969) finding that by 7 years, children could notice sudden changes of key in the midst of a tune. By 8 years, the children in Imberty's study could notice changes of mode from major to minor—a change that produces essentially the same kind of changes in intervals as those in the imitations in Figure 5.10. Here again, the 8-year-olds showed the adult ability to notice changes of both key and interval size. This developmental pattern has been further corroborated by Krumhansl and Keil (1982) with methods akin to those of Krumhansl described in Chapter 4.

Training

This review of development has so far been generally true of children with little or no specific training in music. Virtually all of the studies with adults we have mentioned found some improvement in task performance with increased musical training. In most cases, both the amount of training and the performance increment were modest. Further, we have known for some time that adults exposed to special training programs in pitch discrimination and melody recognition improve their test performance for those abilities (Wyatt, 1945). The question remains of how young a child can be and still benefit from training. We believe with the Piagetians that a child can only be effectively taught a skill when ready— when the underlying cognitive capacities are sufficiently developed to learn it. However, we also believe that the child is more ready at even the earliest ages to learn musical skills than our culture typically expects. This should be clear from the above review. Who would have expected the success of Kessen et al. (1979) in teaching infants of 6 months to match pitches? We believe that 3- and 4-year-olds can benefit substantially from musical training suited to their abilities but, unfortunately, have little in the way of solid evidence. We do have good evidence that 6-year-olds develop their skills rapidly with training, and to that we now turn.

Dowling and Goedecke (in preparation) studied first and third graders in inner-city public schools who had been enrolled for about 6 months in a training program in either strings or piano. The training programs were based upon the methods of Shinichi Suzuki (1973); that is, they emphasized auditory processing skills and progressive control over the sounds made by the instrument rather than, for example, learning to read music. Children who had had this training during the year were compared with children in a control group drawn from a waiting list of those who desired training but who, for budgetary reasons, could not receive it. Dowling and Goedecke used two short-term recognition memory tasks involving novel five-note tonal melodies similar to those used in Dowling's studies with adults. In the first task (repetition) the child was asked to distinguish between exact repetitions of melodies and lures having different contours and pitches. As could be expected from the performance of Chang and Trehub's (1977a) infants in recognizing contour changes, even untrained first graders did well on this task, achieving about 75% correct (where chance was 50%). In the second task (permutation), listeners had to distinguish between exact repetitions of melodies and lures in which the pitches of the standard were presented in permuted order. That is, lures in the permutation task differed from targets in contour but not in their component pitches. This task was much more difficult than the first, and neither first nor third graders in the control group attained better than 70% correct.

Figure 5.11 summarizes the performance of the various groups of children. It is clear that even first graders benefit from training in auditory information-processing skills. This can be seen in their improvement on the repetition task from 75 to 90% correct. By third grade, performance on this relatively easy task appears to be approaching asymptote for both trained and untrained groups. Training seems to have little impact on performance of the more difficult permutation task for the first graders, but definite gains can be seen in the performance of the trained third graders. Not that this task, unlike the repetition task, is one that benefits little from simple maturation during this period. Untrained third graders do little better than untrained first graders. Nevertheless, third graders acquire the skill effectively with training. What they have learned is to ignore an obvious, salient source of similarity between targets and lures

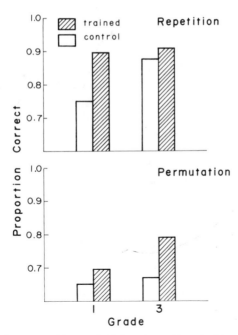

Figure 5.11 Performance of first and third graders with and without training on the two tasks in Dowling and Goedecke's (in preparation) study.

(identity of pitch content) and focus on the musically meaningful feature of melodic contour. The data of Figure 5.11 show that (1) first graders are cognitively ready to benefit from musical training in terms of improvement in their auditory processing skills, and (2) first and third graders are ready to benefit in different ways, as the review of their typical capabilites suggested.

SUMMARY

Melodies seem to be listened to and remembered according to a few perceptually salient features. Mental schemas, developed from early childhood in the course of hearing many of the culture's melodies, search for and extract these features from novel melodic information. These schemas include more general, higher-order information than specific pitches at specific temporal intervals. The context in which a pitch is heard affects memory for that pitch, suggesting that more global features are important. Melodic contour, for example, facilitates the immediate recognition of melodies; however, the relative importance of contour varies with tonal scale context. The most important of these contexts is the key-distance effect, which suggests that intervals—patterns of relative pitch chromas—are important in long-term memory for melodies, where a particular melody must be differentiated from a large number of similar alternatives. We argue that task demands affect which melodic features are important in attending to and remembering melodies. Also, differences resulting from prior musical training point to the role of individual differences in a theoretical model of music cognition.

The child's developing schemas for auditory cognition also involve the use of contour, interval sizes and chromas, and tonal scale system as important features. Infants can recognize changes in melodic contour and can produce a match to a given individual pitch. Over the first 2 years, such behaviors become increasingly integrated into coherently organized songs, although still without stable pitch levels or intervals. By age 5 or 6 a sense of stable key emerges, and children can recognize a change in key. We also argue that children are more ready at even the earliest age to learn musical skills than our culture typically expects.

Having established the importance of schemata in the development and use of melodic perception and memory, we turn, in the next chapter, to the larger perspective of melodic organization—to the temporal patterning of melodies, where cognitive schemas become the foundation for memory and comprehension of more complex musical structures.

6

Melodic Organization

Throughout its history the game was closely allied with music, and usually proceeded according to musical or mathematical rules. . . . In the symbols, ciphers, signatures, and abbreviations of the Game language an astronomical formula, the principles of form underlying an old sonata, an utterance of Confucius, and so on, were written down. A reader . . . might imagine such a game pattern as rather similar to the pattern of a chess game.

(Hermann Hesse, *The Glass Bead Game*, 1943/1969, p. 30)

INTRODUCTION

In Chapter 5, we explored people's memory for melodies in terms of melodic features such as the pitches of notes, the contours of phrases, and the tonal strength and key of a melody. Some of these features are strictly local in that they pertain to just one note (e.g., a pitch), while some features are more global and pertain to larger groups of notes (e.g., the contour that describes a whole phrase). Other features are still more global and describe clusters of phrases (e.g., the key of a whole song). LaBerge (1981) draws our attention to the global–local dimension and provides a good discussion of that relationship in the perception and production of music. In Chapter 6, we look at ways of describing the local and global organization of melodies, focusing on two main issues. First, we address the way local features of melodies are grouped perceptually to form more global patterns. Second, since global musical patterns are extended in time, we look at the possible role of memory in the cognition of musical pattern organization. Finally, we consider hierarchical patterns of organization as a way in which events at the local and global levels might be linked.

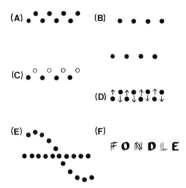

Figure 6.1 Illustrations of gestalt principles of figural organization.

LOCAL PATTERN ORGANIZATION

Recall Example 5a, in which pitch separation between two temporally interleaved melodies allows either melody to be attended to and heard distinctly. If we think of the pitch and time dimensions of Figure 5.1 as dimensions of a musical "space," then such examples become analogous to visual illustrations of perceptual organization formulated by the gestalt psychologists (Köhler, 1929). Gestalt principles can serve as useful rules of thumb, indicating what sort of pattern organization will be perceived given certain stimulus features. They are especially amenable to translation from visual to auditory space where the relatively brief time spans of local stimulus organization are involved. For the most part, they seem to describe aspects of stimulus organization that arise automatically from the operation of the sensory systems, without involving more complex cognitive systems such as memory. Some visual illustrations of the principles are shown in Figure 6.1.

Proximity can lead a set of eight dots to be seen as one wiggly row (A) or as two separate rows (B). *Similarity* leads us to see a row of four filled dots and a row of four open dots in (C). If we imagine the arrows in (D) as indicating direction of movement, then that configuration as well splits into two rows—one moving up and the other down—distinguished by *common fate*. *Prägnanz* (good continuation) leads us to see a curved line and straight line in (E). And when extended in time with notes instead of dots, the pattern in (E) illustrates organization according to common fate as well, with the trajectory of one melody passing through the path of the other. Figure 6.1F is more complicated, as meaning and memory enter into our perception of both the whole pattern and its elements. Proximity predicts the perception of the word FONDLE, while similarity suggests that the two patterns F N L and O D E will be seen. In fact, both of those organizations are by turns likely to occur. Moreover, when the organization breaks down into the two smaller patterns ODE is more likely to be seen as figure (the pattern to which the perceiver is attending at the moment) because it is a meaningful word, while FNL is likely to become ground (everything else in the stimulus). The organizational principles of proximity, similarity, common fate, and *prägnanz* indicate which aspects of a stimulus are likely to be attended to as a figure. And to these four gestalt principles we can add *meaning* as a fifth source of pattern organization.

Chapter 5 provides auditory analogs of all of the principles in Figure 6.1 with the exception of common fate (to which we return below). Examples 5a, b, c, and d illustrate perceptual grouping based on pitch, timbre, loudness, and location. And in Examples 5e and 5f, we see that the listener could attend to the notes of a familiar melody even though they are not differentiated from their background on any other basis than being parts of a meaningful configuration. In the visual analogy, this would be as though the word ODE in Figure 6.1F were written in the same color letters as the background and yet remained perceptually salient. Now we turn to a discussion of further phenomena related to pitch proximity as a grouping principle.

Proximity

The importance of pitch proximity in audition is reflected in the fact that melodies all over the world use small pitch intervals from note to note. Figure 6.2 shows the distribution of intervals in melodies from all of those societies for which we could find data (Dowling, 1968, 1978c). Cul-

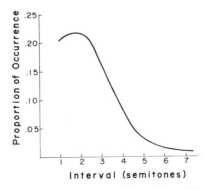

Figure 6.2 Proportionate occurrence of pitch intervals of different sizes (means across numerous cultures). (After Dowling, 1968.)

Figure 6.3 Two passages from J. S. Bach's Partita No. 3 for violin solo.

tures differ somewhat in which interval sizes they use (Merriam, 1964), but all agree in avoiding intervals larger than 4 or 5 semitones. This tendency toward small intervals is truly a cross-cultural universal and very likely derives from the physiological structure of the auditory system. (Remember that violations of the proximity rule, as in the octave-scrambled melodies in Chapter 5, led to patterns that were difficult to follow.)

Violations of proximity have been used in various periods and genres of both Western and non-Western music for a variety of effects. For example, in the Baroque period of Western music, a predilection for polyphonic counterpoint converged with a tradition of writing solo pieces for a single melody-instrument playing alone. Fission based on pitch proximity was used to enrich the texture so that out of a single succession of notes, two melodic lines could be heard. Example 6a is from the Prelude of Bach's Third Partita for violin solo. In it, passages that violate proximity and produce fission (Figure 6.3A) alternate with passages that do not (Figure 6.3B), but nowhere does the violinist play more than one note at a time. Dowling (1968) counted the intervals in a number of such pieces by Bach and Telemann and found that intervals in fission-producing passages were rarely smaller than 3 semitones.

Three semitones is, in fact, the interval at which a rapid trill of two alternating pitches typically split apart perceptually. Miller and Heise (1950) presented listeners with trills analogous to the wiggly pattern in Figure 6.1A. Then the upper notes gradually increased in pitch, approaching the pattern of Figure 6.1B. At some point, the smooth ripple of the trill split apart perceptually into two sets of beeping tones. This fission usually occurred at a separation of about 3 semitones, a distance Miller and Heise called the trill threshold. Example 6b presents such a gradually widening trill at 10 note/sec. Van Noorden (1975) explored this phenomenon further and found that the fission threshold of 3 semitones held for fast sequences of 8 or 10 notes/sec (as in Example 6b). However, as the sequence is slowed, the listener has more discretion—being able to hear it as one coherent pattern or as split, depending on the way his or her attention is directed. That is, at 8 tones/sec, a sequence with a 4-semitone interval almost always splits apart, while at 3 tones/sec the listener can hear it either way—attending to it now as a coherent, single pattern, now as split in two. Example 6c presents such a slower sequence with a 4-semitone interval at 3 notes/sec. Try listening to it first one way, then the other. When you listen to a split-apart stimulus like that of Example 6b, you can attend to either the upper series of notes or the lower but not both at once. The line you attend to becomes figure, the other line ground.

6c

A curious phenomenon occurs here: The temporal relationships between the notes of the figure and those of the ground become lost. Norman (1967) noticed this phenomenon, and the temporal derangement led him to call the effect rhythmic fission. Van Noorden (1975) constructed a compelling demonstration of the degree to which temporal integration between the separate lines is lost. In Example 6d, we first hear two alternating tones, together in pitch and evenly spaced in time (Figure 6.4A). The temporal spacing of the notes is then changed to produce a halting rhythmic pattern (Figure 6.4B). Then the pitch separation is increased to more than an octave (Figure 6.4C). The halting rhythm is still clearly heard. Then the tempo is increased (Figure 6.4D), and the halting rhythm disappears perceptually. The sequence is going too fast for the listener to follow note for note over such large changes of pitch. The temporal integration of the two streams breaks down. Last, the pitch difference is reduced to the original interval (Figure 6.4E). The halting rhythm, never physically absent, reappears. This demonstrates an interaction between tempo and pitch separation. At slow tempos, the rhythm can be integrated over large pitch intervals, while that integration breaks down at faster tempos. Rhythmic integration can be restored at the fast tempo by reducing the pitch interval.

6d

Figure 6.4   Focal stimuli in Example 6d.

McAdams and Bregman (1979) provide a very useful review of a number of phenomena related to the proximity principle and fission. Among the most interesting of these is the result of Bregman and Dannenbring (1973) that introducing glissandos between the tones—that is, by having the frequency slide from one to the next rather than switching abruptly—reduced the tendency for fission and made it more likely that the sequence would be heard as continuous rather than split. This was true to some extent even if only the suggestion of a glissando, just the beginning and end of a slide but not the middle, was present.

The kind of figure–ground effect produced with interleaved melodies in different pitch ranges can also be produced with brief melodic fragments embedded in longer tone sequences. Divenyi and Hirsh (1978) gave listeners the task of detecting a three-note sequence embedded in a longer sequence. When the target sequence and the background tones were in separate pitch ranges, the target was easy to identify, even at very rapid rates, but not when the two sets of tones were in the same region. As we might expect from the proximity and similarity principles, targets using relatively small pitch intervals between tones such as in music were easier to identify than targets with very large intervals. It is curious that embedding the very rapid target in a long sequence (eight tones) did not make the task much more difficult than embedding it in a short sequence (four tones—only one extra tone). This suggests that a rapid tone sequence is processed as a unit or chunk and that the extra tone cannot simply be ignored by the listener unless it is in a separate pitch region.

Good Continuation and Common Fate

It is difficult, both conceptually and operationally, to arrive at a good definition of *prägnanz* (good continuation), and good continuation seems to be a rather weak organizing principle when brought into conflict with proximity. Bregman and Dannenbring's (1973) example of reducing fission by linking alternating pitches by glissandos is, in a sense, an instance of good continuation. But the auditory analog of Figure 6.1E, in which alternating melodies cross each other, is another type of example. Van Noorden (1975) constructed such sequences in which a scale was interleaved with a repeating tone. The scale proceeded at half the rate of the repeating tone, as shown in Figure 6.5. As you can hear in Example 6e, the scale notes are "captured" by the pattern of the repeating notes as they pass through that frequency region, and the sense of the scale as a pattern is lost.

Similarity of timbre also easily overrides pitch-organization *prägnanz;* otherwise it would not be so difficult to follow the continuity of a

6e

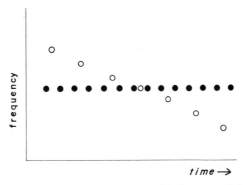

Figure 6.5 Stimulus pattern in Example 6e, in which the notes of the scale (open symbols) are "captured" by the repeating notes (filled symbols).

Klangfarbenmelodie (literally a "melody of tone colors," that is, a musical passage in which the sounds are organized as a pattern of timbres, rather than as a pattern of pitches). A study by Warren, Obusek, Farmer, and Warren (1969; Warren & Warren, 1970) gives some indication of the relative difficulty of auditory processing of rapid timbre shifts. Warren et al. presented listeners with recycling patterns of four different timbred sounds, for example, "beep," "hiss," "eeh," and "buzz," over and over. Even at only five sounds/sec, and after listening to numerous repetitions of the pattern, listeners performed only at chance in identifying the order of the sounds. This poor performance with timbre sequences can be contrasted with the much better performance of listeners identifying four-note sequences of pitches in the musical range after only one presentation at five notes/sec (Warren & Byrnes, 1975). It can also be contrasted at the extreme with the performance of Divenyi and Hirsh's (1978) highly trained listeners' identifying three-note pitch sequences at 50 notes/sec. Rapid shifts in timbre are simply more difficult for the ear to follow than rapid changes in pitch.

The principles of perceptual organization outlined above help decide how a particular local pattern element—a particular note or phrase, for example—will be perceived in relation to its local context. They help us predict the perceptual grouping into which a given note will fall. A single note taken out of context is meaningless, and it gains meaning only from its contextual relationship with other notes. In most of the above examples, the local meaning of a particular note is given directly by the local organization of the musical stimulus. Except for Examples 5e and f, the melodic figure could be distinguished from ground just on the basis of the present organization of the stimulus, without the listener's needing to remember either previous events in the piece or aspects of the piece's style. In this sense, most (but not all) local features of a piece are accessible to the listener without using memory. The organization of local features in music are, for the most part, determined by the straightforward and automatic operation of the listener's sensory systems. In contrast, the apprehension of global features of a piece almost always involves memory for earlier events in the piece (as perceptually organized in terms of local features) as well as knowledge of other pieces in the same style. Thus, the problem of the relationship between human memory and musical form appears.

We have found certain recent conceptual developments in perceptual and cognitive psychology useful in developing our account of memory and form. In the following sections, we develop a rather eclectic perspective that draws on two theoretical traditions that are not usually mixed: Gibson's (1979) approach to perception and Tulving's (1972) approach to memory. In doing this, we find it useful to think of pieces of music as sequences of events (Pick, 1979)—events that can be experienced as unitary occurrences and as embedded in larger events.

Global Organization

A useful way to think of the listener's apprehension of the global aspects of a piece of music is in terms of what Gibson (1979; Cutting, 1983) calls invariants—structural constancies underlying surface change in local pattern features. Invariants that might occur over relatively long time periods in a piece are regularities of temporal organization such as the beat, of tonal scale organization such as the key, and of instrumentation and density of note spacing in pitch and time. The invariants that the listener apprehends need not be literally represented in the surface pattern. The listener knows when the beat occurs even when it is not explicitly stated in the audible rhythmic pattern (Weaver, 1939). And the listener can infer the pitches in the scale of a tonal key after hearing only a few notes (Cohen, 1982). The listener's apprehension of the whole piece lies precisely in the perception of the long–time-span invariants of its structure. And the listener's prior experience with sets of similar pieces provides for the building up of schematic knowledge that allows for the filling in of aspects not explicitly stated (Neisser, 1976).

Some invariants are specific to a certain piece, such as the pitch and rhythm contour of the initial theme of Beethoven's Fifth Symphony. Other invariants heard in a particular piece are common to a large family of similar pieces, for example, the characteristic repeated rhythmic pattern of certain dances such as beguine and tango. In terms of scale-structure invariants, a piece may exhibit a particular shift between keys in the middle. Like Beethoven's Minuet in G, it may start out in one key and then toward the middle, shift (modulate) to a new key, for example, the dominant (with a scale built upon the fifth degree of the original scale). Then before the end, it may shift back again to the original key. Such a pattern involves variation within the single piece, but if the listener has heard many such pieces with the same pattern of modulation, then that pattern constitutes an invariant that the listener can perceive in each piece he or she hears, even pieces not heard before. Such invariants across sets of pieces constitute what we mean by a style. Experience with pieces in a particular style facilitates the listener's comprehension of the stylistic invariants of a new piece.

The listener's understanding of a piece on any but the surface level of local features involves the apprehension of invariant structures of considerable complexity. In fact, it is that complexity that makes a piece meaningful. A local phrase or note in the midst of a piece of music is the nexus of a multidimensional grid of invariants. That grid includes multidimensional pitch and time structures as well as all of the multiple dimensions involved in timbre, consonance, loudness, and so forth suggested in the preceding chapters. Consider a note in even a simple context: the note on the third beat of the fifth measure of the tune "Three Blind Mice" (denoted by the arrow in Figure 6.6). That note is involved in several simultaneously operating invariants of the musical structure. There are invariants underlying the linear melodic pattern, for example, motion by small pitch intervals, and here specifically, the continuation of the upward melodic succession of the preceding two notes. The temporal invariants of the rhythmic pattern require an accented note on the third beat of the measure. The key, C major, limits the notes of a simple melody like this to those of the C-major scale. The temporal harmonic pattern consists of the repeated sequence tonic-dominant-tonic (I–V–I) in every measure—a pattern appropriate to a round (in which new voices can enter at the beginning whenever the lead voice passes a bar line). This harmony requires a member of the tonic (I) chord on the first and third beats (namely, C, E, or G), and a member of the dominant (V) chord on the second beat

Figure 6.6 "Three Blind Mice."

(G, B, or D). The particular consonance relationships of the note to those sounding with it (in this case, when the melody is sung as a round) constitute another set of invariants. Timbre, loudness, general pitch range, and spatial location, as more or less global invariants, apply to the particular note and remain relatively constant over several notes if not the whole piece.

The meaning of the note lies in the sets of invariants it invokes. Note that every note need not literally instantiate every invariant bearing on its place in the piece. (That is, invariants *generally* hold over a large number of cases but do not hold *absolutely* in each particular case; see Cutting, 1983.) The meaning of a note arises from those invariants whose tendencies it violates as well as those whose tendencies it expresses. The note indicated by the arrow in "Three Blind Mice" is the resolution of a melodic and harmonic progression leading to the tonic on an accented beat; hence, the tonic note C is directly in keeping with that set of tendencies. However, the melodic contour of all four preceding measures has been that of two downward steps, from the first beat to the second and from the second to the third. Setting aside the eighth notes as passing tones, the upward move to the C violates that pattern. The global downward contour of the measure is restored in the latter part of the beat by the descent to the G. (That elaboration of melodic motion solves the problem that the melodic pattern B–G with the chord progression dominant–tonic (V–I) sounds awkward compared with the pattern B–C.)

The conflict of different sets of invariants impinging on a given point sets up structural tensions that add to the aesthetic interest of the piece. This inner tension is different from the tension (noted above) introduced by the departure of a specific note from the expectations invoked by invariants. That is, the tension of sets of invariants running at cross-purposes to each other should be apparent even before that conflict forces a choice in the selection of an element. The selection of an element in a sense resolves the conflict, but the resolution itself introduces a new conflict between the note and an invariant. Such structural tension is present in a simple way in "Three Blind Mice" and operates in complex ways in more elaborate pieces. Meyer (1956) discusses varieties of ambiguity used in the Western classical style. Ambiguity may be produced and tension heightened by avoiding the strong invocation of stylistic invariants, as, for example, by avoiding a clear tonality. Ambiguity and tension may also be produced by introducing conflicting tendencies among invariants. In Chapter 8 we discuss ways such cross-cutting tendencies and the expectancies they invoke could give rise to listeners' emotional responses.

Memory and Form

The above discussion suggests that there is an immense amount of structure in musical stimuli. This is no surprise for the musicologist devoted to the study of musical structure. For the psychologist, the description of the stimulus structure is only the beginning of the solution to the problem. The psychological questions start with the given structure and ask what aspects of that structure are relevant to cognition—which of the many dimensions of a musical stimulus structure have psychological reality, and how fine a grain of discrimination on those dimensions is relevant. In Chapter 5, we review evidence that listeners remember certain aspects of melodies better than others, and they remember different aspects under different conditions. Memory encoding and retrieval processes select among available stimulus aspects. The question of the relationship between the stimulus and what is remembered arises. Here, in its broadest sense, is the question of the relationship between memory and musical form. For complex pieces, ordinary listeners do not literally remember every detail, nor would they be able to reconstruct such a piece flawlessly from a combination of details and invariants. The listener understands a complex piece through just those aspects that have filtered through the listener's own cognitive systems, taken in conjunction with what the listener already knows of the piece and its style.

The role of memory in hearing a piece of music is somewhat like the role of memory in listening to a conversation. To understand present utterances or events, one needs to have a notion of the gist of what went before but need not be able to recall literally all that was said. Usually, one comes away from a conversation with a knowledge of its overall meaning but with little exact recollection of details. Sometimes, however, a surprising or vivid phrase sticks in the mind and can be literally recalled. That sometimes happens with music, too, when a particularly felicitous tune or turn of phrase is remembered. In Chapter 5, we show that memory for such phrases is likely to be very precise in that they are not likely to be confused with highly similar imitations.

To illustrate both kinds of memory process, consider the listener's experience of a speech in a play, for example, Mark Antony's Funeral Oration in Shakespeare's *Julius Caesar*. Most of Antony's words after the initial "Friends, Romans, countrymen" are forgotten after the first hearing, but the overall meanings of what Antony says are remembered—his intentions of arousing the crowd as well as his more plainly stated love of Caesar. In fact, as in music, tensions arise from conflicts among the underlying meanings the speech invokes, since Antony carefully skirts the overtly seditious while nevertheless inciting sedition. These meanings are remembered by the listener even though the particular phrases in which they are expressed may be forgotten. However, in this speech, at least one phrase stands out and is remembered literally, namely, "Brutus is an honorable man." Part of the cumulative effect of the speech derives from the repetition of this phrase. It is repeated three times literally at the start and later paraphrased some five times. This repetition is an invariant of the speech. Here not only is the invariant apprehended, but also the phrase itself is literally represented in memory and the listener is able to remember when he or she heard the phrase and could give a good guess as to how often it occurred.

Analogous patterns of repetitions of memorable phrases occur commonly in musical compositions, and standard patterns of formal organization provide for their use. Two common forms of the Classical and Romantic periods in Western music (1750–1900), the rondo and the sonata allegro, are based on repetition patterns that can easily incorporate the recurrence of memorable phrases. Simple schematic versions of the overall repetition of melodic material in those two forms are: rondo (*ABACA-DAZ*) and sonata (*ABABXABZ*), where *X* represents a reworking, or development, of *A* and *B,* and *Z* represents a coda (tail) that may incorporate aspects of any of the foregoing elements. In rondos, the A melody is often a brief, catchy tune, while the contrasting interspersed sections are more discursive and diffuse (as in the Rondos of Mozart's four Concerti for Horn and Orchestra, where the formal pattern is immediately apparent to the listener). The *A* and *B* patterns in sonata movements are typically more extended and not usually the sort of self-contained units that could be called tunes. In fact, they are often best thought of as clusters of melodic patterns that appear in various arrangements through the rest of the piece. But in some cases, composers have used the recurrence of an initial, highly memorable phrase in the *A* cluster as a recurring guidepost throughout the piece. Outstanding examples are Beethoven's opening melody for cello in the Sonata for Cello and Piano, *op. 69,* the opening of his Fourth Piano Concerto, and the French horn melody at the start of Brahms' Second Piano Concerto. Throughout the musical cultures of the world and in Western jazz and popular music, forms like rondo as well as theme and variations abound, in which memorable material is repeated with unfamiliar material interspersed. As in memory for the verbal material of a play, the pattern of memory processes through the development of a piece seems to include both rather specific memories for particular salient phrases as well as less specific memories for broader pattern invariants.

These two kinds of memory processes—memory for overall meanings and memory for the occurrences of specific events—are much like what Tulving (1972; Tulving & Thomson, 1973) refer to as semantic and episodic memory, respectively. In one sense, memory for a piece is organized into a series of episodes of varying length. The length of the memory record of an episode depends on musical structure. Rhythmic and *Episodic* melodic features often mark the starts and finishes of such phrases, and *Ep* local phrase organization appears to be well characterized by the gestalt principles outlined above. (This application is complicated somewhat by the fact that phrase boundaries often overlap on different levels of a complex musical structure.) The listener's experience of a piece in terms of its local phrase episodes is analogous to viewing a series of snapshots. If this were all that is important to understanding the meaning of a piece of music, then a *Readers Digest* version of a piece that preserved all the memorable episodes would be entirely satisfactory. (The *Readers Digest* in the 1950s actually published such a version of the "classics.") In fact, there is more involved in understanding a piece than making memoranda *Semantic* of its local phrases, and that "more" we are now lumping together under the label of semantic memory for the piece, with the suggestion that it concerns a grasp of the broad pattern invariants of pieces and styles.

Episodic musical memory is much better understood than semantic. Rhythm—the pattern of temporal relationships in the stimulus—is centrally important at this level. As has been well documented with verbal materials (Bower, 1972), local rhythmical organization can determine what is remembered. As an illustration of this, Dowling (1973b) presented listeners with sequences 20 notes long divided rhythmically into 4 five-note phrases. Following each sequence, listeners were tested with five-note fragments—coherent phrases marked off rhythmically as in the initial sequence—or five notes that crossed a phrase boundary (the last three notes of one phrase plus the first two notes of the next). Recognition was significantly better in the five-note fragments, suggesting that the 20-note sequence was stored in memory as four phrases rather than as 20 notes with no breaks (see Handel, 1973, for a similar result). Jones, Boltz, and Kidd (1982) demonstrated that such predictable rhythmic patterning can serve to call the listener's attention to structurally significant pitches and, hence, improve performance in detecting deviations from pitch pattern regularity.

Deutsch (1980) provides a subtle example of the effects of phrasing on memory for melodies, in which she shows that phrase boundaries can be marked by melodic pitch structure even without explicit temporal breaks or literal repetition. Attneave (1965) demonstrated a similar effect of phrasing on memory by giving listeners the task of discriminating between random tone sequences and ones with regular structure. Listeners found this task to be relatively easy when the regular sequences consisted of repetitions of subsequences 6 or 8 or 10 notes long. Listeners had more difficulty when the subsequences repeated at intervals of 20 or 30 notes. These studies show that what is remembered in a piece is influenced by its temporal grouping.

Set

When we begin to think about the listener's comprehension of global properties of a piece, we also need to take into account the listener's attitudes to listening and the listening strategies those attitudes invoke— the listener's *set*. Two dimensions along which those attitudes might be differentiated are (1) depth of cognitive understanding, and (2) degree of subjective (vs. objective) involvement. Along the first dimension, we can contrast the listener who simply accepts each local feature as it appears and says, "Oh, wow!" or "Ah, how beautiful!" with the listener who integrates each local feature into a meaningful global pattern, understanding (usually implicitly, not explicitly) its relationship to the whole. Wittgenstein (1966) contrasts a person commenting on clothing styles who can say only, "Oh, how charming," with one who can make astute comments on the design. The first attitude is often the only one we can use for a piece from an unfamiliar style or culture when we do not have the implicit semantic knowledge that makes deeper understanding possible. And certain pieces have been produced with such a high degree of repetition as to discourage the involvement of memory, for example, Terry Riley's *In C* (Columbia album MS-7178) or the improvisations of Keith Jarrett (e.g., ECM album 1064/65). As Boulez (1984, p. 14) comments, such "minimalist and repetitive music appeals to an extremely primitive perception, and it reduces the elements of music to one single component—periodicity." We should note, however, that a listener could well have deep cognitive understanding without the sort of *explicit* knowledge Wittgenstein requests. In that case, the behavioral evidence for *implicit* understanding would lie in the pattern of pieces the person chooses to listen to and so forth.

The second dimension, subjective versus objective listening, applies whenever the listener goes deeper than the superficial level of local features. As Meyer (1956) points out, the listener can become immersed in the piece, losing the sense of being a separate critic (the subjective mode), or he or she can identify with the composer or performer, retaining a self-conscious and detached critical attitude (the objective mode). The extreme of the objective form of cognition is exemplified by the young Mozart's going home and writing out the score of the symphony he had just heard. But in most listening, and certainly in the most enjoyable listening for the majority of listeners, the subjective attitude is more typical, involving the implicit cognition of global properties of the piece.

Expectancy

One way in which the comprehension of global invariants of structure might function as we listen to a piece is by affecting our expectancies from moment to moment. Recall from Chapter 5 the role of mental schemata in guiding the listener's expectancies in the perception of a piece. A schema facilitates the processing of events that match expectancies and provides a standard for evaluating moderate deviations. In Chapter 5, we discuss the role of schemata principally in terms of memory for melodies built on tonal scales. Here we view the global organization of a piece as a cluster of schemata that guides perception dynamically through time, generating expected paths through musical time and space (pitch and timbre). Jones expresses this view well:

> I propose that people actually generate subjective space–time paths of their own in response to certain features of the external stimulus pattern. These mental "paths" function as psychological expectancies. And it is through extrapolation of these mental spatio-temporal patterns that a person comes to anticipate "where" in space and "when" in time future events may occur. Expectancies, at least initially, are typically ideal or simplified paths. They are continuous, rhythmically generated paths that allow us to guide our attention to approximately correct neighborhoods. But what is most important is that organisms possess subjective generators that resemble those outlined in the representation of world patterns. . . . The responsive person dynamically generates trajectories that cast . . . attentional thrusts into space and forward in time. (Jones, 1981b, p. 571)

Jones with Meyer (1956; see Chapter 8, this volume) believes that such expectancies must be nonspecific. Here the analogy of a path seems apt. As we walk along a forest path, we are not very surprised if it detours around a newly fallen tree, as long as it continues in the general direction we intended to go. Our expectations are not so specific as to lead to great surprise in such a case. We construct a model of the world not unlike Tolman's (1948) cognitive map. Just as the rats in Tolman's study learned the general layout of the room and not a set of specific responses at turns in the maze, we have a general idea of the layout of the forest that allows for moderate variations of detail. In fact, we would be surprised if everything were *exactly* as we saw it a year before. With sufficient experience, the structure of our revised schemata comes to resemble the structure of the world more and more closely. As our schemata converge with the world, our perceptions change in the direction of greater richness and subtlety. We notice small changes in a familiar forest—we notice nuances of expression in a familiar piece.

The effectiveness of expectancies in even the simple task of detecting a single pitch in noise has been well documented (Swets, 1963). Knowing the pitch range in which the target will appear aids perception. A musical context can establish such expectations, and the expectations vary with the musical sophistication of the listener. Dewar, Cuddy, and Mewhort (1977) found that repetition of melodic context improved recognition of single tones. Krumhansl and Shepard (1979) presented listeners with a scale (C–D–E–F–G–A–B) and asked listeners to rate the suitability of notes from the octave above as completions of the sequence. They found that inexperienced listeners rated completions on the basis of similarity in pitch height to the next note in the scale (C), while more experienced listeners tended to take into account the suitability of members of the harmonic triad based on C, namely, C, E, and G. The more experienced people had more than the simple schema of scale-wise motion to guide them. And the particular experiences people have with the music of their culture lead them to different expectancies. Carlsen (1981b) asked music students in Germany, Hungary, and the United States to sing completions of melodies and found that the completions were very different for the three groups, even though they came from closely related musical subcultures.

Jones, Kidd, and Wetzel (1981) provide a demonstration of how expectancies can be responsive to rhythmic invariants of a tonal sequence, suggesting that attention is under rhythmic control. Bregman and Rudnicky (1975) had shown that recognition of a two-note target flanked by distractor tones could be improved if additional distractor tones were included before and after the flanking tones and in the same frequency region. However, if the additional tones were in a separate frequency region, they did not help. When the additional tones were near the flanking tones in frequency, all the distractor tones were grouped perceptually (according to pitch proximity) into a separate pattern from the target, facilitating target recognition. Jones et al. showed that this effect depends on the rhythmic grouping of target and distractors. Under conditions where the distractors were closely grouped in pitch, the rhythmic relationships of target and background were important. When the target tones had their own rhythm, distinct from the distractors, listeners achieved 62% correct recognitions. But when the whole sequence, including targets and distractors, was presented in a uniform rhythm, performance fell to 48%. Thus listeners are able to use the rhythmic information in melodic sequences to control their allocation of attention and to improve their recognition.

Expectancies are related to accuracy of perception and memory for actual music. Carlsen (1981a) had musically sophisticated listeners perform a melodic dictation task in which they tried to write down the notes they heard. He compared their dictation performance with their expectancies, using common seven- or eight-note melodies from the Western tradition. He found that the incidence of dictation errors was correlated negatively ($r = -.69$) with expectancy successes. Expectancies based upon the operation of more than one schema at a time are typical. Jones (1981a) points to the simultaneous use of harmonic schemata and those based on scale-wise motion (the second being the mental representation of implicit knowledge of the facts summarized in Figure 6.2). Jones, Maser, and Kidd (1978) provide evidence for the use of more elaborate schemata in which higher-order structural properties of melodies overrode even pitch distance in determining expectancies and memory performance.

HIERARCHICAL ORGANIZATION

Thus far we have left open the question of exactly how global and local aspects of our memory representation of a piece might be integrated. That they are linked in some way is clear. Local features, however memorable, are not always remembered independently, in isolation from global context. They *can* be so remembered, as when suddenly a memorable phrase pops into consciousness and we cannot get it out of our heads. But the more usual case is for episodic memories to contribute to our comprehension of an ongoing piece by serving as guideposts to global structure, as suggested above. This raises the question of how local features are related to each other and to global patterns.

One proposal of numerous theorists from music, psychology, and linguistics is to represent those local–global relationships in a hierarchical tree structure. Figure 6.7 represents the first four phrases of "Three Blind Mice" by means of a structural tree. The notes of each phrase are joined together under a node representing that phrase. Within each phrase, each succeeding note is shifted downward along the scale with respect to the preceding note. The node label representing this transposition is labeled T−. The first two phrases are closely related: The second is a repetition of the first. This is indicated by their connection to a common node (labeled R). The third and fourth phrases are similarly related. At a still higher level the node indicates the relationship between the first pair of phrases and the second pair. That relationship has at least three components: (1) The second pair of phrases repeats the contour of the first pair, but (2) the second note of the phrase is rhythmically elaborated, and (3) the second

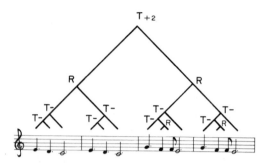

Figure 6.7 Hierarchical structure of "Three Blind Mice."

note of the phrase is at a higher pitch level (denoted by the label T + 2, for a transposition of two diatonic scale steps). The highest node in Figure 6.7 is in turn connected to even higher levels in the structure of the whole song. (We are here using the term *hierarchical* to mean "having elements related by superordinate–subordinate relationships" and do not mean to imply that the structures described are symmetrical.)

Local properties of "Three Blind Mice" in Figure 6.7 are represented in lower levels in the hierarchical structure (for example, the pitches and durations of single notes). More global properties are represented at higher structural levels. For example, the contour of the first phrase is a relatively global property pertaining to the node representing that phrase. Other global properties involve the overall harmonic and rhythmic structure of a piece and the place a particular phrase occupies in that structure.

Basic questions in the study of perception arise over the relationship between global and local properties of stimuli. The gestalt psychologists (Köhler, 1929) focused on this problem, maintaining that the perceptual whole is different from the sum of the parts, that is, that global properties of stimuli often emerge that are not related in some simple, direct way to their local properties. Rather, the same local set of stimulus elements might, because of a change of context, take on very different global properties. The beginning and ending phrases of "Three Blind Mice" provide a very mild example of such an effect. These changes in meaning are related to the way in which the phrase satisfies prior expectations and to the expectations that it in turn invokes. A more dramatic example can be found in the Gloria of Haydn's *Theresa* Mass (Figure 6.8), where the same contour is repeated in a different position on the scale with a different harmonic meaning. The first presentation begins and ends on the tonic of B-flat major. The second presentation begins where the first left off but ends on the tonic of E-flat major, a modulation to a nearly related key. This pair of phrases is presented in Example 6f, where you can hear the

6f

Figure 6.8 Two phrases from the Gloria of Haydn's *Theresa* Mass in B-flat (1799).

rather static feeling of the first phrase transformed into the dynamism of the second. Although their local contours and rhythmic patterns are identical, these phrases differ in global properties linking them to the larger tonal structure in which they appear. (Kubovy & Pomerantz, 1981, provide a collection of highly stimulating chapters concerning the recent history of issues of perceptual organization raised by the gestaltists.)

Tree Structures

The hierarchical tree structure in Figure 6.7 is an intuitively appealing representation of the melodic pattern in "Three Blind Mice." We think of that melody as beginning with a repeated phrase, followed by a translation of the whole pattern to another level of the scale with a slight rhythmic elaboration. These relationships among the components of the pattern are clearly represented in the tree diagram, called in linguistics a phrase structure representation. Such relationships among the parts of melodic patterns have led some theorists (Bernstein, 1976; Deutsch, 1982; Deutsch & Feroe, 1981; Jones, 1976, 1981c; Lerdahl & Jackendoff, 1983; Restle, 1970) to suggest that important aspects of melodies might be well represented by tree diagrams. Rules are applied at each node in such a diagram in the generation of a melody. Thus, at the topmost node in Figure 6.7, the first two phrases are translated along the scale to form the basis of the second two. The nodes at the next level down involve the repetition of the first and third phrases to form the second and fourth phrases. And the nodes at the lowest level of analysis within the phrases involve scalewise movement from note to note (applied twice within each phrase in a right-branching fashion). This sort of rule structure could be used to generate melodies, and we could look at relationships between properties of rule structures and the difficulties people have in learning patterns.

The operation of such rules in the generation of melodic patterns is illustrated for "Three Blind Mice" in Figure 6.7. We call the transposition rule T. T transposes whatever falls under the left branch of the node to a new level along the diatonic scale. In case of single notes, T+ indicates that the next note will be one step up from the present note; T− indicates one step down. R is short for T0 and indicates a repetition. Dowling (1978b) found that skips along the scale are relatively rare in songs, but when they occur, skips are indicated by marking with a number, such as T + 2, T − 3, and so forth. A similar relationship holds for phrases, using the starting pitch of the phrase to determine distance of translation. Repetition of a phrase is indicated, as with notes, by R. One remaining rule in most systems, but not illustrated in Figure 6.7, is inversion (I), which produces the mirror image of each pitch with respect to the other end of the scale: C remains C, D becomes B and vice versa, E becomes A and vice versa, and so forth. (Technically, this is called taking the complement *modulo* 7; Babbitt (1962) provides a useful explication.) Restle (1970), Jones (1976, 1981c; Jones et al., 1978), and Deutsch (1980, 1982; Deutsch & Feroe, 1981) use somewhat different notation for highly similar types of system. (The main difficulties in applying these structural descriptions to note sequences arise from the fact that they are often ambiguous in the sense that a given sequence can be given more than one description with no clear means of deciding which is to be preferred. See the discussions by Jones, 1981c, 1982, and Deutsch, 1982.)

Restle's (1970) early results on the effects of hierarchical structure (such as displayed in these tree diagrams) on learning of temporal sequences of events were obtained with a row of lights that flashed one at a time. The viewer's task was to anticipate which light would flash next. Over a series of repetitions of the sequence, the viewer came to learn the pattern and to anticipate correctly. The questions Restle investigated concern the effects of sequence structure on rate of learning and on the types of errors that occur. A sequence of flashing lights is closely analogous to a sequence of melodic pitches, and Restle's results are interesting for the musician. As we would expect, errors were most prevalent following breaks between constituents in the phrase structure. The more major the constituent—the higher the node—the more errors occurred. This is analogous to listeners' producing the most errors anticipating the first and seventh elements in the sequence diagrammed in Figure 6.7, somewhat fewer for the fourth and eleventh elements, and fewest for the elements falling within the shorter phrases. Furthermore, the errors tended qualitatively to anticipate a continuation of the sequence along the scale (as in anticipating that the third element of Figure 6.7 would be a C) or to anticipate continued alternations (Restle & Brown, 1970a, 1970b). Restle (1972) found that if viewers were allowed to preview sequences, then that experience was especially helpful if the sequence was temporally phrased in a way consonant with its phrase structure, that is, if brief pauses were introduced after each constituent. "Bad" phrasing that did not correspond to the phrase structure hindered performance.

Deutsch (1980) studied the effects of temporal phrasing in melodic structures using a task in which music students took melodic dictation. She found that phrasing that conflicted with constituent structure produced many more dictation errors than phrasing consonant with structure. Listeners were apparently trying to learn the sequences in terms of phrases defined by temporal grouping. This is suggested by the fact that the initial elements of *temporal* groups generated the most errors, whether those elements coincided with beginnings of phrase structure constituents or not. Where the boundaries of temporal and phrase structure grouping coincided, errors were relatively low. Where temporal phrasing departed from phrase structure, errors increased. Thus, phrase structure is psychologically real in representing stimulus propertied the listener uses in organizing perception and production.

Limitations of Phrase Structure

It is clear that musical expectancies at a global level encompassing extended melodic sequences can be influenced significantly by phrase structure. Yet purely symmetrical structures such as those we have just been discussing are too simple to represent actual music. This is shown even in the first four phrases of "Three Blind Mice" (Figure 6.7), which are diagrammed by an *inhomogeneous* tree. The second two phrases in that diagram contain a rhythmic elaboration not contained in the first two phrases. Therefore, the topmost node in Figure 6.7 cannot just be represented as a T + 2 rule. This is what Restle means when he says,

> In [such] trees . . . every part could be generated from the previous part (at some level) by a single [rule]. Such structures are too simple for communication, and even for aesthetic purposes. The sonata allegro, in music, traditionally uses two contrasting themes. This has several advantages, one of which is that the two contrasting themes are highly distinguishable, so that [the listener] is not easily confused as to where he [or she] is in the sequence. Inhomogeneous patterns may be either easier or more difficult than homogeneous ones. It is more difficult to generate an inhomogeneous pattern, but easier to discriminate the parts. (Restle, 1970, p. 490)

There are a number of ways in which musical structures depart from strict homogeneity. The first, just mentioned with regard to "Three Blind Mice," is that complications are often introduced into phrases that are otherwise copies of phrases that went before. A second source of inhomogeneity could be relationships of phrase repetition or similarity that span intervals filled with different material. This is one thing Restle means in referring to sonata allegro form (described above), in which earlier material is repeated after digressions into other material. Even in a simple song like "Three Blind Mice" (Figure 6.6), this type of relationship occurs between the last phrase and the first. Such remote relationships cannot be expressed handily using phrase structures.

Third, it often seems natural to analyze music in terms of overlapping constituents. The end of one phrase is often the beginning of another (Bernstein, 1976). Examples of such patterns range from folk music (in the Irish jig "Nora Creina," for example) to the imitative forms of the baroque. Figure 6.9 shows a portion of Bach's Three-Part Invention in F Minor (Sinfonia IX), in which the contour pattern $[+ - (0) + -]$ is highly influential. The brackets indicate the parsing of phrases in the three parts.

6g (Example 6g).

Fourth, each element in a song could be thought of as determined by more than one global structure at a time, as Jones (1981b) indicates and as we discuss above in connection with the note designated by the arrow in Figure 6.6. Such structures that combine with the melodic structure could be rhythmic or harmonic, for example. In the case of the rhythmic elaboration of the second pair of phrases in "Three Blind Mice," this would involve imposing a rhythmic structure (here determined by the poem) on the melodic structure and doing so with a minimum of melodic disruption (T0). In fact, the fifth phrase of "Three Blind Mice" (Figure 6.6) can be viewed as a further rhythmic elaboration the initial three-note descending contour. The harmonic structure of "Three Blind Mice" is shown in Figure 6.10. The harmony is tightly constrained by the fact that the song can be sung as a round, with different singers starting every two measures. Thus, each two-measure group must be compatible with all the others. Each, in fact, repeats the tonic–dominant–tonic pattern shown in Figure 6.10.

The problems with a simple homogeneous phrase structure model of melodic organization lead one to believe that some elaboration of such

Figure 6.9 The structure of a passage from J. S. Bach's Three-Part Invention in F Minor, showing overlapping phrase structures.

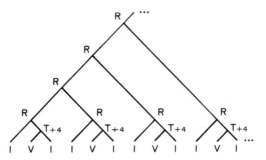

Figure 6.10 Harmonic structure of "Three Blind Mice," involving repetitions represented by a right-branching tree structure.

models would be desirable. The elaboration that immediately suggests itself is the use of transformational grammar, since that is the solution used in linguistics to solve parallel problems (Chomsky, 1965) and that Bernstein (1976) suggests might be useful in describing musical structures. However, Lerdahl and Jackendoff (1983; Jackendoff, 1977) have serious doubts about the usefulness of that type of solution, and we have to await future developments to see how hierarchical models are brought into closer compatibility with actual musical structures. Nevertheless, evidence such as we have reviewed here suggests that phrase structure models will play a fundamental role in future cognitive theories.

Levels of Reality

In the following chapter, we take a closer look at the organization of time in music and extend our range of examples to non-Western musical structures. Before closing this chapter, though, we wish to comment on one more aspect of the use of structural descriptions such as those we have been considering, namely, the levels of reality they can be supposed to represent. Like grammatical descriptions of language (see Chomsky, 1965), structural descriptions of music can be thought of as applying to one or another of three levels. First, the description may be applied simply to the musical structure itself, apart from any psychological considerations. This is the aim of the musicologist. Second, the structural description may be taken as describing the knowledge the listener (or performer) has and uses in understanding or producing music. This is the level at which most of our discussion in this chapter is aimed and corresponds to Chomsky's description of competence. It is this knowledge that is described in terms of invariants of piece and style and that represents more than just memory for particular instances. Finally, there is the description of the process by which musical information is handled by the mind (brain). The structural description taken at this level needs not only to represent the knowledge the listener has, but to represent it with the actual structural properties of a brain representation and to represent as well the processes by which that knowledge is put to use. This is the goal of our theories and experiments, and the issue of whether a given structural description would make a suitable basis for an account of processing remains an important one in evaluating theories (Collard & Povel, 1982). Nevertheless, we seem far from achieving an account of musical information processing in that sense and must settle for now with partial descriptions of knowledge representations.

SUMMARY

This chapter has presented an account of certain aspects of musical structure relevant to perception and memory. One question underlying this account is, given that a structural pattern exists in the music, whether that pattern is psychologically important. The immense amount of information transmitted in the sound wave is selected and organized by the cognitive systems of the listener, and it is the result of that cognitive processing that is experienced and remembered. Thus, one of our first tasks is to determine what those cognitive-processing systems do and what aspects of musical sound structure are psychologically real in the sense of making a difference to cognition.

In considering cognition and musical structure, we found it useful to distinguish between local and global features. Local features were seen as combining in larger and larger groups to form global features. We agreed with the gestalt psychologists that local features in combination typically take on properties that they did not exhibit in isolation and that global properties of whole patterns are often different from local features of their components. We explored local features of pitch and rhythmic organization that tend to make patterns difficult or easy to perceive and remember, and we continue the exploration of rhythmic organization in Chapter 7. We considered some proposals for characterizing the relationships between local and global properties as organized in hierarchical structures.

In considering global properties of patterns, we found Gibson's concept of pattern invariants quite useful. Invariants are abstract properties that hold over larger or smaller regions of patterns. The tonality of a musical passage is an invariant, and so is the temporal arrangement of melody contrasts characteristic of a style. A listener's knowledge of a piece or of a style is stored in semantic memory, and that knowledge is integrated with specific episodic memories of local events in the cognition of a passage. The listener's understanding of the ongoing sequence of events within a piece of music depends on the cognition of the way those events are related to one another and to the broader scheme of pattern invariants. That type of cognition is not usually explicit and conscious, but rather functions subconsciously to provide the listener with the conscious experience of the music.

7

Rhythm and the Organization of Time

*Ultimately the delight [in rhythmic portrayals and presenta-
tions] springs from the fact that such things are instances of
the relationships that determine the course of life, natural
and achieved.*

(Dewey, 1934, p. 150)

INTRODUCTION

In Chapter 6, we looked at some broad, overall conceptualizations of
the organization of time in music. Here we turn more specifically to some
empirical results bearing on the perception of rhythmic patterns. In the
psychology of music, rhythm has not been as thoroughly studied as pitch.
After an auspicious beginning in the nineteenth century, work in the
experimental psychology of time and rhythm perception tapered off until
revived by Fraisse (1956, 1974) in the 1950s. There are probably several
reasons for the half-century lapse. First, as Gabrielsson (1973d) notes,
after some early successes, the study of rhythm after the turn of the
century quickly led researchers into considerable amounts of puzzling
complexity. Part of this complexity undoubtedly mirrors the elaborate-
ness of humans' information-processing capacities for time and rhythm,
while part of the complexity may be intrinsic to the way brief time intervals are processed. There is probably more than one perceptual system
involved in the processing of temporal and rhythmic information. And it
may be, as Idson and Massaro (1977) suggest, that temporal judgments
are reflexive in that the judged duration of a time interval is based in part

on the processing time used to produce that judgment. Second, the study of pitch perception since Helmholtz has been bound up with basic questions concerning sensory analysis in the periphery of the auditory system, outlined in Chapter 2. Researchers' success with those problems focused attention on pitch rather than rhythm. And the behaviorist movement of the 1920s and 1930s had the effect in psychology generally of emphasizing the study of simpler, more peripheral processes in the nervous system as opposed to more complex central processes like those concerned with rhythm.

The neglect of rhythm was especially unfortunate for the psychology of music because rhythmic information is, if anything, more fundamental to music cognition than pitch information. William James (1890) observed that we can recognize familiar tunes from their rhythmic patterns alone, a fact now well documented (White, 1960). And when listeners are given an array of brief melodies in a multidimensional scaling task designed to find the important stimulus dimensions, rhythmic information tends to dominate pitch information in their judgments (Carterette, Monahan, Holman, Bell, & Fiske, 1982; Monahan, 1983). The neglect of rhythm is fortunately ending. The stimulus control and complex data analyses afforded by computers, coupled with a renewed interest of psychologists in complex cognitive processes, are leading to a resurgence of rhythm research in the second half of the twentieth century.

TEMPORAL EXPERIENCE

Two of the more successful nineteenth-century investigations of time perception dealt with the psychological present, that part of our ongoing experience currently accessible to consciousness, and psychological pace, involving the question of whether there is some natural rate at which psychological events take place and at which environmental events are most efficiently processed.

The Psychological Present

William James characterized the psychological present as a temporal span of attention, a sort of window opened on experience, continually shifting its view along in time. "The practically cognized present is no knife-edge, but a saddle-back, with a certain breadth of its own on which we sit perched, and from which we look in two directions in time" (James, 1890, p. 609). The question arises as to the temporal extent of this window. Undoubtedly, its size varies with attention and with characteristics of the material being listened to. Fraisse (1978, 1982) has assembled a variety of converging evidence indicating that the psychological present typically extends for a few seconds and is rarely more than 5 sec long. Fraisse found that listeners were able to reproduce accurately simple sound sequences 3 or 4 sec long. He also found that listeners "chunk" long sequences of clicks into subsequences, and in that way, are able to perceive accurately sequences as long as 25 clicks by chunking them as five groups of 5. James had noted that the listener spontaneously divides even a uniform sequence of clicks into rhythmic groups in that way and cited Wundt and Dietze to the effect that the extreme upper limit of accurate recognition of a click series is about 40 over a period of 12 sec, which could be chunked into either five groups of 8 or eight groups of 5.

Five or eight chunks agrees, of course, with Miller's (1956) estimate that 7 ± 2 items can be held concurrently in immediate memory. In fact, it seems reasonable to associate the experienced psychological present with the cluster of various auditory information processes usually called immediate or sensory memory. (Sensory memory briefly stores complex information that is difficult or impossible to verbalize.) The time estimates of a few seconds with the longest possible durations around 5 or 10 sec converges with other evidence on the persistence of events in sensory memory. For example, Kubovy and Howard (1976) used tone clusters such as those described at the end of Chapter 2 to arrive at an estimate of how long precise auditory waveform information remains available in the auditory system. The tone clusters were each 0.3 sec long, and they were presented dichotically with one component phase-shifted between the two ears. In successive sound bursts, the shifted component was either higher or lower in pitch. Kubovy and Howard argue that if the auditory system was preserving information permitting the identification of the shifted component, then a series of such shifted components could be compared for pitch by the system. The perceptual effect of such a series would then be that of an ascending or descending pitch scale. Kubovy and Howard found that listeners were about 70% accurate in identifying scale direction when the time delay between bursts was about 1 sec, a period that they characterize as "a lower bound on the average half-life of echoic [sensory] memory" (1976, p. 531). One extraordinary subject succeeded at this task with interburst intervals of 9.7 sec, which is in the same ballpark as the upper estimates derived from click-series recognition.

Another kind of evidence Fraisse (1982) cites bearing on the duration of the psychological present is from phrase lengths in songs and poetry, giving durations ranging between 2 and 5 sec. Data available from a study of the spontaneous songs of two children gave us the opportunity to look at phrase length developmentally. Dowling (1984) had analyzed songs from two age ranges (around 18 months and around 3 years) into phrases. For analysis, the songs had been dubbed onto tape in consecutive fashion without pauses between songs. We measured the length in time of each child's tape and divided by the total number of phrases in all the songs. The result was an upper estimate for the length of phrases, since pause time between phrases was included in the total time. The average time devoted to a phrase was 5.50 sec around 18 months and 4.47 sec around 3 years. The decrease is probably not due so much to shortening of actual phrase length, but rather to minimizing pauses between phrases as part of a general tightening of song structure.

When we applied the same method to adult songs, we obtained a variety of results. The singers on a tape accompanying a children's song book (Beall & Nipp, 1982) produced simple songs at a rapid rate without pauses between phrases, giving a mean time per phrase of 2.52 sec (range, 1.87–3.88 sec for the first ten songs in the book). In contrast, Joni Mitchell on the album *Miles of Aisles* used an average time per phrase of 4.32 sec (range, 2.54–5.36 sec for the 10 songs on sides 2 and 3). Long instrumental interludes were eliminated from the measurements; however, these performances, like the children's, often had brief pauses between sung phrases. Further evidence on individual differences in phrase length is provided by comparing Joni Mitchell's performance of her popular "Both Sides Now" with that of Judy Collins. Collins (on *Wildflowers*) used 4.31 sec/phrase, while Mitchell on the above album used 4.76 sec/phrase, and on her earlier *Clouds* used 5.22 sec/phrase.

All of these estimates from a variety of methods are in good agreement with a psychological present normally lying in the 2–5 sec range but occasionally stretching out to 10 or 12 sec. Those figures do not appear to change radically with development from early childhood. The length of the psychological present varies with context and can be manipulated by composers and performers in particular contexts within stylistic limits. These estimates of the extent of the temporal window provide us with a good idea of the range of time periods involved in the "snap-shot" episodes discussed in Chapter 6.

Psychological Pace

Nineteenth-century researchers also focused on the issue of whether there is a natural pace, or "spontaneous tempo" (Fraisse, 1982), to the sequence of psychological events. If there is such a pace, then it should appear as a preferred rate for tapping and listening, stimuli presented at that rate should be relatively easy to perceive and remember, and stimulus sequences at neighboring rates should be assimilated to the preferred pace (with slower rates perceived as relatively faster, and vice versa). Since the late 1800s, researchers have collected a variety of converging evidence on these points (James, 1890; Fraisse, 1978, 1982; Woodrow, 1951). Though the evidence is often weak, it points in the direction of a natural pace for psychological events of 1.3 to 1.7 per second (i.e., events spaced about 0.6 to 0.75 sec apart, or metronome settings between 80 and 100 beats/min). This agrees roughly with the intuitions of musicians regarding a moderate tempo, neither noticably fast nor slow (e.g., Hindemith, 1961). The natural pace varies considerably in different contexts and from person to person (see, e.g., Oshinsky & Handel, 1978). Pace does not seem to be related to any obvious physiological timing mechanisms (such as heart rate). We incline toward Woodrow's (1951) judgment that though the various lines of evidence converge, timing as measured in the different tasks is probably mediated by different psychological mechanisms. Those complications, however troubling to the psychologist, would not prevent a weakly felt natural pace from being used effectively in music as a baseline rate defining the cross-over region between fast and slow.

Ontological versus Virtual Time

A composer can vary perceived pace not only by varying the presentation rate of events in a piece, but also by varying the predictability of those events. As James says, "In general, a time filled with varied and interesting experiences seems short in passing, but long as we look back. On the other hand, a tract of time empty of experiences seems long in passing, but in retrospect short" (James, 1890, p. 624). Ornstein (1969) has documented the longer retrospective judgment of time intervals filled with interesting events, both auditory and visual. Time intervals filled with continually varying note patterns seem to pass more rapidly than those filled with repeated patterns.

Composers can control the variability of pace within a piece as well as rate and predictability of content. Time within a piece can be made to move along at a relatively constant pace in direct correspondence with time on the clock; or it can go at times slower, at times faster, and at times halt altogether. Stravinsky (1956, p. 32). discussing ways in which a piece of music establishes its own temporal world, notes that some pieces exist more or less in the "normal flow of time" while others are "dissociated" from that normal flow. Pieces closely related to the normal flow are said to be based on "ontological" time, closely paralleling clock time. Those that depart from the normal flow are based on what we here call virtual time. The degree of dissociation from the normal flow of time seems to be related to the degree of ambiguity of rhythmic events in the piece. Stravinsky suggests that pieces in ontological time are usually based on strong principles of similarity among their elements, while those in more subjective, virtual time are usually based on dramatic contrasts. We can find good examples of the use of ontological time in the baroque style often used by Bach and Vivaldi, as in several movements from the *Brandenburg* Concerti and *The Four Seasons*. In those pieces, the beat chugs along at the same measured rate throughout, and the listener is continuously in touch with the regular progress of time in the music, paralleling the progress of time in the world. In such pieces, psychological pace often remains steady for long periods, and the length of the psychological present remains fairly constant.

Pieces with strong contrasts of pace, rhythm, and emotion provide examples of the use of virtual time. Many pieces by Beethoven come to mind. The opening movement of the Fifth Symphony, for example, begins with a repeated figure that lulls us into a secure atmosphere of ontological time. Then the steady progress halts with a dramatic horn declaration, and time is brought almost to a standstill. The latter part of the movement is dominated by flowing melodic figures that not only contrast with the repeated figure but have an intrinsic rhythm offset in time from its underlying repetitions. Figure 7.1 illustrates that contrast. There both the beat pattern implied by the notation and the beat pattern inferred by the listener are indicated below the score. At the start of the movement, those patterns coincide, but after the French horn fanfare at measure 59, the two patterns shift apart.

The opening movement of the *Appassionata* Sonata, op. 57, for piano illustrates virtual time in another way. For most of the piece, the psychological pace and temporal window vary continually. At certain points, Beethoven sets up a note repeated in triplets that seems to give us a hold on ontological time. But around that repeated note, he places other figures with displaced accents that prevent us from maintaining an even psychological pace. The piece exists in a virtual temporal world of its own making, moving now faster and now slower than the clock.

Central Javanese *gamelan* music provides an interesting example of stylistic manipulation both of density of acoustic events in real time, and of structural events in more subjective time. A typical style uses as structural divisions temporal cycles of 128 beats, played at a rate of about 60 beats/min. Shorter structural cycles (of 32 beats, for example) occur, but are often spread out in time—at a slower beat tempo—so as to last as long as the cycles containing more beats. This provides for different densities of structural events. A shift in density can be accomplished by slowing the beat tempo until the higher pitched instruments can play their rapid pat-

Figure 7.1 Passage from the first movement of Beethoven's Fifth Symphony illustrating the displacement of heard metric accents from notated ones.

terns twice within a structural unit, by doubling the density of temporal subdivisions—that is, by playing twice as many notes per structural beat. After the shift the upper instruments play at about the same rate as before—the density of events in real time did not change. However, the beat rate of structural events in the temporal cycle has been halved—the subjective pace is slower. Stretching the structural beat left room to be filled in by rapid patterns more complex than before, so that the density of events relative to the structural beat has doubled—an increase of what is called *irama*. The process can be reversed to produce a decrease in *irama* (Example 7a).

7a

There are at least two psychological effects here, both having to do with the perennial question of the relationships between subjective duration and objective time. The first effect arises from the more or less steady motion of a piece—whether it seems fast or slow compared with the natural pace. The second effect involves variations in the progress of subjective time. Both the setting of subjective pace and variations in that pace can serve to dissociate subjective, virtual time from objective time. As Stravinsky observes, some pieces do that to an expecially high degree. The temporal experience of music is like the experience of life, as John

Dewey suggests in the quotation at the start of this chapter. Music provides a good area in which to explore phenomena of subjective time that psychology has too long neglected.

PERCEPTION OF RHYTHM

To this point, we have been discussing the broad overall flow of the listener's experience of music. Now we turn to the listener's perception of rhythmic patterns within that flow. It is first useful to define some terms. *Duration* is the psychological correlate of time. *Beat* refers to a perceived pulse marking off equal durational units. *Tempo* refers to the rate at which beats occur, and *meter* imposes an accent structure on beats (as in "*one,* two, three, *one,* two, three . . . ''). Meter thus refers to the most basic level of rhythmic organization and does not generally involve durational contrasts. *Rhythm* refers to a temporally extended pattern of durational and accentual relationships. Usually, rhythmic patterns are repeated, creating expectancies about future events. Where the events in a piece are of different durations and the beat is hard to determine unambiguously, we use the term *density* to refer to an average presentation rate taken across events of different duration (often expressed in notes per second). Note that in this series of definitions it is possible to conceive of varying tempo, meter, and rhythm independently of one another. Further, it is possible to maintain the same *density* while changing tempo.

The earlier work on time perception was somewhat surprising to musicians because it suggested that humans have a relatively poor capacity for time discrimination. In those early studies, the just noticeable difference (JND) between time intervals was measured in terms of subjects' precision in reproducing isolated intervals and in judging the relative durations of successive intervals in pairs. Performance on these tasks was usually best in the neighborhood of the 0.6 sec time interval noted above. But even at best, the JND size typically fell in the range of 5–10% (Woodrow, 1951). This seemed enormous in comparison with JNDs for pitch, for example, which typically fall well under 1%. The musician correctly concluded that humans must be better at making temporal judgments in music than these discrimination measurements disclosed. In fact, it has become apparent since 1950 that if the task is one of tapping along with a steady beat, listeners' precision is much better. Povel (1981), for example, found that relative precision in such a task was best in the neighborhood of 1.7 beats/sec, with JNDs of the order of 2 or 3%. Performance was at least as good for continuations of a beat sequence after the model had stopped as for synchronization with the model—essentially a tempo-reproduction task. Nonmusicians performed as well as university music students on the task. Povel suggests that the steady beat pattern serves as a cognitive framework with reference to which the listener structures musical time. As well as being precise in reproducing a steady beat pattern, musicians can produce more complex rhythmic patterns with considerable accuracy, as shown by Monahan's (1984) analysis of Gabrielsson's (1974) data. With Povel, Monahan suggests that in music, listener and performer use metric beat patterns as cognitive frameworks with which to judge and produce precise rhythmic patterns. Metric structure thus functions as the temporal analog of the pitch scale schemata discussed in Chapters 4 and 5.

The use of the metric beat pattern as a framework for rhythm appears early in development. In the child's first songs, around the age of 1 or $1\frac{1}{2}$ years, the beat remains steady within phrases. More complex rhythms are superimposed on the regular beat, typically by the adaptation of speech rhythms to conform to the beat pattern. As the child grows older, the regularity of the beat is extended over longer and longer time spans, incorporating more and more phrases without a break (Dowling, 1984). The dual structure of underlying beat and superimposed rhythm is fundamental to the cognitive organization of music from very early ages.

Simple Rhythmic Patterns

As we move into the area of perception of rhythmic patterns, we find that certain simple patterns are easier for the listener to process than others. For example, there is considerable evidence that patterns having temporal ratios of 2:1 between their elements are easy to perceive and reproduce. Fraisse (1982) presented a count of note durations in 15 published European pieces from Beethoven to Bartók showing the prevalence of the 2:1 ratio between note durations. Generally 80 or 90% of the notes in a piece were accounted for by two note durations standing in that ratio. Fraisse noted further that range of timings of the longer notes in those pairs fell between 0.3 and 0.9 sec; that is, the range straddled the preferred pace of 1.7 notes/sec described above.

The 2:1 temporal ratio also seems basic in the sense that other temporal relationships tend to be assimilated to it in perception and production. This effect is well known to music teachers who seem to have to guard continually against the drift of dotted-eighth–sixteenth rhythms (3:1 ratio) into quarter–eighth triplet rhythms (2:1 ratio) in their pupils' playing. Povel (1981) extended his study of listeners' tapping of metric beat patterns to include their tapped continuations of more complex rhythmic patterns. Povel's subjects listened to a repeated rhythmic pattern, and when they felt ready, they tapped 17 repetitions of the pattern themselves. (The first two repetitions were discarded as warm-ups.) In the simplest case, listeners copied rhythmic patterns consisting of alternating intervals in a variety of ratios between 4:1 and 5:4. The repetitions of all the interval ratios tended markedly toward 2:1, demonstrating assimilation toward that pattern. Povel notes that the higher ratios, such as 4:3 and 5:4, were especially difficult as shown by subjects' lack of precision, due to conflicting tendencies to assimilate them to 2:1 and to 1:1 (an isochronous sequence).

When Povel tested listeners' continuations of patterns including two long notes and a short note (e.g., quarter–quarter–sixteenth, 4:4:1, or dotted-quarter–dotted-quarter–quarter, 3:3:2) assimilation toward the 2:1 pattern for the second and third notes still occurred. However, it was apparent that more was influencing the subjects' performance than simply assimilation to a 2:1 pattern. If that had been all that was happening, continuation of the quarter–quarter–eighth (2:1) pattern should have been very precise, but, in fact, it was imprecise. The problem, as musicians will already have realized, was that long–long–short with a 2:1 ratio divides the pattern into five temporal units, an unfamiliar subdivision for Western listeners and one difficult for them to fit into a regular beat structure. Povel went on to show that when more context was provided and the repeating pattern could be heard as dividing into coherent beats, both precision and accuracy improved considerably for both musicians and nonmusicians. For example, quarter–eighth–eighth (long–short–short, 2:1), dotted-quarter–eighth–eighth–eighth (long–short–short–short, 3:1), and half–eighth–eighth–eighth–eighth (long–short–short–short–short, 4:1) were all reproduced precisely and without assimilation by musicians and nonmusicians alike when presented in context.

Povel suggests that there are two steps involved in the listener's encoding of a rhythmic pattern. First, there is an attempt to find a regular beat pattern with a beat rate in a comfortable range. Beat intervals cannot be much longer than about 1.5 sec or tempos much slower than about 40 beats/min. Second, beat intervals are divided, preferably into patterns having equal subdivisions or subdivisions in 2:1 ratios (or they may be left empty). More complex subdivisions are difficult to encode. There are thus two levels of cognitive structure in the representation of a rhythmic pattern: the beat framework and its rhythmic subdivisions.

Monahan (1984) takes this suggestion one step further, suggesting that rhythmic subdivision patterns are laid on the beat framework in a way analogous to the way melodic pitch contours are laid on the scale framework (see Chapter 5). Rhythmic subdivisions can thus be said to be encoded in rhythmic contours of relative, not absolute, temporal relationships. Rhythmic contours are like melodic contours in being able to stretch to fit different frameworks (as with change of tempo) and in being able to slide along a given framework (as in displacement of rhythmic accent). Monahan (1984, Experiment 1) showed that listeners' judgments of similarity of pattern pairs were influenced by both tempo and rhythmic contour. Pairs in which comparison patterns preserved the duration *relationships* of initial stimuli were judged more similar than when comparisons had totally different rhythmic patterns. That result is, in itself, not surprising. What is interesting is that tempo interacted with type of comparison. As the tempo of the comparison stimulus diverged from that of the initial stimulus, comparisons with the same relative (but different absolute) rhythms were judged *more* similar. The shift of tempo freed listeners from a reliance on the absolute durational content of the pattern and encouraged their use of the relative durational information in the rhythmic contour. Monahan suggests that this use of relative rhythmic information is directly analogous to the use of relative melodic information, discussed in Chapter 5.

More Complex Patterns

The beat framework and more elaborate levels of rhythmic pattern appear quite clearly in the responses of listeners to more complex rhythmic patterns. Handel and Lawson (1983) created complex patterns by having two or three tones at different pitches repeat at different rates, for example, a lower tone repeating twice per measure and an upper tone repeating three times. In that case, the pattern would be a 2 × 3 polyrhythm, and the occurrence of the two notes would coincide once at the start of each measure. Listeners were asked to tap along with the stimulus pattern in any way they wished. This is a very natural task for even musically untrained listeners, and Handel and Lawson found no effects of experience on responses. Different listeners used different strategies in tapping along. A common strategy for patterns such as 2 × 3, 3 × 4, and 3 × 5 was to follow the complex polyrhythm at the slower tempos around 3.0 sec/measure, tapping the cross-rhythm produced by the combination of the pulse rates. As the tempo was increased to 1.6 or 1.2 sec/measure, listeners' tapping shifted to follow the one or another of the steady component beat patterns. In some cases, listeners followed the beat pattern presented in the lower-pitched voice. In other cases, their choice was dependent on tempo. They rarely followed beat patterns with notes more than 0.8 sec apart. Hence, as a 2 × 3 pattern was speeded up to 1.6 sec/ measure they shifted from the 2 × 3 cross-rhythm to the simpler three beats per measure, with the beats now 0.53 sec apart. Then, at 1.2 sec/

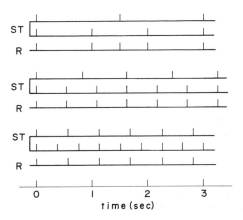

Figure 7.2 Examples of stimulus patterns containing 2 × 3 cross-rhythms with typical responses. ST, stimulus; R, response. (From Handel & Lawson, 1983).

measure they would shift again to two beats per measure, 0.6 sec apart. At 0.6 sec/measure they either continued to follow the two-beat pattern or shifted into one beat per measure. These shifts are shown in Figure 7.2.

These responses reflect the different levels of rhythmic structure we have been discussing: at slow tempos, the level of complex rhythmic patterns, and at faster, tempos the beat structure. Furthermore, the beat chosen tended to reflect the preferred pace of about 0.6 sec/beat (or 1.67 beats/sec) discussed at the start of the chapter. This tendency of preferred beat pattern to shift with tempo leads Handel and Lawson to suggest that as tempos in music slow down, the subjective beat shifts to relatively shorter temporal units to stay within the range of the preferred pace. "In musical instances with a slow metronome tempo, the next smaller denominator (e.g., eighth notes if the tempo specifies quarter notes) may be the true timing element" (Handel & Lawson, 1983, p. 118).

Interesting effects arose from the complications of adding a third level to the patterns, as with 2 × 3 × 7 or 2 × 5 × 7 (shown in Figure 7.3). In those cases there was a sort of rhythmic capture in which the two similarly paced levels would join in a cross-rhythm, contrasting with the different paced level. With the 2 × 3 × 7 pattern at tempos too fast to follow the seven-beat pattern, listeners tended to follow the 2 × 3 cross-rhythm, as shown in Figure 7.3. That tendency was much stronger than it was with just the 2 × 3 pattern alone, as shown in Figure 7.2. With the 2 × 5 × 7 pattern, the 5 and 7 beat pulses grouped together in contrast to the 2, and listeners tended to follow the two-beat rhythm. These effects illustrate the importance of temporal context in determining perceived rhythm. This context dependence involves both complex interactions among structural

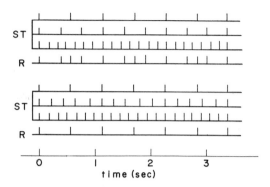

Figure 7.3 Examples of stimulus patterns containing 2 × 3 × 7 and 2 × 5 × 7 cross-rhythms with typical responses. ST, stimulus, R, response. (From Handel & Lawson, 1983).

levels, as in the results just cited, and simpler effects such as those of tempo and beat rate described previously. Handel and Lawson suggest that these complications mean that an adequate theory of rhythmic organization will have to be very complex and may lie some years in the future.

Multidimensional Scaling

The complexity of musical rhythm has led some researchers to use multidimensional scaling techniques in their attempts to delineate its psychological dimensions. We describe applications of multidimensional scaling in Chapters 3 and 4. Here, the method typically involves obtaining listeners' similarity ratings of pairs of stimulus patterns differing in rhythmic content. Rated similarity is taken as a measure of proximity in a psychological space. A computer program then tries to find a way to arrange the distances thus generated among the stimuli so as to disclose a small number of dimensions of the space. The researcher hopes that the dimensions that appear will be psychologically meaningful. If they are, then we can learn something of the important psychological dimensions regarding rhythm.

In a series of studies, Gabrielsson (1973a, 1973b, 1973c; summarized in 1973d) obtained ratings of a variety of stimuli, including monophonic and polyphonic percussion rhythm patterns and piano melodies incorporating those rhythms. The psychological dimensions Gabrielsson found throughout most of his studies converge with the pattern of results reviewed above in their indications of salient properties of rhythms. Some of the main dimensions he found involve differences in meter and tempo, whether or not the first beat were strongly accented, and patterns of

accents and durations. Those dimensions fit closely the layered structure
of musical rhythm we have been describing. Other dimensions seem related to the considerations of ontological versus virtual time discussed
above, for example, uniformity versus variation and rigidity versus flexibility. To illustrate these results let us examine a study in which Gabrielsson (1973b, Experiment 4) used the six rhythmic patterns shown in Figure
7.4. The patterns were presented in pairs. Listeners first heard four measures of one repeated pattern and then four measures of the other. Then
they rated similarity on a 10-point scale. The ratings were used to generate the distances among stimuli you see represented in Figure 7.4. Dimension I distinguishes two groups of stimuli on the basis of a prominent
feature of their rhythmic pattern: Stimuli 1, 3, and 5 begin with a quarter
note followed by two eighths, while Stimuli 2, 4, and 6 begin with two
eighths followed by a quarter. Dimension II represents meter, distinguishing Stimuli 1 and 2 (with four-beat measures) from the others (with three-
beat measures). Dimension III represents tempo, distinguishing the
slower stimuli (5 and 6) from the other faster stimuli. Gabrielsson notes
that individual differences among listeners were apparent in the data.

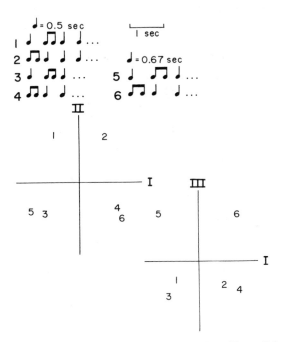

Figure 7.4 Stimuli and multidimensional scaling solution. (From Gabrielsson, 1973b,
Experiment 4).

Different listeners, though agreeing on the basic dimensions, weighed them differently in making their similarity ratings.

The above dimensions fit quite well into the layered structure of meter, tempo, and rhythmic pattern. Gabrielsson also found dimensions of rhythmic similarity that were more closely related to affective meaning, such as excited versus calm, vital versus dull, and dimensions related to the character of movement, such as graceful versus thumping and floating versus stuttering. We return in Chapter 8 to affective meanings and their relationship to properties of music.

Monahan (1984, Experiment 2; Carterette et al., 1982) carried out a study along the same lines as Gabrielsson's, but with melodic pattern systematically varied. Figure 7.5 shows the component patterns of Monahan's stimuli. There were four different rhythmic patterns combined with eight melodic contours formed from four distinctive contours and their inversions, giving a total of 32 stimuli. Comparison stimuli were always in different keys from initial stimuli in the pairs to insure that listeners were rating melodic *pattern* and not just pitch similarity. There are 32 × 32 = 1024 pairs of 32 stimuli, and listeners rated all the pairs for similarity. Figure 7.5 shows the distances derived from the ratings for the two most important dimensions for a group of experienced ensemble musicians.

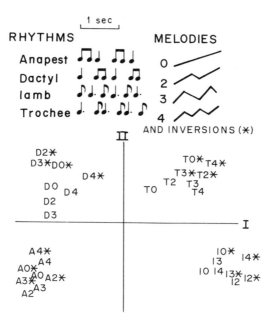

Figure 7.5 Stimuli and multidimensional scaling solution (From Monahan, 1984, Experiment 2.)

The stimuli clustered into four quadrants. The first major dimension separated two-element patterns (iambic and trochaic) from three-element patterns (anapestic and dactylic). The second dimension separated initial-accent patterns (trochaic and dactylic) from final-accent patterns (iambic and anapestic). These dimensions are thus consonant with Gabrielsson's dimensions in differentiating patterns on the basis of meter and accent.

It was not until arriving at the third dimension in order of importance that melodic features of the patterns began to be apparent in the data. The third dimension distinguished patterns with rising global pitch contours from those with falling contours. And the fourth dimension distinguished between contours with inflections—corners—and those without. It is noteworthy that the rhythmic aspects of these stimuli overode their pitch-pattern aspects in determining listeners' responses. This clearly demonstrates the importance of rhythm in music cognition.

We turn now to consider the development of rhythm perception, where we will see that children's development of rhythmic sensitivity follows a pattern parallel to that described for the development of melodic perception in Chapter 5.

DEVELOPMENT

Sensitivity to basic features of rhythm appears very early in the infant's life, followed by increases in sophistication throughout childhood. As children grow older they are able to extend rhythmic comprehension and control, imposing increasing subtleties of organization over longer and longer time spans. And the levels of organization that characterize adult cognition—beat and rhythmic pattern—prove useful in describing cognitive development from even the youngest ages.

Infancy

Evidence has been accumulating that young infants notice rhythmic differences. Demany, McKenzie, and Vurpillot (1977) played a rhythmic pattern for 2- to 4-month-olds whenever they looked at a simple patterned figure. The sounds stopped whenever the infant looked away. The infants tended to habituate to the sound pattern and to stop looking at the figure associated with it. Then Demany et al. switched rhythmic patterns and observed whether the infants started looking at the figure again, in order to bring about more presentations of the novel rhythm. That is exactly what the infants did, indicating that they were noticing the change of rhythm. In a converging study, Chang and Trehub (1977b) used a heart-rate habituation method parallel to that reported in their studies of melodic contour described in Chapter 5. They found habituation to repeated rhythmic patterns, followed by deceleration to a novel pattern. Allen, Walker, Symends, and Marcell (1977) obtained similar results with 7-month-olds. Like changes of melodic contour, changes of rhythmic pattern are noticed at the earliest ages.

Infants notice not only changes of rhythmic pattern, but also changes in tempo and beat. This is shown by infants' responses to the temporal synchrony of simultaneous sequences of events as well. Spelke (1979) devised an imaginative series of experiments using what could be called the "hoppy kangaroo" paradigm. Spelke presented 4-month-olds with a pair of movies side by side. In one case, for example, there was a kangaroo hopping once every 2 sec next to a donkey hopping about four times as fast but out of phase (i.e., they seldom landed at the same time). Each hop of the kangaroo was accompanied by a "bong," and those of the donkey by a "thump." Spelke found that when only one sound track was presented, the infants tended to look more at the movie that was synchronized with it, looking at the kangaroo for bongs and the donkey for thumps. Spelke reasoned that this result would occur whether the infants were noticing the simultaneity of bongs and bounces or the common tempo in each movie/sound-track pair or both. She did further experiments separating those features and found that the infants were able to respond on the basis of either type of cue. Infants were able to produce a match on the basis of speed as well of synchronization, demonstrating sensitivity to tempo.

Childhood

The importance of rhythmic pattern and beat can be seen in production as well as in perception as the child emerges from infancy. Around the age of 1 year, the child begins singing spontaneously. Two main features that distinguish singing from speech are stable pitches of sustained vowels and regular temporal organization. Even in the child's earliest songs, there is a steady beat pattern within phrases. During the second year of life, children impose the regular beat on longer and longer time spans, a trend that continues throughout childhood. Rhythmic patterns of some complexity are superimposed on the steady beat already in the second year, and it seems reasonable to suppose that the more complex patterns are based on the rhythms of speech. Regular subdivision of the beat probably does not occur as a general principle until the learning of standard nursery songs, such as "Twinkle, Twinkle," during the third and fourth years. On a broader level, children organize the temporal pattern of variety and repetition in whole songs across longer and longer time spans as they develop (Dowling, 1984) and by the age of four or so can reproduce entire nursery songs more or less intact (Davidson et al., 1981).

Piaget (1970; Piaget & Inhelder, 1969) offers perhaps the most comprehensive theory of the child's developing conception of time. In accordance with other domains of intelligence, Piaget found that the child's ability to organize temporal sequences of events develops in stages, with class inclusion, a stable durational unit, and seriation of events appearing by 5–8 years of age. Piaget dealt with broad overall categories of temporal organization that function in music at a global level. There have also been studies, inspired by Piaget's work, of the more local features of time and rhythm in musical contexts.

Pflederer (1964; Pflederer & Sechrest, 1968) collected many responses of 5- to 13-year-old children on a series of musical tasks. Among other results, she found Piagetian conservation for rhythm. In her study, children in an experimental group listened to a series of transformations of familiar songs like "America" and discussed them. (The transformations involved changes of instrumentation, tempo, harmony, mode, rhythm, and melodic contour as well as other changes of pitch intervals.) The children then heard pairs of phrases from Bartók's folklike *For Children*. In each pair, the second phrase was a transformation of the first along one of the above dimensions. The children were asked whether the two selections were the same or different, and why. *Conservation* was defined as the ability to recognize the tune as the same through the transformation and to specify the source of the changes. Generally speaking, older children were better at recognizing the transformed tunes. Five-year-olds had difficulty recognizing the tunes across any change but recognized the tunes quite well when repeated unchanged. Changes of instrumentation or harmony were most easily handled by the older children. As we would expect, vocabulary limitations made it difficult for the children, especially the younger ones, to specify changes of rhythm. It was clear from the descriptions given that at least some of the children viewed changes of tempo and rhythm as variations in performance practice independent of the tunes themselves.

Serafine (1979) developed a task that addressed the child's conservation of meter more directly. In this task, children heard a sequence of eight equally spaced clicks and were asked whether they became slower or faster or stayed the same. Most children gave the correct "same" response. The children then heard the initial click sequence simultaneously with another sequence having the same beat structure but varying in rhythmic density. The children were then asked the same question: Did the sequence get faster or slower or stay the same? Metric conservation was indicated by "same" responses. Serafine pretested 103 children aged 4–9 years for conservation with both the above task and a combined auditory–visual task that duplicated the click patterns with blinking lights. Nonconservers were then assigned to an ineffectual half-hour training session, to no training at all. A week later all the children were tested again. Serafine found that the older the children were the more likely they were to conserve meter: 33% of the 4-year-olds conserved as compared with 68% of the 7-year-olds and 76% of the 9-year-olds. Metric conservation correlated more strongly with nonmusical Piagetian conservation tasks than with chronological age, suggesting a link in development to more general intellectual abilities.

This link is increasingly evident as the child grows older. The child's increased rhythmic ability serves as an organizing factor not only in music production but also in a broader range range of intellectual tasks. For example, Huttenlocher and Burke (1976) showed that rhythmic organization can play a role in memory for verbal materials. In that study they presented children 4—11 years old with series of digits that were (1) sung rhythmically to a familiar melody such as Brahms's "Lullaby," (2) rhythmically grouped, or (3) said without any grouping. They found that rhythmic grouping improved memory for the digits at all age levels and that adding melody to the rhythmic grouping improved memory only a small amount over that. That is, even at 4 or 5 years, the child is able to use the rhythmic grouping of events to organize them cognitively and remember them better. The general applicability of rhythmic organization in life is one of the things John Dewey was pointing out in the quote at the start of this chapter. Such correspondences are especially interesting to observe in cultures where the rhythms of both life and music are different from our own, and to those studies we now turn.

CROSS-CULTURAL STUDIES

As with pitch organization, details of rhythmic organization differ from culture to culture; and as with pitch, certain general principles seem to apply. In particular, the tendency for rhythmic structure to be organized in layers involving beat, tempo, and rhythmic pattern, which we have already encountered in European music, are apparent in the following examples. The examples we discuss, drawn from Africa, India, and Indonesia, illustrate a wide variey of rhythmic organizations.

Africa

Locke (1982) describes the complex polyrhythms of dance drumming by the Eve of Ghana. Locke argues that cross-rhythms and syncopation combine with basic beat patterns to generate the rhythmic density that typifies various West African traditions. Locke suggests that the underlying meter of much Eve drumming is 12:8, since musicians and dancers often appear to feel and to express the rhythm in alternate and simultaneous groups of three, four, six, and eight beats. By emphasizing critical off-beats in asymmetrical accent patterns, ensemble players produce cross-rhythms (as in the polyrhythm experiments discussed above; see Figure 7.3) and syncopation (accents falling consistently off the main beats). As an additional complication, cross-rhythms can be played out of phase with the main beat sequence, creating an additional level of cross-rhythm.

Example 7b, which is transcribed in Figure 7.6, illustrates such shifted **7b** beats and phrases. Note the on- and off-beat drum patterns played against the basic beat in the bell, felt in six. The multilayered complexity of the piece affords the possibility of a number of notational representations, and Figure 7.6 displays two alternative transcriptions provided by Locke. Since complexity seems to be an important part of the musical point here, it would be artificial to choose one view as the "correct" one. Koetting (1979) makes a similar point in his discussion of the *jongo* dance drumming of the Kasena of northern Ghana. The Kasena, like the Eve, make extensive use of three-against-two polyrhythms. Koetting found no reason to believe that either the duple- or the triple-meter component in these patterns is primary. Unlike the Eve ensemble, the typical Kasena ensemble lacks a salient beat line such as that of the bell in Figure 7.6, and so the complexity is even more ambiguous. Koetting believes that there *is* an underlying beat pattern shared by the Kasena musicians but that it is implicit in the structure and hence "abstract" with respect to heard patterns. The problem for the ethnomusicologist is, of course, to find the implicit structure that describes the native musicians' mental representation.

These Ghanaian examples illustrate layers of structure and the interaction of beat and rhythmic patterns. They also raise a mild problem in terminology: If there are two equally important meters going at once, then what is the tempo? As Hood (1971) suggests, it may be preferable in such cases to refer to the average density of the performance in events per second. Such a solution is in keeping with the results of Handel and Lawson (1983) cited above. It is also in keeping with broader historical

Figure 7.6 Lead drum pattern from the Eve dance, atsiagbeko. The pattern is constructed from three motifs, labeled a, b, and c. Panels (A), (B) and (C) represent alternate transcriptions. (After Locke, 1982.)

considerations, since the notion of a single notated tempo and meter has only been characteristic of European music since about 1600 (Yeston, 1976).

India

According to Malm (1977), the theory of rhythm and melody in North Indian music grew out of the tradition of recitation of ancient Sanskrit texts. For example, the basic time unit (*matra*) is defined as the minimum time for one syllable and corresponds to the European term *beat*. The North Indian term for meter or measure is *tal,* and a particular *tal* is defined by the grouping structure it imposes on beats (Wade, 1979). Theoretically a *tal* may define a cycle of from 3 to 128 beats, but as a practical matter, most are under 20 beats long.

The *tal* is divided into subgroups; for example, *tintal* is divided into 4 + 4 + 4 + 4 = 16 beats; *adital* is divided 4 + 2 + 2 = 8. The concatenation of subunits of unequal size is something Western listeners find unusual. Such additive rhythmic structures make possible *tal* lengths of 5, 7, 11, and 14 beats, which would not be possible if (as is usual in European music) the measure were divided into subgroups of equal length. Just as a *rag* specifies not only a modal scale but also a cluster of melodic motifs (see Chapter 4), so a *tal* specifies both metric grouping and a cluster of associated rhythmic patterns. And just as a *rag* specifies a hierarchy of pitch functions in defining a tonality, a *tal* specifies a hierarchy of beat functions. Not only are there accent patterns in the European sense, but also patterns of filled and empty beats, lending rhythmic interest to the metric structure.

The occurrence of empty beats in the *tal* leaves part of the metric information implicit and unstated. In fast movements with complex rhythm, the beat pattern often becomes less and less explicit, as in the Ghanaian examples above. In such cases, a large part of the aesthetic interest lies in the degree to which the musicians and their audience can continue to follow the *tal* accurately across passages of elaborate rhythmic improvisation in which it is only hinted at. Effective musical communication in such cases relies on mental representations maintained in parallel by all the participants through periods of minimal explicit behavioral support.

Indonesia

In the classical *gamelan* music of Java and Bali, time is organized in metric cycles. While it is true that time in typical European music is organized at some level in metric cycles (that is, in recurrent measures), nevertheless Indonesian metric structure is more obviously cyclic in involving less variability across recurrences and in involving cycles that subtend patterns generally longer than the European measure. The cyclic structure of Indonesian meter mirrors the cyclic structure of time in general in that culture, ranging from very short units to very large. As an example in the midrange of unit sizes, Geertz (1973, Chapter 14) provides a fascinating discussion of cyclic "weeks" of five, six, and seven days that define a polyrhythmic cycle of 210 auspicious and inauspicious conjunctions. Conjunctions of a simpler sort define strong and weak beats in Indonesian meters. A typical example from Java is shown in Figure 7.7. Note the pattern of strong and weak subgroups, with the strongest subgroup at the end of each cycle. The subtler rhythmic patterns of a song are superimposed on this underlying meter.

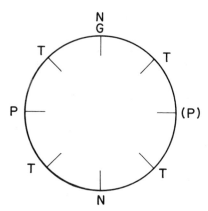

Figure 7.7 The basic cyclic temporal pattern (read clockwise) of Javanese *gamelan* music, marked by a gong and hence called a *gongan*. The relative pitch ranges of the instruments, in descending order, are indicated by the letters. N, kenong; T, kethuk; P, kempul; G, gong. (After Becker, 1979.)

Cross-Cultural Observations

There are two broad conclusions we can draw from these observations of non-Western music. One is that the notion of structural levels is useful in the description of musical time. In particular, the distinction between a level of beat and meter and a level of more elaborate rhythmic events seems appropriate across a wide variety of musical cultures. Second, it is not uncommon among the world's music for meter to be more elaborate than it has been in European music since 1600. In fact, when we speak of the relative rhythmic simplicity of European classical music, we should rather speak of its relative *metric* simplicity. *Rhythmic* complexity, in the sense we have been using the term, is common. However, polyrhythmic meters are rare between 1600 and 1900. When they occur it is usually in isolated passages of two-against-three, most often in the work of Handel and Brahms. A trend toward metric elaboration has been coupled in the early twentieth century with incorporation into mainstream European music of influences from Russia (Mussorgsky, Stravinsky), Spain (de Falla), and Africa (through jazz and Latin American music).

SUMMARY

In this chapter we have considered a variety of phenomena involved in the psychological organization of musical time. We looked at some basic aspects of time perception and suggested that there is a natural psychological pace with reference to which a musical tempo can seem fast or slow. There also appears to be a time interval of the order of a few seconds over which perceptual events (such as the contents of a musical phrase) tend to be integrated into what William James called the "psychological present." Composers manipulate steadiness of tempo and the constancy of other rhythmic factors to keep a piece within the real-time framework of the world outside or by creating temporal ambiguity, dissociate time within the piece from time in the world.

We gave evidence for the psychological reality of multilayered rhythmic structures in which complex rhythmic patterns are overlaid on an underlying beat sequence. The same type of mental representation appears to operate with rhythm as we encountered in Chapters 4 and 5 for tonal organization, namely, a solid framework (beat or tonal scale) on which more elaborate patterns (rhythm or melody) are laid. The development of these mental representations appear to follow a closely parallel course for both pitch material and rhythm.

The chapter closed with a brief survey of rhythmic usage across several cultures, presenting complications that a psychological theory of time and rhythm perception will ultimately need to confront.

8

Emotion and Meaning

Only the butterfly itself can give us joy by unexpectedly alighting on our shoulder.

(Ellen Berscheid, 1983, p. 156)

INTRODUCTION

When we discuss our work with nonpsychologists, the questions that most often arise concern music and emotion. Music arouses strong emotional responses in people, and they want to know why. Emotional responses to music have puzzled psychologists as well. There are several sources of this puzzlement. First, emotional phenomena in general are complex and have defied psychological explanation for a very long time. Second, the easiest emotional responses to understand are those tied directly to biological survival, for example, the reaction of fear in the face of a life-threatening situation. Reactions to music are not obviously of such direct biological significance; thus, the strength of those reactions is harder to account for. Third, there is the great variety of responses and experiences that people group under the category of emotion. Emotional responses to music run the gamut from laughing and crying and chills going up and down the spine to cool appraisal of technique. Though we have no definitive answer concerning the psychology of emotional responses to music, we do have a better grasp of this area than psychologists did in the late 1950s. Therefore, in this chapter we provide a framework for thinking of the issues involved, as well as our best notions as to the kinds of answers that are most useful.

The relationship between emotions and music is complicated in another way. Not only do listeners have emotional reactions to music, but pieces of music also *represent* emotions in ways that can be recognized by listeners. Indeed, one of the oldest aesthetic theories, that of Aristotle (1961), holds that works of art represent emotional processes as well as induce them. It may be that often the emotion represented is also the emotion induced, though this is not always the case.

INDEX, ICON, AND SYMBOL

It seems reasonable to suppose that music represents and induces emotions in many of the same ways. The nineteenth-century philosopher Charles Peirce (1931–1935, Vol. 2) developed a classification of the various ways in which signs could represent other things and events. We have found Peirce's outline useful in our exploration of the ways in which music can represent emotion. Peirce describes three types of sign: index, icon, and symbol. An index represents its referent by having been associated with it in the past, as lightning and thunder with a storm. An icon represents through formal similarity to the referent, as a wiring diagram represents a circuit. Symbols represent by being embedded in a formal system, such as a language. The meaning of a sentence in a language (for example, *That is a bird*) depends on interpretation through the syntactic rules of the language and not on association or resemblance. The meaning of some of the words in the sentence may be bound up with indexical or iconic meanings, as in the association the listener makes between *bird* and actual birds. But the meanings of other words are clearly dependent on their being embedded in a conventional system of syntactic rules, for example, *is* and *a*. We suggest that many of the meanings of musical events depend on this symbolic mode of representation and that musical symbols often depend for their meaning on being embedded along with other musical symbols in a structure of musical syntax.

In the following discussion, we consider each of Peirce's categories of sign in turn, first considering examples of its use to represent emotion and then how it can induce emotion. This is quite straightforward for index and icon, but for symbol we need to provide more elaborate psychological machinery to account for the effects. Also, Peirce did not intend these categories of signs to be mutually exclusive. Musical events are typically so complex that they are involved in more than one sign function at a time. For example, the national anthem in the midst of an elaborate piece evokes patriotism as an index, is vigorous and stirring in character as an icon, and is in a specific key with specific harmonies and arouses particular expectations in the listener concerning the future course of the melody as a symbol (embedded in syntax).

Index

Indexical representation involves the direct association of a musical event with some extramusical object or event, so that emotions previously associated with the extramusical object come to be associated with the music. Students of psychology will recall the famous experiment by Pavlov (1927), who introduced food powder on a dog's tongue immediately after ringing a bell. The dog, who previously would salivate only to the food powder, learned to salivate to the bell even without the food powder. Here, music is analogous to the bell, and food powder to some extramusical event already associated with emotional responses, for example, a happy mood, sexual excitement, or religious enthusiasm. This process was well described by Spinoza 300 years ago: "If the mind has once been affected by two emotions at the same time, it will, whenever it is afterwards affected by one of the two, be also affected by the other;" and, hence, "anything can, accidentally, be the cause of pleasure, pain, or desire" by first being associated with something that previously elicited those emotions (Spinoza, 1677/1955, Vol. 3, xiv-xv).

The use of indexical association to represent emotion is illustrated in Puccini's use of the first phrase of "The Star Spangled Banner" in *Madama Butterfly* to indicate the American protagonist's patriotic feelings in his toast "America forever!" and by Tchaikovsky's use of the Russian and French anthems in *Overture 1812* to indicate the two sides in the war. Indexical induction of emotion is even more common than representation, since the device is so immediately effective. For example, rehearing an old popular song may wistfully remind one of a former romantic relationship; or, in case the relationship has matured, "Listen, dear, they're playing our song." A classic description of that reaction is found in *Swann's Way,* where Proust (1934) recounts Swann's reaction to hearing again a melody he had associated with an earlier love affair:

> And before Swann had had time to understand what was happening, to think: "It is the little phrase from Vinteuil's sonata. I mustn't listen!", all his memories of the days when Odette had been in love with him, which he had succeeded, up till that evening, in keeping invisible in the depths of his being, deceived by this sudden reflection of a season of love, whose sun, they supposed, had dawned again, had awakened from their slumber, had taken wing and risen to sing maddeningly in his ears, without pity for his present desolation, the forgotten strains of happiness. (Vol. 1, pp. 264–265)

A powerful use of indexical associations in nineteenth-century opera was provided by the *leitmotif* developed by Wagner and utilized by Verdi, Massenet, and Puccini. A leitmotif is musical theme associated with some element in the drama, such as a character or a feeling or a location. Some of its most effective uses run closely parallel to the process just described by Proust. For example, in Verdi's *La Traviata,* Massenet's *Manon* and Puccini's *La Bohème,* the hero and heroine at their last meeting recall the earlier, happier days of their love by singing musical phrases associated with those earlier scenes. Those recollections have a powerful emotional impact on the audience and are vividly representations of the mental states of the characters as well. (We return to consider the symbolic—as distinct from the indexical—uses of leitmotif below.)

Music can evoke conditioned emotional reactions simply by incorporating elements to which emotional responses have already been conditioned. Tchaikovsky's use of cannon shots in *Overture 1812* is an example. The use of this technique is common in *musique concrète,* in which a typical method for constructing a piece is to start with natural sounds recorded on tape and then transform them by various electronic means. Sometimes the sounds are presented relatively untransformed, as in the case of the fire sirens in Varèse's *Poème Electronique,* and those can evoke previous reactions to sirens with considerable emotional impact. Beethoven's use of bird songs in his Sixth Symphony falls in this category.

Powerful though these conditioned reactions can be, we agree with Hanslick (1854/1957) that there is nothing particularly *musical* about the process. It is not obvious that we have a very different reaction to the siren when we hear it in the *Poème Electronique* than when we hear it in real life. In fact, we suppose that the composer is using the siren to evoke the previously conditioned response. There is nothing morally wrong with that—at least every composer from Bach to Brahms as well as from Telemann to Tchaikovsky has used elements having strong extramusical associations. These effects can, however, border on the meretricious—or, when they fail, the silly. Hindemith (1961) joked about a string quartet of one of his contemporaries that imitated jack hammers, suggesting that it would have been more cost-effective to hire a quartet of jack-hammer operators to produce the effect.

Icon

With iconic representation we turn to effects that depend upon patterns within the music itself. Music can represent emotions iconically because the ebb and flow of tensions and relaxations in the music mirror the form of emotional tensions and relaxations. Helmholtz (1877/1954) cites Aristotle to this effect:

> Why is sound the only sensation that excites the feelings? Even melody without words has feeling. But this is not the case for color or smell or taste. . . . But we

feel the motion which follows sound. . . . These motions stimulate action, and this action is the sign of feeling. (p. 251)

Actually Aristotle (or one of his associates) here combined indexical and iconic representations in noting both the iconic relationship between tonal motion and action and the prior indexical associations of actions and feelings. Helmholtz goes on to discuss the relationship between the form of rhythmic motions in general and the forms of our emotional life.

Langer (1951, 1953) develops this view very carefully and persuasively. "Because the forms of human feeling are much more congruent with musical forms than with the forms of language, music can *reveal* the nature of feelings with a detail and truth that language cannot approach" (Langer, 1951, p. 199). Beethoven provides perhaps the best examples of the process of tension and release for the contemporary American listener. If you have not done this already, listen to a recording of Beethoven's Fifth or Sixth Symphony, for example, and let yourself be carried away with the flow of emotional energy. You can notice cycles of energy buildup, followed by partial relaxation, followed by greater buildup, in a sawtooth sort of pattern, leading to a final resolution of which you can say, "Well, I'm glad that came out right in the end!"

But the musical icon does not represent specific, verbalizable emotions, such as pity or fear. Music represents the dynamic form of emotion, not the specific content, as both Langer and Helmholtz point out. Langer quotes Wagner's essay *Ein glücklicher Abend* to the effect that

> what music expresses, is eternal, infinite and ideal; it does not express the passion, love, or longing of such-and-such an individual on such-and-such an occasion, but passion, love or longing in itself, and this it presents in that unlimited variety of motivations, which is the exclusive and particular characteristic of music, foreign and inexpressible to any other language. (Langer, 1951, p. 188)

But the iconic representation of music is less specific even than this. Music mimics the form, not the content, of emotional life. As Langer says, "It is a peculiar fact that some musical forms seem to bear a sad and a happy interpretation equally well" (Langer, 1951, p. 202). An often cited example is Orfeo's aria "Che farò senza Euridice" from Gluck's *Orfeo ed Euridice*, where Orfeo laments his loss of Euridice via a beautiful, flowing melody in a major key that could easily serve as a serenade or expression of quiet joy. As Brown (1981) points out, it is generally true of iconic signs that they require some context for their disambiguation. The nineteenth-century Viennese critic Edouard Hanslick in his monograph *The Beautiful in Music* argued vehemently against the notion that music represented emotions at all, yet was willing to grant that

> there are ideas which, though not occurring as feelings, are yet capable of being fully expressed in music; and conversely, there are feelings which affect our minds but which are so constituted as to defy their adequate expression by any ideas music can represent. . . . What part of the feelings, then, can music represent, if not the subject involved in them? . . . Only their dynamic properties. It may reproduce the motion accompanying psychical action, according to its momentum: speed, slowness, strength, weakness, increasing and decreasing intensity. But motion is only one of the concomitants of feeling, not feeling itself. (Hanslick, 1854/1957, p. 24)

In fact, the effort to achieve too precise a conceptual determination of musical meaning runs the risk of missing the point entirely. As Imberty remarks, "It is exactly the *meaning* that when explicated in words gets lost among the verbal significations—too precise and too literal—and gets betrayed. . . . Music doesn't *signify*, it *suggests*; that is, it creates forces in the imagination that stimulate and orient verbal associations" (Imberty, 1975, p. 91). The verbal responses of listeners cannot be taken as refering literally and precisely to emotional states, but rather as pointing in a general way to differences in emotional representation among pieces of music.

Though the representation of emotion in musical icons is necessarily vague, listeners find it quite natural to attach general emotional labels to pieces of music (Francès, 1958, Experiment XIV). There is considerable evidence that listeners are quite consistent in their broad characterizations of the emotional import of music. Hevner (1935, 1936) presented listeners with five pieces of widely differing character, ranging from Debussy's *Reflects dans l'eau* for solo piano, to the middle of the first movement of Tchaikovsky's Sixth, to the Scherzo from Mendelssohn's *Midsummer Night's Dream*. She had the listener respond via a checklist of 66 adjectives for each piece. The adjectives had emotional connotations and had meanings that fell into eight clusters; for example, *merry, joyous,* and *gay* fell into one cluster, while *pathetic, doleful,* and *sad* fell into another. Listeners were consistent in their responses, checking adjectives in the *spiritual, lofty, dignified* and *dreamy, tender, yearning* groups for the Tchaikovsky excerpt and adjectives in the *dreamy, tender, yearning* group plus the *exhilarated, dramatic, passionate* group for the Debussy. Thus, in a general way listeners agreed on broad distinctions concerning the emotions represented in a disparate sample of pieces.

The next logical step was to attempt to link emotional properties of the pieces to particular iconic features of the music, while holding other musical features constant. This Hevner (1936) did by producing different versions of the same brief piano pieces, much as a composer writing a set of variations might do. Hevner explored contrasts involving richness of harmony (simple vs. complex), rhythmic character (firm vs. flowing), mode (major vs. minor), and melodic direction (ascending vs. descending). For each contrast she selected 6 to 10 pieces that could plausibly be altered to illustrate the contrast. For example, for the contrast in rhythmic character she used one of Mendelssohn's *Songs without Words*, played with a rippling sixteenth-note pattern (the way he wrote it) for the *flowing* condition and played with block chords under each melody note for the *firm* condition. Thus the other properties of the piece remained roughly constant while the character of its rhythmic activity changed—it would still have the same melody, with the same harmony, going at the same speed, played on the same instrument at roughly the same loudness, and so forth. Hevner collected listeners' responses with the adjective checklist as before, looking for effects of the varied features on the relative choice of the eight adjective clusters—especially effects consistent across the pieces.

Of the features Hevner studied, melodic direction had the least effect. It made little difference to listeners' responses whether the predominant direction of the melody was up or down. The other three variables had consistent effects. The minor mode led listeners to select adjectives in the *pathetic, doleful, sad* and *dreamy, tender, yearning* clusters, while the major mode led to a shift of choices toward the *merry, joyous, gay* and *playful, sprightly, graceful* clusters. Firm rhythm led to choices in the *spiritual, lofty, dignified* and *vigorous, robust, emphatic* clusters, while flowing rhythm was characterized by choices in the *merry, joyous, gay* and *dreamy, tender, yearning* clusters, and somewhat less consistently in the *playful, sprightly, graceful* cluster. Simple (vs. complex) harmony led to choices in the *merry, joyous, gay* and *playful, sprightly, graceful* categories. Thus, in a broad way, the features Hevner studied appear to be systematically related to listeners' judgments of emotional representation.

Corroboration for Hevner's results comes from a study by Scherer and Oshinsky (1977) using even simpler stimuli. Scherer and Oshinsky used brief eight-note sequences produced on a MOOG synthesizer. They varied features such as tempo, evenness of rhythm, major versus minor mode, rapidity of attack and decay, melodic direction, and amount of pitch variation. Like Hevner, Scherer and Oshinsky found a definite effect of major versus minor on perceived happiness, though with these brief synthesized fragments the minor mode was associated more with disgust and anger than with sadness. Ascending versus descending melodic direction had little effect, except perhaps to connote fear. Not surprisingly, faster tempos, sharper attacks, and greater variation of pitch were associated with happiness and activity.

More can be learned about the structure of the emotional contrasts afforded by music by applying the techniques of factor analysis and multidimensional scaling, described in Chapter 4 in connection with the structure of pitch relationships and in Chapter 7 in connection with rhythm. Here, instead of assuming the dimensions along which responses would be structured (as Hevner did by assuming that the adjectives to which listeners respond were clustered in some reasonable way), the researcher first has listeners use the adjectives in responding to a large number of pieces of music and then sees if the pieces of music and the adjectives fall naturally into clusters. This method of data analysis finds clusters of musical selections for which listeners' responses are strongly correlated. Two pieces are grouped together if listeners respond to them with similar patterns of adjective choice. If listeners tend to check both *glad* and *playful* in response to the same pieces and to check neither in response to other pieces, then those items are clustered together. The computer program by which the analysis is carried out finds clusters of pieces within which correlations between response patterns across the adjectives are very strong and among which there is little correlation. That is, if two pieces consistently draw the responses *glad* and *playful* (and, in contrast, not the response "ominous"), then they are grouped together on a dimension we could call gaiety versus gloom.

Wedin (1972) applied this method to listeners' ratings of 40 musical excerpts using a checklist of 125 adjectives. The pieces of music were varied widely in character, including excerpts (each about a minute long) from a Bach Adagio for organ, an accordion polka, *The Merry Wives of Windsor* overture, Dodgson's Guitar Concerto (twentieth century), and the Beatles' "Revolution" from the *White Album*. Wedin's analysis disclosed three main dimensions along which the peices grouped themselves. In terms of the adjectives that characterized it, the first dimension contrasted energy versus relaxation—at one end was a cluster including *lively, inspiring, elated, energetic, powerful,* and at the other end a cluster including *peaceful, melancholy, dreamy, soft, lyrical*. (That is, when listeners checked adjectives in the former cluster, they tended *not* to check adjectives in the latter cluster.) The second dimension contrasted gaiety versus gloom, with clusters *glad, airy, playful, cheerful, light* versus *dramatic, fateful, powerful, ponderous, ominous*. The presence of *powerful* on two of the dimensions means that the dimensions were not completely independent; and this is even more evident with the third dimension, which shared a whole cluster of adjectives with the second. The third dimension contrasted trivial and light versus solemn and serious: *glad, airy, playful, cheerful, merry* versus *powerful, grand, solemn, serious, dignified*.

Wedin went on to relate listeners' adjective choices with features of the music. Each of the 40 musical excerpts was placed in the three-dimensional space on the basis of the ratings it received on the dimensions energy–relaxation, gaiety–gloom, and trivial–solemn. The excerpts were also rated independently for their musical features. Thus Wedin could find out if possession of certain musical features was correlated with position along the dimensions. The main features associated with energy (vs. relaxation) were staccato (vs. legato) articulation and loud (vs. soft). Gaiety (vs. gloom) was characterized by consonant harmonies, flowing (vs. firm) rhythm, major mode, and relatively high pitch level. Seriousness (vs. triviality) was associated with having the cultural labels *serious* or *old*, as well as with being loud, slow, low in pitch, and avoiding the major mode. These characterizations fit our previous notions and fit well with what Hevner, in a less systematic way, found. They show that there is a definite pattern to the way listeners characterize a wide variety of pieces of music in emotional terms, supporting our belief in the effectiveness of emotional representation in music. This pattern operates at a very broad and general level. The next step is to see if, under some conditions, finer emotional discriminations are possible.

In the search for finer discriminations among the emotions represented by music, Brown (1981) decided to move away from the total reliance on verbal responses that characterized the broad-guaged studies reported above. Brown's technique was to ask listeners for judgments of synonymy, on the plausible supposition that listeners know more about the subtleties of emotional representation than they are able to verbalize. We suppose that listeners will be able to match two musical excerpts according to their similarity of emotional tone and their difference from other excerpts, even though all the excerpts fall into the same *verbal* category. To see how Brown's method works we first illustrate it with a broad-guaged study that replicated the qualitative results of the studies described above, in addition to providing some baseline data against which to compare the results of Brown's fine-grained studies.

In Brown's broad-guaged study, he selected six pairs of classical and romantic European pieces that spanned a wide range of emotional qualities, for example, the Lullaby from Canteloube's *Songs of the Auvergne* (soprano and orchestra) and the Largo from Beethoven's Piano Sonata No. 7 as representing a *tender, hushed* mood, or the opening of Haydn's *Lark* Quartet and Leoncavallo's song "Mattinata" representing *spring morning buoyancy*. The selections were mostly 3–5 min long. By pairing pieces that were similar in mood though different in superficial musical characteristics (such as the impressionist orchestral color of the Canteloube vs. the more spare solo piano of the Beethoven), Brown hoped to show that listeners were indeed able to delve beneath the surface and retrieve the underlying emotional meanings. Brown told his listeners:

"Try to penetrate to the emotional essence of each piece, setting aside as far as possible style, composer, artist, tempo, etc." (Brown, 1981, p. 245). Listeners heard the set of 12 selections twice. Their task was to pair mood-matching pieces with each other and with the appropriate adjective cluster (out of the six given). Listeners' success at the task was indicated by how consistent they were in their choices, measured by the number of choices that agreed either with the predetermined pairings or with the group's modal choices. The probabilities of accidental agreement with group choices are quite low—.09 for picking one pair, .01 for two pairs, .001 for three pairs, and so on—so the choice of even two or three pairs in agreement with the group represents better-than-chance performance.

Listeners were relatively successful with this task. Thirteen nonmusicians had an average of 2.7 matches apiece with the group choices, and a group of 16 of what Brown calls "nineteenth-century knowledgeables" achieved 2.9 matches, and five of those listeners matched 10 of the predetermined set of 12. (Nineteenth-century knowledgeables were selected for being particularly familiar with the musical genres used in the experiment and were typically either graduate students in musicology or obsessive listeners.) Thus Brown's study corroborates those of Hevner and Wedin in finding broad agreement among listeners on the general categories of emotion represented by pieces of music. It remains to be seen whether Brown's method of synonymy judgments can be used to disclose the sharing of fine categories of emotional nuances.

Brown called his fine-grained study "Twelve Variations on Sadness." As in the broad-guaged study, the music was drawn from the orchestral and operatic repertoire of classical and romantic European music, and as before, predetermined "synonyms" were chosen from contrasting genres. For example, the Marschallin's aria toward the end of Act I of Strauss's *Der Rosenkavalier*—a meditation on time and aging—and the Andante from Mozart's Piano Concerto No. 21—the piece used for the movie *Elvira Madigan*—were paired as representing a *wistful, delicately regretful* mood. Another pair was Berlioz's aria for soprano and orchestra "Le Spectre de la Rose" from *Les Nuits d'Eté* and the Adagio from Bruch's Violin Concerto No. 1 for *sadness tinged with romantic mystery*. The other sad moods represented were *funereal, strong but sorrowful; depression, the 'pits'; poignant, plaintive;* and *relaxed, somber, reflective*. Brown presented the task to different groups of listeners, either with or without his predetermined adjective pairs. In both cases listeners were encouraged to take notes, especially during the first hearing of the pieces, to help them in making their pairings. Thirty-two nonmusicians and 22 musicians (conservatory students) were divided between the with- and without-words presentation conditions.

In the without-words condition, both musicians and nonmusicians achieved only moderate consistency, agreeing with the group pairing only 1.3 and 1.2 times, respectively. More importantly, they failed to respond to the nuances of emotional meaning represented in the pieces. Their choices seemed to be determined simply by superficial characteristics of the music; for example, they grouped the two soprano arias together, the Mozart concerto excerpt with another Mozart concerto, and the Bruch concerto with another late romantic concerto. The degree of consistency they did achieve, then, was not in response to the underlying meanings that formed the basis of the original selection. While in the broad-guaged study reported above, it did not make a drastic difference whether subjects' choices were scored in relation to the group's modal choices or in relation to the predetermined selection of pieces for mood, here it did. The average numbers of choices in agreement with the original pairings were only 0.42 and 0.55 for the musicians and nonmusicians.

The importance of context in aiding listeners to decipher iconic emotional meanings in music is shown in the with-words condition, where Brown also gave listeners the six adjective clusters in terms of which to categorize the pieces. In that condition, the nonmusicians behaved just as in the without-words condition, with 1.6 matches to the modal group choice and 0.56 to the predetermined pairings. However, the musicians group made modal choices that exactly matched the original pairings and had an average of 1.3 choices in agreement. Thus with the added context of the suggested adjective clusters, musicians, but not nonmusicians, were able to solve the task of retrieving the underlying meanings at better than chance accuracy. Brown suggests that the musicians' success in the with-words condition was due to the fact that the words indicating target moods freed the musicians to concentrate on activities that would help them remember the selections better. During the first playing of the pieces in the without-words condition, both musicians and nonmusicians tended to take notes that described the emotions represented (as they did in a comparable condition of Francès's (1958, Experiment XIV) study). In the with-words condition the nonmusicians took the same type of notes or just used the adjective clusters provided. Seventy percent of the musicians in the with-words condition, however, took notes indicating technical aspects of the music, which Brown thinks aided them in identifying the pieces on the second hearing and in imagining them for comparison. This helped them achieve greater consistency and freed them to attend to subtler aspects of emotional representation. Thus, the method of synonymous pairings provides evidence that under certain circumstances experienced listeners are able to make quite subtle distinctions among the emotions represented in music.

Brown points out an important aspect of iconic representation in general: that contextual support is almost always necessary for the perceiver to understand the sign unambiguously. Icons are typically vague enough so that without context we are often bewildered as to the intended meaning of the sign. With context we suddenly understand, "Oh, now I see why it means that!" This is especially relevant to our understanding of the iconic representation of emotion in music. In an opera or ballet, the story provides sufficient context so that we are unlikely to misunderstand, even on a first hearing. Other music in which the context is not explicitly provided requires greater familiarity before we can delve into the underlying meanings. For musicians this familiarity with particular pieces is usually provided by the rehearsal process—by the time a piece reaches performance it is so familiar that it is understood through and through by the musicians playing it. The increasing quality and availability of recordings since the 1930s has made it possible for average listeners to become thoroughly familiar with whatever music they choose and thus to understand the deeper meanings of music that would be opaque in a single hearing at a concert.

Symbol

By symbol, Peirce meant a sign that derives its meaning from its relationships in a network with other signs. Where musical signs are indexical or iconic, the meaning can often be read from the sign directly—as with thunder and the pitter-patter of raindrops in Beethoven and Rossini, or even the firm footsteps of faith in Bach. The meaning of musical symbols arises from their place in the syntax of a piece and, more broadly speaking, of a style. This is true of some iconic signs as well. The play of tension and release over time that mirrors the ebb and flow of emotional excitement depends on syntactic relations for its expression, and so such icons also function as symbols. Wagner's leitmotifs, too, which were initially introduced as indices of characters and plot themes, when heard again in the symphonic texture, provide a unifying principle in the syntactic structure of the opera (Janik & Toulmin, 1973) and thus function symbolically. A symbol thus depends for its significance on its place in the musical pattern in relation to other symbols.

In order to consider the emotional significance of symbols, we first need to explore a more elaborate account of emotion than those based simply on conditioned reactions. We need to examine the way the patterns that link symbols together in music and cognition function in relation to emotion. Specifically, we need to consider how the interruption of patterns can lead to the generation of emotional meaning. Because of the active involvement of the listener in following the musical pattern at the symbolic level, we expect that musical symbols will typically induce emotion, rather than merely represent it. We turn now to the presentation of a cognitive theory of emotion and return below to a consideration of musical symbols.

A COGNITIVE THEORY OF EMOTION

The theory we rely on is that of Mandler (1984). We find its presentation by Berscheid (1983) especially apt and useful for our purposes, and so in what follows we rely on it to a great extent. Like most theories of emotion, Mandler's attempts to account for the biological adaptive value of emotional reactions, for the function of biological arousal and its relation to the other aspects of emotion, and for what is known about human emotional experience and behavior. The essentials of Mandler's theory of emotion are as follows: Human cognition operates by means of perceptual–motor schemata through which (largely unconscious) expectancies are generated for upcoming events and by which future behaviors are planned. The interruption of an ongoing schema or plan brings about biological arousal—a signal that something has gone wrong. This reaction in turn triggers a search for a cognitive interpretation of what happened— a search for meaning. The arousal and the interpretation join together in producing an emotional experience of a particular quality. Now we look at these stages in detail and apply them to the experience of music.

The characterization of cognition in terms of schemata and plans is quite consonant with the picture of musical experience developed in Chapters 5 and 6. There we suggest that in following a piece of music, the listener develops expectations for where it is going; and we draw the analogy of the person walking through a forest on a well-known but not recently trodden path. Unexpected events will occur, such as a newly fallen tree blocking the way, but generally, these occasion only small detours, and the walker will resume the path. As long as the events on the walk do not violate expectancies, the walking itself does not require conscious attention and proceeds automatically. Attention is activated by the unexpected, and with it a cognitive appraisal of the novel situation.

Unconscious Schemata

The unconscious nature of many sets of expectancies and the cognitive consequences of violating them can be handily illustrated by an experience familiar to everyone who drives a car. Driving is a good example of a skilled activity at which people receive considerable practice. Other activities would do as well—hitting a tennis ball, playing the piano, or riding a bicycle. When we drive a well-known route—from work to home for example—we decide where we want to go at the start, and then mostly automatic and unconscious processes take over to execute the plan. How automatic these processes are becomes apparent if we try later to recall specific routine events from the trip. And just after we move to a new home, we can easily find ourselves driving home quite efficiently to our old house before we consciously intervene and revise the plan. The unconscious execution of such a behavioral plan leaves our minds free to attend to other things—listening to the radio or carrying on a conversation. And the interruption of the plan immediately affects our ability to carry on the concurrent activity. A sudden emergency in the road, such as a car pulling out in front of us, leads our attention to be directed to our driving and away from our conversation. We are consciously attending to the task and assessing the novel situation. Moreover, we are emotionally aroused. In fact, Mandler's account of emotion holds that it is our arousal that serves as a signal to set the processes of cognitive assessment in motion.

In listening to music, the schema we are following is the plan of the work—or rather, plans, since a complex work involves the simultaneous execution of several plans: melodic, harmonic, rhythmic, and so forth, all operating on several levels at once. We follow most of these plans unconsciously; in fact, there is usually much too much going on for us to attend consciously to everything. As described in Chapter 6, we project these plans forward in time, generating expectancies for coming events. Insofar as the composer was creative, these plans are continually interrupted with somewhat novel events, and that brings about physiological arousal. The arousal in turn triggers cognitive activity aimed at an interpretation of the novel event—an interpretation that integrates the event into the meaningful pattern of the piece.

Arousal

At this point we should be more specific about the type of physiological arousal Mandler's theory supposes, namely, arousal of the autonomic nervous system (ANS). The ANS if the control system for many automatic bodily functions, including the circulation of the blood, breathing, and digestion. It has two main divisions—the sympathetic and parasympathetic nervous systems—of which the sympathetic is mainly involved in emotional arousal. It seems plausible that ANS arousal evolved as a fast-acting warning system to initiate activation of the organism in the face of potential danger. ANS arousal accelerates breathing and heartbeat and increases the blood supply to peripheral muscles by vasodilation. It also produces piloerection (in which the hair "stands on end") as a social signal of activation. (Humans, who have less hair than their mammalian cousins, get "goose bumps.") The involvement of ANS arousal provided the basis of the James–Lange theory of emotion. James (1890) supposed that the experience of emotion arose when a person "read" the physiological symptoms of arousal. The person who experiences increased heart rate and piloerection and sweating knows he or she is afraid. For James, each experienced emotion had its distinctive pattern of physiological symptoms.

Mandler's account agrees with James' in supposing that ANS arousal is the first stage in an emotional reaction. However, Mandler (1984) reviews evidence suggesting that ANS arousal is essentially contentless—that emotional qualities cannot be read directly from the qualities of arousal. Arousal requires cognitive interpretation before a specific emotion can be experienced. (There is some dispute about whether this is always literally true—see Lang, 1984—but it seems true in many instances.) The central experiment bearing on this issue is that of Schachter and Singer (1962), who covertly administered an ANS-arousing drug to subjects and then provided a social context suggesting one or another emotional reaction— euphoria or anger. Subjects tended to experience the emotion suggested by the context, leading to the conclusion that ANS arousal itself is relatively contentless and that content is provided by subsequent cognitive analysis. Thus Mandler's theory proposes that interruptions of ongoing plans and schemata produce ANS arousal, which in turn triggers a cognitive search for an interpretation of the interruption.

This account many strike the reader as somewhat counterintuitive, since the question arises of how the brain can know the correct ANS reaction until cognitive analysis has told it what the stimulus is: lion-behind-the-bush or pussycat-in-the-tree. But much of the adaptive value of the activation system must lie in how fast it acts: We jump first and think later. ANS arousal seems to involve a fast-acting system that depends on very rough first approximations to stimulus identities, noticing primarily departures from the expected. And evidence for the arousal-then-interpretation sequence is rapidly accumulating (Zajonc, 1980, 1984).

There is considerable evidence that strong emotional reactions to music involve ANS, especially sympathetic arousal. Binet and Courtier (1895, cited in McLaughlin, 1970) found that hearing such pieces as the "Ride of the Valkyries" from Wagner's *Die Walküre* and the "Soldiers' Chorus" from Gounod's *Faust* led listeners' pulse and breathing rates to increase.

The effect seemed not to depend necessarily on the martial tempo of those selections—the spring song "Winterstürme wichen dem Wonnemond" from *Die Walküre* and the love duet from *Faust* produced effects just as great. Goldstein (1980) has assembled persuasive evidence that ANS arousal figures in the emotional thrills listeners experience to music. Listeners' reports certainly reflect the symptoms of ANS arousal, and those symptoms characterized the responses of listeners in a laboratory situation experiencing thrills to self-selected music (such as the final scene of *Faust*). Furthermore, administering a drug that is supposed to block sympathetic arousal tended to lessen the number of thrills, at least in some cases. Thus, Mandler's theory seems applicable to the experience of music insofar as ANS arousal is an important component of emotional response to music.

The notion that ANS arousal may be triggered by interruptions of unconscious schemata in the musical pattern is also supported by a considerable amount of evidence. Meyer (1956, 1967) provides numerous examples of such interruptions, tracing the emotional import and meaning of music to sequences involving interruption-of-schema-plus-resolution. The interruptions can arise from very simple phenomena. Jones (1976) argues that the range of expected continuations of a melody are constrained by how far in pitch the melody can move in a limited period of time. Leaps, as contrasted with scale-wise motion, of a melody can provide subtle surprises. Consider one of the melodies used by Mahler in the finale of his Second Symphony, two instances of which are shown in Figure 8.1. The arrows point to critical places in the melody, at which either a step or a leap can occur. Most of the time, as in (A), there is a small leap. Mahler saves the most marked leap versions for dramatic moments in the piece, as in (B). Examples 8a and b present schematic **8a, 8b** versions of the two examples in Figure 8.1.

Verdi plays similarly on our expectations with a theme in *La Forza del Destino* (Act II, scene 2) associated with spiritual tranquility, shown in Figure 8.2 and presented in Example 8c. Here expectations are generated **8c**

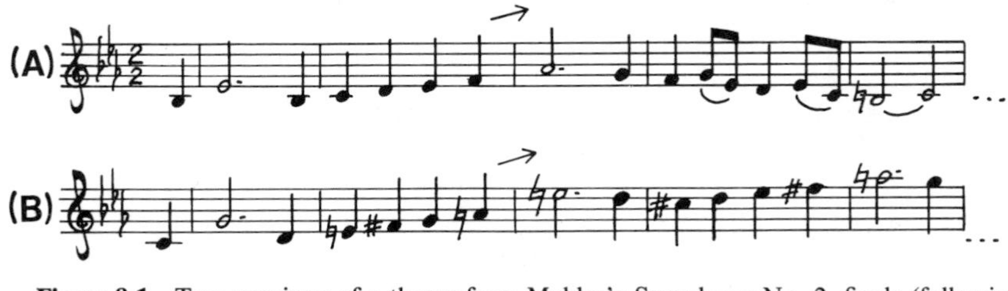

Figure 8.1 Two versions of a theme from Mahler's Symphony No. 2, finale (following Rehearsal Number 46 in the alto and soprano parts).

Figure 8.2 Theme from Act II, scene 2, of Verdi's *La Forza del Destino*.

for motion along the chord. The melodic leap (arrow) occurs after expectations for motion along the chord pattern have been set up and are ripe for interruption. The note (G♯) that would have been expected is denoted by the x. The leap produces a slight emotional lift. A third example, showing how such patterns can be so hidden in the musical texture as to operate only subconsciously, is provided by Chopin's Waltz in C♯ minor, **8d**   op. 64, no. 2 (Figure 8.3, Example 8d). Beginning in measure 25 the middle line (Arrow 1) follows a downward chromatic scale, moving to a new pitch in each measure (shown in bolder notation). The second note in this series—the E♯ in measure 26 (Arrow 2)—is the first that attracts the listener's attention, since it is different from the corresponding note in the initial presentation of the waltz melody. Then there is an interruption of the descending line when the seventh pitch in the series (Arrow 3) is delayed two beats, creating a slight increase of emotional tension just before the end of the phrase. (Note also in this example that the slow, descending melodic line iconically suggests relaxation and perhaps resignation.) It is obvious in this example that the descending chromatic scale

Figure 8.3 Passage beginning at measure 25 of Chopin's Waltz, Op. 62, No. 2.

is not the only, or even the main, pattern being developed in the passage. There are the melody in the top line and the oom–pah–pah waltz rhythm in the bass. Music generally involves several overlapping schemata operating simultaneously so that subconscious interruptions are occurring by turns on different levels. The subconscious information-processing machinery of the brain is kept very busy by an attentive listener.

Meaning

Once ANS arousal occurs, a search for an interpretation of the interruption begins. This search is like the mental activity initiated by finding the forest path blocked by a fallen tree. First, the interruption is noted for what it is. Then an evaluation of alternative courses takes place. A very large tree blocking a narrow defile simply brings the walk to an end. Composers generally try to avoid interruptions so severe that the piece simply ends. Interruptions in the underlying schemata of music are more like those caused by small trees where there is a detour at hand. Cognitive activity is directed to finding the alternative route. The happiest outcome occurs when, in the course of the detour, we come upon an especially beautiful wildflower that we would have missed on the main path. Meyer (1956) argues persuasively that especially meaningful moments in music arise from the violation of schematic expectations followed by creative and felicitous resolutions of the disruption. The pleasant surprise described by Berscheid at the start of this chapter is of the same form.

It is important to keep in mind that the schematic processes whose interruption causes arousal are mostly subconscious. As shown in Chapter 5, the average listener not only has much structural information about music stored in the mind, but is largely unaware of its presence and the ways it operates in the solution of perception and memory tasks. Even the musically untrained listener subconsciously marks deviations from the tonality he or she is used to, is aroused by them, and subconsciously finds meaning in their resolution. In fact, Meyer suggests that too conscious an attention to any one detail of this pattern of interruption and resolution may distract us from emotional responsiveness and enjoyment of the music:

> Conscious awareness of the mental activity involved in the perception of the response to the stimulus situation is by no means inevitable. Intellectual experience (the conscious awareness of one's own expectations or, objectively, of the tendencies of the music), as distinguished from intellectual activity, is largely a product of the listener's own attitude toward his [or her] responses and hence toward the stimuli and mental activities which bring them into existence. That is to say, some listeners, whether because of training or natural psychological inclination, are dis-

posed to rationalize their responses, to make experience self-conscious; others are not so disposed. If intellectual activity is allowed to remain unconscious, then the mental tensions and the deliberations involved when a tendency is inhibited are experienced as feeling or affect rather than as conscious cognition. (Meyer, 1956, p. 31).

The subconscious nature of most sources of emotion in music at the symbolic level provides us with the solution of a puzzle posed by Wittgenstein (1966). Wittgenstein notes that we may be very familiar with a favorite piece, say a Haydn minuet and yet want to hear it again—want to hear specifically that piece and not another one similar to it. Wittgenstein asks why we should want to hear just that piece. After all, it holds no surprises for us. Here we suggest that though it might hold no surprises for us on the conscious level, it is full of schematic violations on the subconscious level. Now of course it would be possible to listen to it so often (several dozen times consecutively for example) that we would habituate even these subconscious reponses to it. That is, our schemata for the type of piece and the style would simply come to mirror this particular piece as the prototype. But in the normal course of events, that is unlikely. The familiar pieces we enjoy hearing often are not *merely* prototypical: They are creative elaborations of prototypes (Meyer, 1967). If the meaning of music were entirely accessible at explicit verbal levels, we would not actually have to listen to it—we could just talk about it. As Seeger (1977) suggests, words name things, but music does not name. Rather it conveys meaning in the relationship among signs embodied in a complex semiotic system.

Individual Differences

It is partly this verbal inaccessibility of the musical symbol that gives it its power. Jung (1971) suggests that this is true of symbols in general, that as soon as their meanings become fully explicated, they lose their power as symbols. And Jung goes on to suggest origins in the structure of personality for the individual differences in response to musical symbols noted above by Meyer—the attitude of enjoyment of the emotional import of music without seeking to attain explicit verbalization versus the attitude of seeking to explain everything and, in the process, rob the symbol of its power to affect us. Machotka (1981) provides a model of the way individual differences in personality can be subtly related to preference for visual art. This has yet to be done for music. Wallach and Greenberg (1960) made a start on this project, using broad categories of personality in connection with a limited range of musical materials. They found that high-anxiety introverts tended to find higher levels of sexual imagery in music than other listeners, suggesting (not implausibly) that for those listeners, music provided a substitute for human contact. The problems of investigating the relationship of persons' need structures to musical choice are exacerbated by the wide range of musical training in Western urban populations, leading to cognitive as well as psychodynamic differences. And there are undoubtedly interactions between need structure and the kind of training sought, as Machotka notes in connection with the visual arts; that is, different types of personality seek training as performers versus musicologists versus psychologists of music and so on.

Relationship to Other Accounts

Mandler's (1984) and Berscheid's (1983) theory of emotion provides us with a plausible account of the genesis of emotional response to the symbolic (syntactic) content of music. Perceptual learning throughout the listener's life has led to the formation of structural schemata. Subconscious information processing in the brain traces current musical structure using those schemata. The schemata embody expectancies that novel music violates. (And even familiar music is somewhat novel with respect to the subconscious schemata.) Those interruptions trigger ANS arousal, which serves to activate further cognitive activity in a search for an interpretation of the interruption—a search for meaning. The meaning, when found, merges with the arousal in an experienced emotion.

This account links the emotions of real life with those experienced with music at the symbolic level. But there is an important difference. As Berscheid points out, emotions experienced in life are more likely to be negative than positive. This is because the schematic interruptions that set them off typically involve the frustration of an ongoing plan, and that is usually an unpleasant experience. (About the only way such interruptions can be positive is through the premature completion of a plan, as when our plan of saving up for a new car is interrupted by a person at the door who gives us $1,000,000.) The interruptions afforded by music are not often materially frustrating, and composers search for satisfying resolutions. Thus music serves as a marvellous cultural invention for providing positive emotional experiences in a more or less unsatisfying world.

A closely related account of emotional response to music is that of Berlyne (1971). Like Mandler, Berlyne emphasizes the role of arousal in musical experience. However, for Berlyne, the arousal itself is the goal sought in listening. This contrasts with Mandler's empahsis on the search for meaning that arousal initiates. For Berlyne, the main process underlying the person's choice of music is the need of every organism to keep itself at some moderate level of arousal. The more complex and less

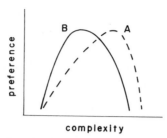

Figure 8.4 Inverted-U–shaped relation between stimulus complexity and preference. More sophisticated listeners should prefer higher complexity Curve A to Curve B.

predictable the music (that is, the more the music produces interruptions of cognitive schemata), the more arousal it will produce. On this point, Mandler's and Berlyne's theories are in agreement. For Berlyne the listener seeks arousal, but only up to a point; beyond that point the listener seeks to avoid further arousal. Thus the listener's preference in relation to musical complexity will follow an inverted-U–shaped function, as shown in Figure 8.4. The more sophisticated the listener's cognitive structures are, as a result of perceptual learning with similar materials, the less the tendency for additional complexity to be arousing. Hence, more sophisticated listeners should have preferred levels of complexity that are higher than those preferred by less sophisticated listeners—Curve A versus Curve B in Figure 8.4. Much research has been directed at the testing of this relationship of stimulus complexity and preference predicted by Berlyne's model. We review some of it below.

Before proceeding, however, we should note that both Mandler's and Berlyne's accounts of emotion are compatible with the inverted-U–shaped function of Figure 8.4. In pieces of moderate complexity, the schematic interruptions caused by surprising events usually admit of resolutions that are comprehensible to the listener. With increasing complexity, two difficulties for the listener emerge: The sheer number of interruptions increases, making it difficult for the listener to follow all of them, and the resolutions become more complex and inscrutable themselves in terms of the listener's existing schemata. Thus the listener will prefer music of what for him or her is moderate complexity. If it is too complex, it will be incomprehensible; if it is too simple, no arousal will occur. In spite of the agreement of Mandler's and Berlyne's accounts with the data we can present, we nevertheless prefer Mandler's account as applied to emotion in music. This is because of its emphasis on meaning and qualitative differences among arousing stimuli. In terms of Berlyne's theory, all arousing stimuli are more or less equivalent. Subtle and even unsubtle differences of meaning are lost—one thrill is as good as another. One receives the same arousal from a roller coaster as from a Mahler symphony. Many listeners find music highly meaningful in ways they find difficult to verbalize (Brown, 1981; Dowling, 1981; Imberty, 1975), and Mandler gives a very plausible account of why that should be true.

Complexity and Arousal

Smets (1973) presents good evidence that complexity is related both to arousal and to preference as shown in Figure 8.4 for visual materials whose properties varies over a fairly wide range. There are fewer studies dealing with auditory materials, but they lead to the same general conclusion. For example, Overmier and Schuck (1969) found that the time listeners spent listening to tone patterns was an inverted-U–shaped function of the complexity of those patterns. Vitz (1966) varied stimulus complexity by controlling variation along the dimensions of pitch, loudness, and duration of tones in brief sequences. He found that listeners preferred moderate levels of complexity to either extreme. Listeners with more musical training and interest in music preferred higher levels of complexity, as in Figure 8.4. Vitz (1972) even found that certain midrange frequencies (400–750 Hz) and intensities (50 dB SPL) were preferred over lower and higher values, presumably because more and more extreme values produce higher and higher levels of arousal.

One study that used stimuli closer to actual music was that of Werbik (1969). Werbik selected a number of European folk melodies, all 40 notes in length, and modified the intensity and duration of each note so that the only variable dimension was pitch. An initial group of listeners then listened to part of each melody and tried to predict the next note. (They indicated their predictions by tuning an oscillator.) Each of these listener made predictions for all the notes of the melodies in that way. The complexity of a melody was taken as its average uncertainty as indicated by the listeners' predictions; that is, the more difficult to predict, the higher the complexity. Werbik then had a second group of listeners hear the same melodies and rate them. He found an inverted-U–shaped function just as Vitz did. In line with our emphasis on the resolution of schematic interruptions, Kraehenbuehl and Coons (1959; Coons & Kraehenbuehl, 1958) showed that listeners liked the places in patterns where their expectancies were confirmed, rather than places where they were interrupted. Interruption followed by resolution was more pleasing than resolution followed by interruption. And the inverted U of Figure 8.4 occasionally shows up in in developmental studies of auditory pattern preferences (e.g., Duke & Gullickson, 1970).

Stylistic Change

These accounts of emotion based on the perceived complexity of the music provide an attractive explanation of stylistic change over time, parallel to that suggested in Chapter 3 concerning changes in the use of consonance and dissonance. As listeners' schemata accomodate to a style—that is, as they include more and more of its novelties and subtle nuances—the composer finds it more and more difficult to produce the schematic interruptions necessary for emotional arousal. The composer then needs to go outside the existing style for interruptions, and so the style inevitably changes. One byproduct of this sort of change is that some listeners whose schemata have not yet caught up with those the composer is trying to surprise find the novel interruptions to be too far removed from what they expect for them to achieve satisfactory resolutions and meaningful interpretations. This leads them to believe (correctly) that they do not understand the new music. Gradually, the average listener accomodates to the new patterns, and the once avant garde composers are incorporated into the mainstream. One has only to read what the contemporary critics of Bach or Beethoven or Stravinsky said about their music when it was new to see this process in action. Art must change in order to maintain its power to move us.

SUMMARY

In this chapter we have examined some of the ways by which music represents and excites emotion. We used Charles Peirce's outline of functions of signs to suggest that music *indicates* emotions previously associated with it, that it *iconically* mimics the form of emotional experience, and that syntactic relationships among musical *symbols* are closely related to emotion and meaning. Concerning symbols, we invoked Mandler's theory of emotion to describe the way emotional experience can arise out of stylistically embedded expectancies. The violation of (largely unconscious) expectancy brings about nonspecific arousal, which in turn triggers a search for an interpretation of the arousing event. That search provides the content of the emotional experience—the musical meaning. In our discussion of emotion and meaning, we reviewed evidence that listeners agree on the emotional meanings of pieces of music in styles with which they are familiar. Indeed, they were able to agree on very subtle shades of meaning when provided with sufficient context.

9

Cultural Contexts of Musical Experience

> *When one day an arctic traveler played a recorded song by one of the most famous European composers . . . to an Eskimo singer, the man smiled somewhat haughtily and stated: "Many, many notes, but no better music."*
>
> (Curt Sachs, 1965, p. 218)

INTRODUCTION

Anthropology exerts a healthy influence on psychology in providing a wide range of evidence, drawn from people in widely varying circumstances, against which to test generalizations derived from laboratory studies done within one culture. There is a good example of this in Chapter 4, where cross-cultural comparisons provide a means of deciding which of the psychological constraints on musical scale construction are truly general and which were peculiar to European scale structures.

The study of musical experience across cultures typically pursues one of two complementary goals: either the description of general psychological processes shared by people throughout a wide range of societies or the description of real-life behavior of people in rich and complex social contexts. Psychologists typically pursue the first goal, looking to cross-cultural studies to provide converging evidence for what they have found within their own cultures. Anthropologists typically pursue the second goal, seeking as deep an understanding of their particular cultures as possible. Though we cannot pursue both simultaneously, we need answers along both paths in our construction of a complete view of humanity. Campbell (1961) observes:

> Cooperation between these orientations is often difficult—but it is helped rather than hindered by the explicit recognition of the great difference in goals: Too often those in one camp regard those in the other as the wilful practitioners of a wrong-headed approach, implicity assuming a common goal. (p.338)

And Campbell goes on to note:

> Common cause joining the abstracting–generalizing orientation . . . and the descriptive–humanistic orientation [is that] both stand in opposition to the undisciplined generalizations often found in the more dramatic efforts to interpret man and culture. Both look askance at the more sweeping generalizations of a Spencer, a Spengler, a Toynbee, or a Nietzsche when offered as established scientific truth. This common ground is not always noted, and, indeed, each orientation tends to attribute undisciplined generalization to the other. (p.339)

Psychologists will recognize in this complementarity between abstract category schemes and richly detailed description a version of Allport's (1961) contrast between nomothetic and idiographic approaches to the study of persons—between approaches that strive to find commonalities true of people in general and approaches that strive to capture the rich detail of a unique personality.

In this chapter, we consider results gained from both of these approaches, contrasting what can be learned from the one with what can be learned from the other. Lomax (1968) provides a prime example of the cross-cultural generalization approach. He categorized a large number of societies according to two kinds of dimensions: dimensions describing musical style and performance practices and dimensions describing economic and social organization. He then attempted to find broad overall generalizations linking those two types of cultural pattern across all of the societies. Lomax's cross-cultural application of category schemes can be contrasted with what Geertz (1973) calls thick description. Thick description is done from the point of view of the participant–observer and attempts to present the "native's world view," providing an interpretation of behavior patterns from within the cultural context of an unfamiliar society. There are advantages and disadvantages at each end of the continuum: Thick description provides a wealth of meaningful detail, but there is a danger of losing sight of the theoretical forest among the fascinating empirical trees, while too coarse a category scheme does violence to the data by forcing together things that belong apart.

CROSS-CULTURAL RESEARCH

One of Lomax's early studies was of folk singing in Spain and Italy, where he found traits of song performance to be related to aspects of social interaction (Lomax, 1959). In the northern districts of Spain and Italy, he found relaxed vocal quality in songs, much choral singing in highly cohesive groups, and little melodic ornamentation. In the soughern regions of those countries, singing was basically a solo endeavor, with elaborate ornamentation and a tight, constricted vocal quality. Lomax's acquaintance with the two cultures led him to assert that song performance and cultural life-style varied together as a coherent whole. Cultural life-style involves such features as methods of food production, degree of political centralization, and rules governing sexual relationships and childrearing.

Clearly, the claim of general patterns relating singing style and culture would have to be based on the study of more than two societies. To provide better grounds for generalization, Lomax (1968) and his colleagues carried out a large survey of the folk song styles in 233 cultures throughout the world. As examples of the kinds of song-style/culture relationships they were looking for, consider two hypothetical cultures:

1. A culture with a highly individualized song performance, in which a solo singer commands attention by means of complex song production— complex text, highly ornamented melody and/or rhythm, noisy voice, and precise enunciation: Such a culture is stratified politically, socially, and economically, practices highly organized agriculture, has severe sexual sanctions, and shows male dominance and low social cohesiveness.

2. A culture with a choral, multileveled song performance that is highly cohesive and group-involving, with repetitious text that is organized simply; the voice is clear, and enunciation is slurred. Such a culture is highly cohesive politically, socially, and economically, hunts and gathers food, shows more male–female equality, and has reduced levels of sexual tension.

To obtain data on the social and cultural variables, Lomax's group relied primarily on the *Ethnographic Atlas* of the Human Relations Area Files (Murdock, 1962–1967). The *Atlas* is a topic-indexed data bank of information concerning societal traits and institutions gleaned from anthropological reports. Lomax selected cultural indices like those used in describing our hypothetical societies and devised rating scales for them that could be applied to a sample of the world's cultures.

Next, Lomax designed a rating system for attributes of musical behavior, which he calls *cantometrics*. The most important of these dimensions are the following:

1. Social organization of the vocal group: one singer, one singer with audience, social unison with leader or with no leader, simple alternation, overlapping alternation, or interlocking parts.

2. Social organization of the instrumental group (examples similar to the vocal group scale).
3. Level of cohesiveness of the vocal group or of the orchestra.
4. Explicitness in text: words dominant, words dominant but with some repetition, half of performance repetitive, or performance entirely repetitive.
5. Rhythmic organization of the vocal group or of the orchestra: rhythmic unison, heterophony, polyrhythm, or counterpoint.
6. Melodic complexity: canonic, litany, litany with variation, strophe, strophe with variation, or through-composed.
7. Melodic embellishment: from little or none to extreme amounts.
8. Vocal stance: including glottal activity, width of vocal cavity, register, nasalization, and raspiness.

Lomax trained coders to categorize song styles using these features. Independent coders listened to unlabeled recordings from the societies in the sample and rated them.

Lomax found that a major cultural variable was the complexity of a society's economic subsistence system—how they produce their food. Going from simple to complex, a society's economy can range from hunting-and-gathering to simple agriculture to animal husbandry to plow agriculture to irrigation. With more elaborate economic organization came more elaborate political organization and the stratification of society into social classes. It is perhaps not surprising that elaborate songs and variety of instrumentation were associated with economic complexity and social stratification. The European symphony orchestra provides a good example: Stratification in the orchestra mirrors stratification in society.

A more surprising result related harsh and constricted vocal quality to restrictions on female premarital sexual activity: The more permissive the society, the more open and relaxed were the vocal chords in singing. More permissive societies were also given to greater synchrony in dancing and public communication. African hunter–gatherer societies, such as the Mbuti pygmies of the Ituri forest (Turnbull, 1961), typify that pattern. In contrast, Middle Eastern Islamic societies typify cultural systems with severe premarital sexual sanctions, male dominance in community life, and a vocally tense, predominantly solo song style. However, the relationship between sexual restrictions and constricted vocal production appeared to hold across a variety of societies in different areas of the world; and hence reflected an intrinsic relationship between societal patterns and song style and not merely fortuitous historical influences. Lomax (1968) concludes:

> The main findings of this study are two. First, the geography of song styles traces the main paths of human migration and maps the known historical distributions of

cultures. Second, some traits of song performance show a powerful relationship to features of social structure that regulate human interaction in all cultures. (pp. 3–4).

The publication of these findings generated considerable comment and controversy (see Downey, 1970; Driver, 1970; Hill, 1969; Kolata, 1978; Laban, 1969; and Maranda, 1970, for a range of review and analysis from varying perspectives). Much of the discussion of the research from outside ethnomusicology stressed the advent of a new age in cross-cultural research, an age in which statistical modeling would emerge as a powerful analytical tool for cross-cultural comparison. In contrast, much of the criticism from among ethnomusicologists suggested that those very procedures did violence to musical reality within particular cultures and that Lomax's conclusions were too sweeping to be useful.

For a psychologist, the main value of Lomax's work is in its broad blocking out of an area and its dimensions. Further, Lomax's conclusions are tantalizing. The possibility that some features of music may be directly related to other aspects of social behavior in ways that hold across cultures is a very attractive one, especially to the nomothetically oriented psychologist. There are, however, some difficulties of which the reader should be aware in the interpretation of cantometric data. We briefly point out some of these difficulties and then turn to alternative formulations.

Statistical Significance

Some of the criticisms of Lomax's (1968) book centered on his use of statistical tests. The cantometrics study used one particular test—the chi-square test—repeatedly on the same data, testing for so many differences that the results of the entire cluster are brought into question. That is because statistical tests rely on a stated probability that the results in question could have occurred simply by chance. That probability applies meaningfully to only one independent application of the test to a given set of data. Repeated applications of the same test to rearrangements of the same data can lead to spurious results. Consider flipping a coin to see if you can get three heads in a row. The probability of success on one trial (with the random data of coin flips) is low; namely, $.5 \times .5 \times .5 = .125$. However, if you are allowed numerous trials, you are almost certain to get a run of three heads sooner or later. Repeated use of the same test on the same data takes advantage of the same type of fortuitous occurrence.

Reanalyzing the Cantometrics Results

In response to this criticism, new studies were made of the cantometrics and societal data using factor analysis techniques similar to those described in Chapters 4 and 7. The aim was to find clusters of social and musical features that varied together. Lomax and Berkowitz (1972) found some of the same relationships as before. However, many of the relationships observed now appeared to be due to historical and geographical continuities of the cultures involved, rather than to universal relationships between musical and nonmusical cultural patterns. (We return to this point below.) General relationships between cultural and musical features that held up in this more careful analysis were those between cohesive choral singing and social cohesion in other areas and between harsh, constricted vocal production and sexual restrictiveness.

E. E. Erickson (1976) made an extensive analysis of Lomax's data using sophisticated techniques designed to focus on specific clusters of variables while holding constant the effects of other variables such as geographic region. Erickson found that a number of the relationships among the cultural variables (apart from relationships to musical variables) were in fact universal in that they appeared to hold across diverse geographical–historical regions. For example, Erickson (like Lomax & Berkowitz) found a strong cluster of variables related to economic and technological complexity: population of typical communities, intensity of agricultural cultivation, social stratification into classes, inheritance of property rights, and political units transcending the merely local. This complexity appeared to be related to number of musical instruments employed—probably a reflection of technology—but not to other musical features. Other clusters grouped musical features together, without regular relationships to the nonmusical variables, for example, the cluster of features involving tonal blend and rhythmic cohesiveness. Nevertheless, there were a few strong relationships between societal and musical variables that held, which were independent of geographical region. These were the previously mentioned relationships between sexual restrictions on young women and an "uptight," constricted style of vocal production, between polyphonic singing and male–female equality and between the use of interlocking, contrapuntal choral parts and a small-scale gatherer type of social organization. Thus at some broad level of analysis, certain cantometric features do appear to be related to features of society, and that relationship holds across societies in diverse regions of the world, unrelated by historical cultural ties.

Let us return now to one of the most striking results of these last two studies, namely, that patterns of singing style appear to be extremely stable in spite of changes in the social and economic organization of society. This is shown in the strong relationships observed between patterns of musical features in geographically and historically related societies that had diverged in economic organization. As E. E. Erickson

(1976) notes, American Indian groups differing in type of economic organization can produce nearly identical profiles of song features, for example, fairly noisy, raspy vocal production. This suggests that as human groups migrate and change their economic and social organization, they tend to maintain basic features of their musical style. An outstanding example is the stability of the pentatonic (do, re, mi, sol, la) scale that remained intact in central Asia—China and Tibet—as well as across the migrations that radiated out to the east and west. The same scale predominates in American Indian music, having been brought to North America 20,000–40,000 years ago; and it is also central to the music of the Celts, who had traveled in the opposite direction. Lomax and Berkowitz (1972, p. 229) conclude that "main song performance patterns seem to be extremely stable (as well as very audible) aspects of regional cultures and, on the whole, do not migrate unless a whole people or culture also migrates." As E. E. Erickson (1976, p. 307) says, "Song style appears to be less directly reflective of the institutions of society than of something whose definition is far more elusive: cultural identity." The music of a culture provides a focus for the representation of cultural identity. Songs are emblems of society and culture, and they form an important part of the self-image of members of society. This is as true of urban teenagers who think of rock-and-roll (in its current form) as their music as it is of the Mbuti hunter–gatherers, for whom song expresses the relationship of the individual to the world (Turnbull, 1961).

Grain

A second type of criticism of Lomax's approach is that cross-cultural research carried out with such broad-grained categories misses some important facts about human cultures and societies. Lomax's categories are of the order of whole societies, leaving little room even for broad distinctions among genres, for example, within a culture, let alone subtler nuances. This coarseness of grain is inevitable at the start of a line of investigation. Which grain of category system to use is a problem that faces every scientist. The grain of Lomax's categories is at the coarse end of the scale, lumping together things that on closer inspection need to be separated. As such, it is very useful as a first step in blocking out a new field of study. However, it should be followed by finer-grained analysis. The coarse-grained nomothetic cross-cultural approaches need to be complemented with more idiographic studies of particular cultures and of the functioning of music in actual cultural contexts. That is, we are not saying that the cantometrics approach is wrong, but that a complementary approach is also necessary.

DESCRIPTION FROM WITHIN CULTURES

In this section, we describe a few examples of music as it is experienced in cultural context to illustrate the context-dependence of musical meaning and the potential richness of meaning within a cultural tradition—two aspects that tend to be lost in the more coarse-grained approaches. Our first example is of a particular genre from Bali that has been recently put to several different cultural uses. In Lomax's category scheme, it would be scored the same regardless of cultural context. However, it actually means different things in those different contexts.

The Balinese *Ketjak*

The *ketjak* (pronounced "ketchóck") is an especially dramatic piece of music. In performing it a group of men sit in a circular pattern and sing in chorus. They sing rhythmically interlocking parts similar to those of an instrumental *gamelan* piece, including the rapid higher-pitched parts and the intermittent larger and lower-pitched gongs. The piece itself is dra-
9a matic in dynamic (loudness) contrasts and tempo changes (Example 9a). An extended sample of it can be heard on Nonesuch recording H-72028 (Lewiston, n.d.). McKean (1979; see also Bandem & DeBoer, 1981) points out that the *ketjak* can have several distinct meanings for the Balinese, depending on the context, the intention of the sponsors of the performance, and the audience. At the extremes of its range of use a *ketjak* performance can be a religious exorcism, or a lavish tourist attraction.

In the (probably ancient) religious role, the *ketjak* chorus accompanies the *sanghyang* trance dancing of young girls who represent heavenly nymphs. Prayers are offered for the exorcism of evil spirits associated with danger or disease in the village. Here, the *ketjak* clearly has a serious ritual meaning. Singers, dancers, and audience all cooperate in interlocking roles to produce a successful ritual. A successful performance leads to a definite outcome: an oracular pronouncement. Here the *ketjak* serves an essentially sacramental function of making manifest the latent sacred reality. Musical time expresses cosmological time—in Indonesian cosmology cyclic and finely subdivided. In such a serious religious context the propriety of performers and audience in contributing to the effective realization of the ritual is essential.

The second context for the *ketjak* is distinctly secular, being performed mainly for tourists. These versions consist of relatively short dance segments. The tourist version of the *ketjak* was suggested by a Westerner living in Bali and has become immensely successful since the 1940s. The tourists, of course, are not participants in the ritual, neither knowing the proper behaviors nor being part of the social system in which the ritual has meaning. The focus of such *ketjak* performances has naturally shifted away from ritual propriety and efficacy toward elaborate showmanship. The tourist versions are often elaborately choreographed, involve exceptionally large groups of singers (70 or 80 men), have lavish costumes, and are elegantly staged. To provide meanings that are accessible to the tourists, these versions often tell a story. For example, in a popular episode from the Hindu epic *Ramayana*, the monstrous villain Ravana has abducted Sita, the beautiful consort of the god Rama. Rama enlists the help of the monkey army led by Hanuman to attack Ravana's island fortress. At length the attack is successful and Sita is saved. Here the *ketjak* portrays the attack by the monkey army, providing the Western listener with an iconic representation of the chattering of the monkeys. It is clear that the meaning of the *ketjak* is entirely different when performed as a tourist attraction than when performed as a serious religious ritual. This change in meaning depends on the social context of the performance, the way in which the piece is performed, and the manner of perticipation of the audience.

In Chapter 8 we emphasize factors intrinsic to the music and its stylistic context as determinants of emotional reaction and meaning. The foregoing example shows the importance of extramusical factors in the broader cultural context in affecting emotion and meaning. It is clear that the "very same" music can evoke different reactions and carry different meanings depending on the circumstances in which it is heard. The next example demonstrates the effects of cultural context in a somewhat different way, using prior indexical associations to evoke strong emotional reaction. These emotional reactions are probably stronger when evoked in the cultural setting of a musical event than they would otherwise be (e.g., by the simple presentation of the place-name stimulus).

Kaluli Longhouse Ceremony

A striking example of the emotional power of musical experience in social context is provided by the Kaluli of Papua, New Guinea. Schieffelin (1979) describes the *Heyalo* longhouse ceremony, which visitors to the longhouse perform at dusk. The visitors enter, dancing and singing songs referring to various landmarks and places in the hosts' clan territory:

> After a while, the audience (the hosts) become very deeply moved. Some of them burst into tears. Then, in reaction to the sorrow they have been made to feel, they jump up angrily and burn the dancers on the shoulders with the torches used to light the ceremony. The dancers continue their performance without showing any sign of pain. The dancing and singing and the concommitant weeping and burning con-

tinue all night with brief rest periods between songs. In the morning the dancers, who often carry second- or third-degree burns on their arms and shoulders, pay compensation to those people whom they made cry (Schieffelin, 1979, p. 128).

There are more profound ritual implications (see Feld, 1982, and Schieffeling, 1976, for more detail), but here we focus on certain key elements in the song: the place names. Mention of the place names themselves generates nostalgia and sorrow, invoking thoughts of past events and dead relatives, without explicit reference. The visitors may not know who will be moved by a particular reference until a member of the audience reacts. Land and landmarks invoke metaphorically an individual's identity. The Kaluli identify with their lands "because they are reflected in them" (Schieffelin, 1979), and ceremonial song has the power to touch that identity quite profoundly.

Text and Tradition

As a third example of important aspects of music and society captured by a finer-grained analysis, let us consider the use of textual content of songs to communicate significant material. Genealogy chants are important in many of the world's societies. For example, the Maori of New Zealand perform *patere,* the subject of which is a recitation of the genealogical history of the tribe and the individual. Such performances rely on strict vocal unison and rhythmic coordination, since breaking the continuity of the song performance may "invite death or disaster" (Malm, 1977). The *ko'ihonua mele* of Hawaii is likewise a geneaolgical chant retelling royal history and accomplishments. Again, great care is taken for accuracy, and the chant is performed under strict taboos, which are extended to the places where they were composed (Roberts, 1967, p. 59). These historically focused and ritually performed songs are common throughout Oceania, where highly complex social and political structures dictate the individual's inherited place in the society. In the absence of writing systems, genealogies both preserve an individual's descent lines and record a society's routes of migration. The songs of Polynesian societies recounting migration histories suggest that such accurate recounting was a necessary ingredient for guiding other voyagers. Clearly, a "map chant" serves an ecological purpose, storing for the seafarers important astronomical and navigational knowledge. The Hawaiian *mele* refers to geographic, floral, and faunal aspects of the surrounding environment. These references often evoke a time, an event, an emotion, or perhaps even convey a double entendre. Closely related to such symbolism in ancient Hawaiian song is the symbolic gestural language used in some hula dances and in other contexts (Roberts, 1967). This dance gesture system also conveys geographic references and double meanings. Herskovits (cited in Merriam, 1964, p. 280) describes a similar example of both music and the musician as "keeper of records," in the African Dahomey, Waterman (1955) describes one role of the *karma* songs of the aboriginal Australian Yirkalla as that of "text-books in natural history, cosmology, and religion," which also reaffirm the individual's kinship and totemic attachments, emphasizing the "antiquity, continuity, and permanence of his family line" (p.46).

From these examples, and from the reader's own experience, it should be clear that the meanings of music are subtly (and not so subtly) determined by cultural context. The same musical content can mean different things in different contexts. Extramusical associations can be used within a musical context to evoke strong emotional responses. And extramusical aspects of cultural context can determine properties of musical style. We turn now to broader questions of the place of music in society and the issue of how music evolved in human societies.

THE FUNCTION OF MUSIC IN SOCIETY

The evolution of human musical abilities has been a puzzle for biologists since the late 1800s. The problem has been that musical ability seems to have no clear adaptive value. The musically adept seem to have no more offspring than the musically inept, and so it is not clear why musical ability should be preserved in the genetic endowment. Humans contrast with songbirds in this regard, since a songbird without musical ability would fail to have offspring. Granit (1977) states this problem dramatically:

> There is no explanation of the talent that made possible the creation of the Ninth Symphony or the *Marriage of Figaro*. Why has musical creativity turned up at such high levels of excellence? A possible answer is that this talent has proved harmless in the process of natural selection and so has escaped annihilation. (p. 13)

This is essentially the "fortunate spinoff" explanation—musical ability is of no adaptive value in itself but is the result of happy accidents in human evolution that left us with a delightful means of whiling away our leisure hours and that fortunately is relatively harmless. Granit goes on to suggest that, in fact, the abilities used in music may have evolved in "happy symbiosis with some more useful characters." The obvious candidate for a more useful ability is speech, and it is clear from the evidence reviewed in Chapters 2 and 3 that many of the auditory mechanisms used in speech perception are almost certainly involved in music perception as well. It does appear that musical abilities developed hand in hand with speech abilities. However, at the earliest ages when children begin singing—between 9 and 12 months—their singing is easily distinguished from their speech. In particular, vowels are sustained on discrete pitch levels, and rhythm is controlled with reference to a more or less steady beat (Dowling, 1984). Thus, although music uses some of the same brain mechanisms as speech, it appears to involve other mechanisms as well, or at least other ways of using them.

We believe that now a better case can be made for the adaptive value of musical abilities (Dowling, 1983). Music was hard to see as adaptive as long as biologists were focusing on what was adaptive for the *individual*. However, if we conceive of evolution as the adaptation of the *gene pool* rather than the adaptation of individuals (Wilson, 1981), the puzzle of the adaptive value of music becomes easier to solve. It is clear from the evidence reviewed above that music is valuable to human groups. Humans presumably evolved over hundreds of thousands of years in small groups of hunter–gatherers, much more like those described by Turnbull (1961) in *The Forest People* than like those found in the modern city. In those groups, singing and playing music served as a cohesion-facilitating group activity—an expression of social solidarity. Music is capable of serving as a powerful symbol of cultural identity; especially so since musical style is very stable, ranking in stability with language as a culturally transmitted set of shared behaviors. And the music itself can represent central meanings in a culture, ranging from, "We are ——, and this is the way we do things," to, "Just as the musical pattern departs from and returns to stability and rest, so also with other human activities." Music is valuable to human societies, and therein lies its biological adaptive value. Groups that developed music were successful, and they passed on their music to their descendants.

This evolutionary argument would seem to run into a difficulty: If musical abilities were preserved in evolution because of their adaptive value, then why are they not distributed more evenly in the population? In fact, musical ability is not distributed very evenly in contemporary urban industrialized societies (Shuter-Dyson & Gabriel, 1981). There are two arguments to be considered in reply to this difficulty. First, examination of social behavior of existing hunter–gatherer groups (e.g., the Mbuti described by Turnbull, 1961) discloses very general and evenly distributed participation in those social musical behaviors that the evolutionary argument deems important. Thus it would seem that individuals generally inherit quite enough ability to carry out those social musical behaviors that are beneficial. Second, there are two closely related reasons why musical ability, which seems evenly distributed among hunter–gatherers, appears to be so unevenly distributed in urban industrialized societies. One has to do with social structure and the other with psychological development.

A major structural feature of industrialized societies is division of labor. Each person is good at just a limited range of jobs. If your car breaks down, you hire an auto mechanic; if your plumbing breaks, you hire a plumber; if you want music, you hire a musician (perhaps vicariously, as by buying a record). The musician is a music specialist, usually selected for ability and given considerable specialized training. He or she does a job and is paid, just like the mechanic and the plumber. Few people think of producing music for themselves. This is in sharp contrast to the behavior of the hunter–gatherer. In a group of two dozen people who live together all their lives in isolation from other groups, if one wants music, one produces it oneself. There are no music specialists to hire. Everyone is competent enough to perform the music that the group performs. This account is perhaps somewhat exaggerated, since among the Mbuti, for example, there are songs in which a solo singer alternates antiphonally with the chorus, and it is reasonable to suppose that the soloist is selected for ability (just as the best wood carvers carve the most important ceremonial carvings; Turnbull, 1961). But there is nevertheless a big contrast in musical behavior between societies with a great degree of division of labor and those without.

Division of labor has clear consequences for human development. Societies tend to establish mechanisms that widen the gap between the abilities of the specialists and the lay public (Kessen, 1981). Music comes to depend upon high levels of expertise for its performance. Only those with initially high levels of ability and the resources to devote a great deal of time to the development of those abilities become proficient at performance. The rest of the people become spectators, "consumers." Worse, those with initially low levels of ability are encouraged to avoid musical performance. The child who sings out of tune—who needs the most practice—is often discouraged from practicing. A very broad distribution of ability tends to develop in the population. Thus, even though nearly everyone in contemporary urban society may start life with the ability to participate in social musical activities such as the singing of "Happy Birthday," the national anthem, and hymns in church, by the time they reach adulthood many have been discouraged from active participation. This separation of the experts from the laity masks an underlying distribution of ability that is actually as even as in more "primitive" societies.

Thus, we believe that a good case can be made for the adaptive value of music in human society. This argument seems to us to make more biological sense than the argument that sees music as purely fortuitous. But we should also note that, like language, music is realized in an immense variety of ways throughout the range of human cultures. Often the differences are as illuminating as the commonalities in the understanding of human nature.

CROSS-CULTURAL UNIVERSALS

We close this overview of cross-cultural aspects of music cognition with a list of those features of musical behavior and experience that appear to be universal. Most of these are discussed in previous chapters, and we think it would be useful to the reader to gather them together in one place. Some of these features are apparently built into the auditory system, while others are built into more general properties of the brain. All are represented in a sufficiently wide range of human populations for us to believe that they are very likely based on inherited human characteristics.

One cluster of universal features is closely connected with the constraints on the form of musical scales discussed in Chapter 4. The *octave* as a basic relationsip between pitches seems built into the structure of the auditory system. In particular, the slightly stretched melodic octave described in Chapter 4 is found in a wide variety of cultures all over the world. And as discussed previously, from octave equivalence arises the *logarithmic pitch scale,* in which equal differences in pitch correspond to equal ratios of frequency. The octave is divided into stable *discrete pitch levels;* hardly any music in the world uses continuous pitch variations, and children appear predisposed to sing discrete pitches. Further, almost all the world's scales use *five to seven pitch levels* in the octave, a number that fits closely what we know of the cognitive limits on human categorical judgment. Those pitch levels are organized into a *hierarchical structure* with some more important than others, and dynamic tendencies connect them melodically (as, for example, the tendency that leads melodies to end on an important pitch in the hierarchy). Melodies the world over appear to use *melodic contour* as an organizing device: A melodic contour can be repeated at different pitch levels in the scale as a means of providing for subtle variations in its dynamic tendencies. This device is used in the songs of cultures as different as the Flathead Indians and the Balinese, as well as in the songs of Europe and India.

In connection with the discussion of pitch categories, let us note the general value of categorization for cultural communication. As Francès (1958) points out, categorization of pitches into discrete levels makes possible the communication of the musical message in spite of performance difficulties, such a noisy environment and bad intonation. Categorical production and perception have much the same value in music as in speech. And a culture's musical categories appear to have about the same degree of stability across millenia that its linguistic categories do.

Closely connected with the design of mammalian auditory systems is the way we hear timbres. As we discussed in Chapter 3, perceived *timbre differences* seem to depend in large measure on the steady-state specrtum of the sound and on events in the first 50 msec of its onset (as opposed to other possible acoustic features). We have no reason to believe that those sources of timbre differences are not important throughout the world, as well as throughout the animal kingdom.

In rhythmic organization, there seems to be good reason to suppose that the use of a *beat* framework is practically universal. Moreover, children start out singing using a fairly steady beat pattern. On this beat pattern are superimposed *rhythmic contours*—patterns of relative time intervals. Rhythmic contours are often associated with melodic contours as organizing devices.

Finally, one unmistakeable universal is that *people sing*. There is no human culture in which people do not sing, and children being singing as soon as they gain sufficient control over their voice to talk. And, as we argue above, a culture's song is a powerful symbol of cultural identity and an avenue of cultural communication.

These universal properties of human musical ability are partly dependent on other human abilities such as language that are essential for their evolutionary development. Music behavior undoubtedly evolved hand in hand with language, and the two systems share systems for perceptual analysis and vocal production, as well as more elaborate temporal control systems in the brain. But some of the inherent features of music are quite different from those of linguistic systems, for example, the musical insistence on tones of steady pitch and on the organization of those pitches into extremely well-learned perceptual–motor schemata. We believe that the musical uses of brain systems on which music relies, both those shared with language and those that peculiarly musical, evolved as a result of the adaptive value of music in human society. Musical systems of the sort we describe in this book represent a uniquely human capability.

We hope our readers—musicians and nonmusicians—will continue to develop these human abilities. Do not be misled by our industrialized society into thinking that only professionals can contribute. Nonmusicians are continually programming their own brains and developing their own sensitivities—or failing to develop. If you do not sing or play in concerts for others to hear, sing in church or school, sing in the shower, sing while you cook, sing with your children.

References

Allen, T. W., Walker, K., Symends, L., & Marcell, M. Intrasensory and intersensory perception of temporal sequences during infancy. *Developmental Psychology,* 1977, *13,* 225–229.

Allport, G. W. *Pattern and growth in personality.* New York: Holt, Rinehart & Winston, 1961.

Anderson, W. *Therapy and the arts: Tools of consciousness.* New York: Harper & Row, 1977.

Aristotle. *Poetics* (K. A. Telford, Trans.). South Bend, IN: Gateway, 1961.

Attneave, F. Some experiments on the detection of repetition in sequential stimulation. In F. Massarik & P. Ratoosh (Eds.), *Mathematical explorations in behavioral science.* Homewood, IL: Dorsey Press, 1965, pp. 87–94.

Attneave, F., & Olson, R. K. Pitch as medium: A new approach to psychophysical scaling. *American Journal of Psychology,* 1971, *84,* 147–166.

Babbitt, M. Twelve-tone invariants as compositional determinants. In P. H. Lang (Ed.), *Problems of modern music.* New York: Norton, 1962, pp. 108–121. (Reprinted from *Musical Quarterly,* 1960, *46,* 246–259.)

Bach, J. S. *The art of the fugue,* S. 1080. New York: Kalmus, n.d.

Bach, J. S. *Six sonatas and partitas for the violin,* S. 1001–1006. New York: Kalmus, n.d.

Bach, J. S. *Two and three part inventions,* S. 772–801 (H. Bischoff, Ed.). New York: Kalmus, 1943.

Bach, J. S. *Das wohltemperierte Klavier* [The well-tempered clavier] (Vol. 1), S. 846–869. Munich: Henle, 1960.

Backus, J. *The acoustical foundations of music.* New York: Norton, 1969.

Bacon, F. *The advancement of learning and New Atlantis.* Oxford: Oxford University Press, 1974. (Original works published 1605 and 1627)

Bahrick, L. E., Walker, A. S., & Neisser, U. Selective looking by infants. *Cognitive Psychology,* 1981, *13,* 377–390.

Balzano, G. J. The group-theoretic description of 12-fold and microtonal pitch systems. *Computer Music Journal,* 1980, *4*(4), 66–84.

Bandem, I. M., & DeBoer, F. *From Kaja to Kelod.* London: Oxford University Press, 1981.

Bartlett, F. C. *Remembering.* Cambridge: Cambridge University Press, 1932.

Bartlett, J. C., & Dowling, W. J. The recognition of transposed melodies: A key-distance effect in developmental perspective. *Journal of Experimental Psychology: Human Perception & Performance,* 1980, *6,* 501–515.

Beall, P. C., & Nipp, S. H. *Wee sing: Around the campfire.* Los Angeles: Price/Stern/Sloan, 1982.

Becker, J. *Some thoughts about* pathet: *Javanese modal classifications.* Paper presented to International Musicological Society, Berkeley, 1977.

Becker, J. Time and tune in Java. In A. L. Becker & A. A. Yengoyan (Eds.) *The imagination of reality: Essays in Southeast Asian coherence systems.* Norwood, NJ: Ablex, 1979, pp. 197–210.

Beethoven, L. van *Nine Symphonies.* New York: Harcourt, Brace, 1935.

Békésy, G. von. *Experiments in hearing.* New York: McGraw-Hill, 1960.

Békésy, G. von. *Sensory inhibition.* Princeton, NJ: Princeton University Press, 1967.

Benade, A. H. *Fundamentals of musical acoustics.* London: Oxford University Press, 1976.

Beranek, L. L. *Music, acoustics and architecture.* New York: Wiley, 1962.

Berlyne, D. E. *Aesthetics and psychobiology.* New York: Appleton-Century-Crofts, 1971.

Bernstein, L. *The unanswered question.* Cambridge, MA: Harvard University Press, 1976.

Berscheid, E. Emotion. In H. H. Kelley (Ed.), *Close relationships.* San Francisco: Freeman, 1983, pp. 110–168.

Blackwell, H. R., & Schlosberg, H. Octave generalization, pitch discrimination, and loudness thresholds in the white rat. *Journal of Experimental Psychology,* 1943, *33,* 407–419.

Boring, E. G. *Sensation and perception in the history of experimental psychology.* New York: Appleton-Century-Crofts, 1929.

Boulez, P. On new music. *New York Review of Books,* 1984, *31*(11), 14–15.

Bower, G. H. A selective review of organizational factors in memory. In E. Tulving & W. Donaldson (Eds.), *Organization of memory.* New York: Academic Press, 1972, pp. 93–137.

Brady, P. T. Fixed-scale mechanism of absolute pitch. *Journal of the Acoustical Society of America,* 1970, *48,* 883–887.

Bregman, A. S., & Dannenbring, G. L. The effect of continuity on auditory stream segregation. *Perception & Psychophysics,* 1973, *13,* 308–312.

Bregman, A. S., & Rudnicky, A. I. Auditory segregation: Stream or streams? *Journal of Experimental Psychology: Human Perception & Performance,* 1975, *1,* 263–267.

Broadbent, D. E. Attention and the perception of speech. *Scientific American,* 1962, *206*(4), 143–151.

Broadbent, D. E., & Ladefoged, P. On the fusion of sounds reaching different sense organs. *Journal of the Acoustical Society of America,* 1957, *29,* 708–710.

Brown, R. W. Music and language. In *Documentary report of the Ann Arbor Symposium.* Reston, VA: 1981, pp. 233–265.

Burns, E. M. Octave adjustment by non-Western musicians. *Journal of the Acoustical Society of America,* 1974, *56,* S25.

Burns, E. M. Circularity in relative pitch judgments for inharmonic complex tones: The Shepard demonstration revisited, again. *Perception & Psychophysics,* 1981, *30,* 467–472.

Campbell, D. T. The mutual methodological relevance of anthropology and psychology. In F. L. K. Hsu (Ed.), *Psychological anthropology.* Homewood, IL: Dorsey Press, 1961.

Carlsen, J. C. *Musical expectancy: Some perspectives.* Paper presented to Research Symposium on Music Cognition, Unviersity of Western Ontario, 1981. (a)

Carlsen, J. C. Some factors which influence melodic expectancy. *Psychomusicology,* 1981, *1,* 12–29. (b)

Carroll, L. *Alice's adventures in Wonderland and Through the looking-glass.* New York: Macmillan, 1944. (original work published 1865–1871)

Carterette, E. C., Friedman, M. P., Lindner, W., & Pierce, J. Lateralization of sounds at the unstimulated ear opposite to a noise-adapted ear. *Science,* 1965, *147,* 163–165.

Carterette, E. C., Monahan, C. B., Holman, E., Bell, T. S., & Fiske, R. A. Rhythmic and melodic structures in perceptual space. *Journal of the Acoustical Society of America,* 1982, *72,* S11 (abstract).

Cazden, N. The systematic reference of musical consonance response. *International Review of the Aesthetics & Sociology of Music*, 1972, *3*, 217–243.

Chang, H. W., & Trehub, S. E. Auditory processing of relational information by young infants. *Journal of Experimental Child Psychology*, 1977, *24*, 324–331. (a)

Chang, H. W., & Trehub, S. E. Infant's perception of temporal grouping in auditory patterns. *Child Development*, 1977, *48*, 1666–1670. (b)

Chomsky, N. *Aspects of the theory of syntax*. Cambridge, MA: MIT Press, 1965.

Chopin, F. *Waltzes* (C. Mikuli, Ed.). New York: G. Schirmer, 1916.

Cohen, A. J. Exploring the sensitivity to structure in music. *Canadian University Music Review*, 1982, *3*, 15–30.

Collard, R., & Povel, D.-J. Theory of serial pattern production: Tree traversals. *Psychological Review*, 1982, *89*, 693–707.

Collins, J. *Wildflowers*. Elektra 74012.

Coons, E., & Kraehenbuehl, D. Information as a measure of structure in music. *Journal of Music Theory*, 1958, *2*, 127–161.

Crumb, G. *Ancient voices of children*. Nonesuch 71255.

Cuddy, L. L. Practice effects in the absolute judgement of pitch. *Journal of the Acoustical Society of America*, 1968, *43*, 1069–1076.

Cuddy, L. L. Training the absolute identification of pitch. *Perception & Psychophysics*, 1970, *8*, 265–269.

Cuddy, L. L. Absolute judgment of musically-related pure tones. *Canadian Journal of Psychology*, 1971, *25*, 42–55.

Cuddy, L., Cohen, A. J., & Miller, J. Melody recognition: The experimental application of musical rules. *Canadian Journal of Psychology*, 1979, *33*, 148–157.

Cutting, J. E. Four assumptions about invariance in perception. *Journal of Experimental Psychology: Human Perception & Performance*, 1983, *9*, 310–317.

Davidson, L., McKernon, P., & Gardner, H. The acquisition of song: A developmental approach. In *Documentary report of the Ann Arbor Symposium*. Reston, VA: Music Educators National Conference, 1981, pp. 301–315.

Delattre, P. C., Liberman, A. M., & Cooper, F. S. Acoustic loci and transitional cues for consonants. *Journal of the Acoustical Society of America*, 1955, *27*, 769–773.

Demany, L., & Armand, F. The perceptual reality of tone chroma in early infancy. *Journal of the Acoustical Society of America*, 1984, *76*, 57–66.

Demany, L., McKenzie, B., & Vurpillot, E. Rhythm perception in early infancy. *Nature*, 1977, *266*, 718–719.

Denes, P. B., & Pinson, E. N. *The speech chain*. Garden City, NY: Anchor/Doubleday, 1973.

Deutsch, D. Music recognition. *Psychological Review*, 1969, *76*, 300–307.

Deutsch, D. Octave generalization and tune recognition. *Perception & Psychophysics*, 1972, *11*, 411–412.

Deutsch, D. The processing of structured and unstructured tonal sequences. *Perception & Psychophysics*, 1980, *28*, 381–389.

Deutsch, D. The internal representation of information in the form of hierarchies. *Perception and Psychophysics*, 1982, *31*, 596–598.

Deutsch, D., & Feroe, J. The internal representation of pitch sequences in tonal music. *Psychological Review*, 1981, *88*, 503–522.

Dewar, K. M., Cuddy, L. L., & Mewhort, D. J. K. Recognition memory for single tones with and without context. *Journal of Experimental Psychology: Human Learning and Memory*, 1977, *3*, 60–67.

Dewey, J. *Art as experience*. New York: Capricorn, 1934.

Divenyi, P. L., & Hirsh, I. J. Some figural properties of auditory patterns. *Journal of the Acoustical Society of America*, 1978, *64*, 1369–1385.

Dowling, W. J. *Rhythmic fission and the perceptual organization of tone sequences.* Unpublished Ph.D. dissertation, Harvard University, 1968.

Dowling, W. J. The perception of interleaved melodies. *Cognitive Psychology*, 1973, *5*, 322–337. (a)

Dowling, W. J. Rhythmic groups and subjective chunks in memory for melodies. *Perception & Psychophysics*, 1973, *14*, 37–40. (b)

Dowling, W. J. Listeners' successful search for melodies scrambled into several octaves. *Journal of the Acoustical Society of America*, 1978, *64*, S146. (abstract). (a)

Dowling, W. J. Scale and contour: Two components of a theory of memory for melodies. *Psychological Review*, 1978, *85*, 341–354. (b)

Dowling, W. J. Music, meaning, and use. In D. O'Hare (Ed.), *Psychology and the arts*. Brighton: Harvester, 1981, pp. 175–191.

Dowling, W. J. Chroma and interval in melody recognition: Effects of acquiring a tonal schema. *Journal of the Acoustical Society of America*, 1982, *72*, S11 (abstract). (a)

Dowling, W. J. Melodic information processing and its development. In D. Deutsch (Ed.), *The psychology of music*. New York: Academic Press, 1982, pp. 413–429. (b)

Dowling, W. J. Musical scales and psychophysical scales: Their psychological reality. In T. Rice & R. Falck (Eds.), *Cross-cultural perspectives on music*. Toronto: University of Toronto Press, 1982, pp. 20–28. (c)

Dowling, W. J. Review of *Basic musical functions and musical ability*. *Music Perception*, 1983, *1*, 123–126.

Dowling, W. J. Development of musical schemata in children's spontaneous singing. In W. R. Crozier & A. J. Chapman (Eds.), *Cognitive processes in the perception of art*. Amsterdam: North-Holland, 1984, pp. 145–163.

Dowling, W. J., & Bartlett, J. C. The importance of interval information in long-term memory for melodies. *Psychomusicology*, 1981, *1*, 30–49.

Dowling, W. J., & Fujitani, D. S. Contour, interval, and pitch recognition in memory for melodies. *Journal of the Acoustical Society of America*, 1971, *49*, 524–531.

Dowling, W. J., & Goedecke, M. The impact of a Suzuki-based instrumental music program on auditory information-processing skills of inner-city school children. *Psychomusicology* (in preparation).

Dowling, W. J., & Hollombe, A. W. The perception of melodies distorted by splitting into several octaves: Effects of increasing proximity and melodic contour. *Perception & Psychophysics*, 1977, *21*, 60–64.

Downey, J. C. Review of A. Lomax, *Folk song style and culture*. *Ethnomusicology*, 1970, *14*, 63–67.

Driver, H. E. Review of A. Lomax, *Folk song style and culture*. *Ethnomusicology*, 1970, *14*, 57–62.

Duke, A. W., & Gullickson, G. R. Children's stimulus selection as a function of auditory stimulus complexity. *Psychonomic Science*, 1970, *19*, 119–120.

Ellis, C. J. Pre-instrumental scales. *Ethnomusicology*, 1965, *9*, 126–144.

Erickson, E. E. Tradition and evolution in song style: A reanalysis of cantometric data. *Behavioral Science and Research*, 1976, *11*, 277–308.

Erickson, R. *Sound structure in music*. Berkeley: University of California Press, 1975.

Fant, C. G. M. On the predictability of formant levels and spectrum envelopes from formant frequencies. In M. Halle, H. Lunt, & H. MacLean (Eds.), *For Roman Jakobson*. The Hague: Mouton, 1956, pp. 109–120.

Feather, N. *Vibrations and waves*. Baltimore: Penguin, 1964.

Feld, S. *Sound and sentiment*. Philadelphia: University of Pennsylvania Press, 1982.

Fletcher, H., & Munson, W. A. Loudness, its definition, measurement and calculation. *Journal of the Acoustical Society of America*, 1933, *5*, 82.

Fraisse, P. *Les structures rythmiques* [Rhythmic structures]. Louvain: Publications Universitaires de Louvain, 1956.

Fraisse, P. *Psychologie du rythme* [Psychology of rhythm]. Paris: Presses Universitaires de France, 1974.

Fraisse, P. Time and rhythm perception. In E. C. Carterette & M. P. Friedman (Eds.) *Handbook of perception* (Vol. 8). New York: Academic Press, 1978, 203–254.

Fraisse, P. Rhythm and tempo. In D. Deutsch (Ed.), *The psychology of music*. New York: Academic Press, 1982, pp. 149–180.

Francès, R. *La perception de la musique* [The perception of music]. Paris: J. Vrin, 1958.

Gabrieli, G. *The Antiphonal Music of Gabrieli*. Columbia MS-7209.

Gabrieli, G. *Processional & Ceremonial Music*. Vanguard HM 8.

Gabrielsson, A. Adjective ratings and dimension analyses of auditory rhythm patterns. *Scandinavian Journal of Psychology*, 1973, *14*, 244–260. (a)

Gabrielsson, A. Similarity ratings and dimension analyses of auditory rhythm patterns: I. *Scandinavian Journal of Psychology*, 1973, *14*, 138–160. (b)

Gabrielsson, A. Similarity ratings and dimension analyses of auditory rhythm patterns: II. *Scandinavian Journal of Psychology*, 1973, *14*, 161–176. (c)

Gabrielsson, A. Studies in rhythm. *Acta Universitatits Upsaliensis*, 1973, *7*, 3–19. (d)

Gabrielsson, A. Performance of rhythm patterns. *Scandinavian Journal of Psychology*, 1974, *15*, 63–72.

Gabrielsson, A. Music psychology: A survey of problems and current research activities. In *Basic musical functions and musical ability. Publications of the Royal Swedish Academy of Music*, 1981, *32*, 7–80.

Gaston, E. T. *Music in therapy*. New York: Macmillan, 1968.

Geary, J. M. Consonance and dissonance of pairs of inharmonic sounds. *Journal of the Acoustical Society of America*, 1980, *67*, 1785–1789.

Geertz, C. *The interpretation of cultures*. New York: Basic Books, 1973.

Gibson, J. J. *The ecological approach to visual perception*. Boston: Houghton-Mifflin, 1979.

Giles, R. *Ombak* in the style of the Javanese gongs. *Selected Reports*, UCLA Institute of Ethnomusicology, 1974, *2*(1), 158–165.

Goldstein, A. Thrills in response to music and other stimuli. *Physiological Psychology*, 1980, *8*, 126–129.

Goodman, N. *Languages of art: An approach to a theory of symbols*. Indianapolis: Bobbs-Merrill, 1968.

Gordon, J. W., & Grey, J. M. Perception of spectral modifications on orchestral instrument tones. *Computer Music Journal*, 1978, *2*, 24–31.

Granit, R. *The purposive brain*. Cambridge: MIT Press, 1977.

Green, D. *An introduction to hearing*. Hillsdale, NJ: Erlbaum, 1976.

Grey, J. M. Multidimensional perceptual scaling of musical timbres. *Journal of the Acoustical Society of America*, 1977, *61*, 1270–1277.

Grey, J. M. Timbre discrimination in musical patterns. *Journal of the Acoustical Society of America*, 1978, *64*, 467–472.

Grey, J. M., & Gordon, J. W. Perceptual effects of spectral modifications on musical timbres. *Journal of the Acoustical Society of America*, 1978, *63*, 1493–1500.

Grey, J. M., & Moorer, J. A. Perceptual evaluations of synthesized musical instrument tones. *Journal of the Acoustical Society of America*, 1977, *62*, 454–462.

Grout, D. J. *A history of Western music*. New York: Norton, 1960.

Guilford, J. P., & Hilton, R. A. Some configurational properties of short musical melodies. *Journal of Experimental Psychology*, 1933, *16*, 32–54.

Guilford, J. P., & Nelson, H. M. Changes in pitch of tones when melodies are repeated, *Journal of Experimental Psychology*, 1936, *19*, 193–202.

Guilford, J. P., & Nelson, H. M. The pitch of tones in melodies as compared with single tones. *Journal of Experimental Psychology*, 1937, *20*, 309–335.

Handel, S. Temporal segmentation of repeating auditory patterns. *Journal of Experimental Psycholgy*, 1973, *101*, 46–54.

Handel, S., & Lawson, G. R. The contextual nature of rhythmic interpretation. *Perception & Psychophysics*, 1983, *34*, 103–120.

Hanslick, E. *The beautiful in music* (G. Cohen, Trans.). Indianapolis: Bobbs-Merrill, 1957. (Original work published 1854)

Haydn, F. J. *Theresa Mass: Grand mass in B-flat major*. Melville, NY: Belwin Mills, n.d.

Helmholtz, H. von. *On the sensations of tone* (A. J. Ellis, Trans.). New York: Dover, 1954. (Original work published 1877)

Helson, H. *Adaptation-level theory*. New York: Harper & Row, 1964.

Hesse, H. Magister ludi (*The glass bead game*) (R. Winston & C. Winston, Trans.). New York: Holt, Rinehart & Winston, 1969. (Original work published 1943)

Hevner, K. Expression in music: A discussion of experimental studies and theories. *Psychological Review*, 1935, *42*, 186–204.

Hevner, K. Experimental studies of the elements of expression in music. *American Journal of Psychology*, 1936, *48*, 248–268.

Hill, J. N. Singing and dancing: A cross-cultural survey. Review of A. Lomax, *Folk song style and culture*. *Science*, 1969, *166*, 366–367.

Hindemith, P. *A composer's world*. New York: Doubleday, 1961.

Hoffman, S. M. Epistemology and music: A Javanese example. *Ethnomusicology*, 1978, *22*, 69–88.

Hood, M. *Sléndro* and *pélog* redefined. *Selected Reports*, UCLA Institute of Ethnomusicology, 1966, *1*(1), 28–37.

Hood, M. *The ethnomusicologist*. New York: McGraw-Hill, 1971.

Houtsma, A. J. M., & Goldstein, J. L. The central origin of the pitch of complex tones: Evidence from musical interval recognition. *Journal of the Acoustical Society of America*, 1972, *51*, 520–529.

Hunt, F. V. *Origins in Acoustics*. New Haven-Yale University Press, 1978.

Hurni-Schlegel, L. & Lang, A. Verteilung, Korrelate und Veränderbarkeit der Tonhöhen-Identifikation (sog. absolutes Musikgehör). [Distribution, correlation and variance of pitch identification (in absolute pitch)] *Schweizerische Zeitschrift für Psychologie und Ihre Anwendungen*, 1978, *37*, 265–292.

Huttenlocher, J., & Burke, D. Why does memory span increase with age? *Cognitive Psychology*, 1976, *8*, 1–31.

Idson, W. L., & Massaro, D. W. Perceptual processing and experience of auditory duration. *Sensory Processes*, 1977, *1*, 316–337.

Idson, W. L., & Massaro, D. W. A bidimensional model of pitch in the recognition of melodies. *Perception & Psychophysics*, 1978, *24*, 551–565.

Imberty, M. *L'acquisition des structures tonales chez l'enfant* [The acquisition of tonal structures in the child]. Paris: Klincksieck, 1969.

Imberty, M. Perspectives nouvelles de la sémantique musicale expérimentale [New perspectives on experimental musical semantics]. *Musique en Jeu*, 1975, *17*, 87–109.

Jackendoff, R. Review of *The unanswered question* by Leonard Bernstein. *Language*, 1977, *53*, 883–894.

Jairazbhoy, N. A. *The rāgs of North Indian music*. London: Faber and Faber.

James, W. *The principles of psychology* (Vol. 1). New York: Holt, 1890.

Janik, A., & Toulmin, S. *Wittgenstein's Vienna*. New York: Simon & Schuster, 1973.

Jarrett, K. *The Köln concert*. ECM 1064/1065.

Jones, M. R. Time, our lost dimension: Toward a new theory of perception, attention, and memory. *Psychological Review*, 1976, *83*, 323–355.

Jones, M. R. Music as a stimulus for psychological motion: Part I. Some determinants of expectancies. *Psychomusicology*, 1981, *1*, 34–51. (a)

Jones, M. R. Only time can tell: On the topology of mental space and time. *Critical Inquiry*, 1981, *7*, 557–576. (b)

Jones, M. R. A tutorial on some issues and methods in serial pattern research. *Perception & Psychophysics*, 1981, *30*, 492–504. (c)

Jones, M. R. Validating internal hierarchies: Reply to Deutsch. *Perception & Psychophysics*, 1982, *31*, 599–600.

Jones, M. R., Boltz, M., & Kidd, G. Controlled attending as a function of melodic and temporal context. *Perception & Psychophysics*, 1982, *32*, 211–218.

Jones, M. R., Kidd, G., & Wetzel, R. Evidence for rhythmic attention. *Journal of Experimental Psychology: Human Perception & Performance*, 1981, *7*, 1059–1073.

Jones, M. R., Maser, D. J., & Kidd, G. R. Rate and structure in memory for auditory patterns. *Memory & Cognition*, 1978, *6*, 246–258.

Jung, C. G. *Psychological types* (H. G. Baynes & R. F. C. Hull, Trans.). Princeton, NJ: Princeton University Press, 1971. (translation of German edition of 1921 and revisions.)

Kallman, H. J., & Massaro, D. W. Tone chroma is functional in melody recognition. *Perception & Psychophysics*, 1979, *26*, 32–36.

Kameoka, A., & Kuriyagawa, M. Consonance theory part I: Consonance of dyads. *Journal of the Acoustical Society of America*, 1969, *45*, 1451–1459. (a)

Kameoka, A., & Kuriyagawa, M. Consonance theory part II: Consonance of complex tones and its calculation method. *Journal of the Acoustical Society of America*, 1969, *45*, 1460–1471. (b)

Kant, I. *Critique of pure reason* (N. Kemp Smith, Trans.). London: Macmillan, 1933. (Original work published 1787)

Kessen, W. Encounters: The American child's meeting with music. In *Documentary report of the Ann Arbor Symposium*. Reston, VA: Music Educators National Conference, 1981, pp. 353–361.

Kessen, W., Levine, J., & Wendrich, K. A. The imitation of pitch in infants. *Infant Behavior & Development*, 1979, *2*, 93–99.

Kierkegaard, S. *Either/or* (D. F. & L. M. Swenson, Trans.). Garden City, NJ: Doubleday, 1959. (Original work published 1843)

Knudsen, V. O., & Harris, C. M. *Acoustical designing in architecture*. New York: Acoustical Society of America, 1978.

Koetting, J. *Notation as analysis in African music*. Paper presented to the 24th Meeting of the Society for Ethnomusicology, Montreal, Canada, October, 1979.

Köhler, W. *Gestalt psychology*. New York: Liveright, 1929.

Köhler, W. *The place of value in a world of facts*. New York: Liveright, 1938.

Kolata, G. B. Singing styles and human cultures: How are they related? *Science*, 1978, *200*, 287–288.

Kraehenbuehl, D., & Coons, E. Information as a measure of the experience of music. *Journal of Aesthetics*, 1959, *17*, 510–522.

Krumhansl, C. L. The psychological representation of musical pitch in a tonal context. *Cognitive Psychology*, 1979, *11*, 346–374.

Krumhansl, C. L., Bharucha, J., & Castellano, M. A. Key distance effects on perceived harmonic structure in music. *Perception & Psychophysics*, 1982, *31*, 75–85.

Krumhansl, C. L., & Keil, F. C. Acquisition of the hierarchy of tonal functions in music. *Memory & Cognition*, 1982, *10*, 243–251.

Krumhansl, C. L., & Shepard, R. N. Quantification of the hierarchy of tonal functions within a diatonic context. *Journal of Experimental Psychology: Human Perception & Performance*, 1979, *5*, 579–594.

Kubovy, M., Cutting, J. E., & McGuire, R. Hearing with the third ear: Dichotic perception of a melody without monaural familiarity cues. *Science*, 1974, *186*, 272–274.

Kubovy, M., & Howard, F. P. Persistence of a pitch-segregating echoic memory. *Journal of Experimental Psychology: Human Perception & Performance*, 1976, *2*, 531–537.

Kubovy, M., & Pomerantz, J. R. (Eds.). *Perceptual organization*. Hillsdale, NJ: Erlbaum, 1981.

Kuttner, F. A. Prince Chu Tsai-Yü's life and work. *Ethnomusicology*, 1975, *19*, 163–204.

Laban, J. de Review of A. Lomax, *Folk song style and culture*. *Journal of Aesthetics and Art Criticism*, 1969, *28*, 106–108.

LaBèrge, D. Perceptual and motor schemas in the performance of musical pitch. In *Documentary report of the Ann Arbor Symposium*. Reston, VA: Music Educators National Conference, 1981, pp. 179–196.

Lane, H. The motor theory of speech perception: A critical review. *Psychological Review*, 1965, *72*, 275–309.

Lang, P. J. Cognition in emotion: Concept and action. In C. E. Izard, J. Kagan, & R. B. Zajonc (Eds.), *Emotions, cognition, and behavior*. Cambridge: Cambridge University Press, 1984, pp. 192–226.

Langer, S. K. *Philosophy in a new key* (2nd ed.). New York: New American Library, 1951.

Langer, S. K. *Feeling and form*. New York: Scribners, 1953.

Lehiste, I. (Ed.). *Readings in acoustic phonetics*. Cambridge, MA: MIT Press, 1967.

Lerdahl, F., & Jackendoff, R. *A generative theory of tonal music*. Cambridge, MA: MIT Press, 1983.

Levinson, J. What a musical work is. *Journal of Philosophy*, 1980, *77*, 5–28.

Lewiston, D. (Ed.). *Golden rain*. Nonesuch H-72028.

Liberman, A. M., Harris, K. S., Kinney, J., & Lane, H. L. The discrimination of relative onset time of the components of certain speech and non-speech patterns. *Journal of Experimental Psychology*, 1961, *61*, 379–388.

Lindsay, P. H., & Norman, D. A. *Human information processing* (2nd ed.). New York: Academic Press, 1977.

Locke, D. Principles of offbeat timing and cross-rhythm in southern Eve dance drumming. *Ethnomusicology*, 1982, *26*, 217–246.

Lomax, A. Folk song style. *American Anthropologist*, 1959, *61*, 927–954.

Lomax, A. *Folk song style and culture*. Washington, DC: American Association for the Advancement of Science, 1968.

Lomax, A., & Berkowitz, N. The evolutionary taxonomy of culture. *Science*, 1972, *177*, 228–239.

Machotka, P. Aesthetic choice and coping with conflict. In D. O'Hare (Ed.), *Psychology and the arts*. Brighton: Harvester Press, 1981, pp. 102–122.

Mahler, G. *Symphony No. 2*. New York: Kalmus, n.d.

Malm, W. P. *Music cultures of the Pacific, the Near East, and Asia* (2nd ed.). Englewood Cliffs, NJ: Prentice-Hall, 1977.

Mandler, G. *Mind and body*. New York: Norton, 1984.

Maranda, E. K. Deep significance and surface significance: Is cantometrics possible? *Semiotica*, 1970, *2*, 173–184.

Marks, L. E. A theory of loudness and loudness judgments. *Psychological Review*, 1979, *86*, 256–285.

Martin, D. W., & Ward, W. D. Subjective evaluation of musical scale temperament in pianos. *Journal of the Acoustical Society of America*, 1961, *33*, 582–585.

McAdams, S., & Bregman, A. Hearing musical streams. *Computer Music Journal*, 1979, *3*(4), 26–43.

McClain, E. G. Chinese cyclic tunings in late antiquity. *Ethnomusicology*, 1979, *23*, 205–224.

McKean, P. F. From purity to pollution? The Balinese *ketjak* (monkey dance) as symbolic form in transition. In A. L. Becker & A. A. Yengoyan (Eds.), *The imagination of reality: Essays in Southeast Asian coherence systems*. Norwood, NJ: 1979, pp. 293–302.

McLaughlin, T. *Music and communication*. London: Faber and Faber, 1970.

Merriam, A. P. *The anthropology of music*. Evanston, IL: Northwestern University Press, 1964.

Meyer, L. B. *Emotion and meaning in music*. Chicago: University of Chicago Press, 1956.

Meyer, L. B. *Music, the arts, and ideas*. Chicago: University of Chicago Press, 1967.

Miller, G. A. The magical number seven, plus or minus two: Some limits of our capacity for processing information. *Psychological Review*, 1956, *63*, 81–97.

Miller, G. A., & Heise, G. The trill threshold. *Journal of the Acoustical Society of America*, 1950, *22*, 637–638.

Miller, J. R., & Carterette, E. C. Perceptual space for musical structures. *Journal of the Acoustical Society of America*, 1975, *58*, 711–720.

Mitchel, J. *Clouds*. Reprise 6341.

Mitchel, J. *Miles of aisles*. Asylum AB 20.

Monahan, C. B. Parallels between pitch and time: The determinants of musical space. Unpublished Ph.D. dissertation, University of California, Los Angeles, 1984.

Moog, H. The musical experience of the preschool child (C. Clarke, Trans.). London: Schott, 1976.

Mozart, W. A. *Don Giovanni*, K. 527. New York: Kalmus, n.d.

Murdock, G. P. Ethnographic atlas and summary. *Ethnology*, 1962-1967, *1–6*.

Nakaseko, K. Symbolism in ancient Chinese music theory. *Journal of Music Theory*, 1957, *1*, 147–180.

Needham, J. *Science and civilization in China* (Vol. 4, Part 1). Cambridge: Cambridge University Press, 1962.

Neisser, U. *Cognition and reality*. San Francisco: Freeman, 1976.

Neisser, U. The control of information pickup in selective looking. In A. D. Pick (Ed.), *Perception and its development*. Hillsdale, NJ: Erlbaum, 1979, pp. 201–219.

Nettl, B. *Folk and traditional music of the Western continents*. Englewood Cliffs, NJ: Prentice-Hall, 1973.

Norman, D. A. Temporal confusions and limited capacity processors. *Acta Psychologica*, 1967, *27*, 85–94.

Null, C. H. *Symmetry in judgments of musical pitch*. Unpublished Ph.D. dissertation, Michigan State University, 1974.

Olson, H. F. *Music, physics and engineering*. New York: Dover, 1967.

Ornstein, R. E. *On the experience of time*. Baltimore: Penguin, 1969.

Oshinsky, J. S., & Handel, S. Syncopated polyrhythms: Discontinuous reversals in meter interpretation. *Journal of the Acoustical Society of America*, 1978, *63*, 936–939.

Ostwald, P. F. Musical behavior in early childhood. *Developmental Medicine & Child Neurology*, 1973, *15*, 367–375.

Overmier, J. B., & Schuck, J. R. *Relative preferences for auditory patterns*. Paper presented to the 19th International Congress of Psychologists, 1969.

Partch, H. *Genesis of a music*. New York: Da Capo Press, 1974.

Pavlov, I. P. *Conditioned reflexes*. London: Oxford University Press, 1927.

Peckham, M. *Man's rage for chaos: Biology, behavior, and the arts*. New York: Schocken, 1965.

Peirce, C. S. *Collected papers* (Vols. 1–6) (C. Hartshorne & P. Weiss, Eds.). Cambridge, MA: Harvard University Press, 1931–1935.

Perrott, D. R., & Nelson, M. A. Limits for the detection of binaural beats. *Journal of the Acoustical Society of America*, 1969, *46*, 1477–1481.

Pflederer, M. R. The responses of children to musical tasks embodying Piaget's principle of conservation. *Journal of Research in Music Education*, 1964, *12*, 251–268.

Pflederer, M., & Sechrest, L. Conservation-type responses of children to musical stimuli. *Council for Research in Music Education Bulletin*, 1968, *13*, 19–36.

Piaget, J. *The child's conception of time*. New York: Basic Books, 1970.

Piaget, J., & Inhelder, B. *The psychology of the child*. New York: Basic Books, 1969.

Pick, A. D. Listening to melodies: Perceiving events. In A. D. Pick (Ed.), *Perception and its development*. Hillsdale, NJ: Erlbaum, 1979, pp. 145–165.

Plomp, R. *Experiments on tone perception*. Soesterberg: Institute for Perception, RVO-TNO, 1966.

Plomp, R. *Aspects of tone sensation*. New York: Academic Press, 1976.

Plomp, R., & Levelt, W. J. M. Tonal consonance and critical bandwidth. *Journal of the Acoustical Society of America*, 1965, *38*, 548–560.

Pollack, I., & Rose, M. Effect of head movement on the localization of sounds in the equatorial plane. *Perception & Psychophysics*, 1967, *2*, 591–596.

Pope, Alexander. *An essay on man*. London: Cassell, 1911.

Povel, D.-J. The internal representation of simple temporal patterns. *Journal of Experimental Psychology: Human Perception and Performance*, 1981, *7*, 3–18.

Proust, M. *Remembrance of things past* (Vol. 1; C. K. Scott Moncrieff, Trans.). New York: Random House, 1934.

Ravel, M. *Bolero*. RCA LM-1984, published in 1956.

Restle, F. Theories of serial pattern learning: Structural trees. *Psychological Review*, 1970, *77*, 481–495.

Restle, F. Serial patterns: The role of phrasing. *Journal of Experimental Psychology*, 1972, *92*, 385–390.

Restle, F., & Brown, E. R. Serial pattern learning. *Journal of Experimental Psychology*, 1970, *83*, 120–125. (a)

Restle, F., & Brown, E. R. Serial pattern learning: Pretraining on runs and trills. *Psychonomic Science*, 1970, *19*, 321–322. (b)

Révész, G. *Introduction to the psychology of music*. Norman: University of Oklahoma Press, 1954.

Riemenschneider, A. (Ed.). *371 harmonized chorales and 69 chorale melodies by J. S. Bach*. New York: Schirmer, 1941.

Riley, T. *In C*. Columbia MS-7178.

Ritsma, R. J., & Engel, F. L. Pitch of frequency-modulated signals. *Journal of the Acoustical Society of America*, 1964, *36*, 1637–1644.

Roberts, H. H. *Ancient Hawaiian music*. New York: Dover, 1967.

Rosen, C. *The classical style: Haydn, Mozart, Beethoven*. New York: Norton, 1972.

Rosen, C. Battle over Berlioz: Review of J. Rushton *The musical language of Berlioz*. *The New York Review of Books*, 1984, *31*(7), 40–43.

Rossing, T. D., & Fletcher, N. H. Nonlinear vibrations in plates and gongs. *Journal of the Acoustical Society of America*, 1983, *73*, 345–351.

Rupp, R., Banachowski, S. B., & Kiselewich, A. S. Hardrock music and hearing damage risk. *Sound & Vibration*, 1974, *8*(1), 24–26.

Sachs, C. *The wellsprings of music*. New York: McGraw-Hill, 1965.

Saldanha, E., & Corso, J. F. Timbre cues and the identification of musical instruments. *Journal of the Acoustical Society of America*, 1964, *36*, 2021–2026.

Schachter, S., & Singer, J. E. Cognitive, social and physiological determinants of emotional state. *Psychological Review*, 1962, *69*, 379–399.

Scherer, K. R., & Oshinsky, J. S. Cue utilization in emotion attribution from auditory stimuli. *Motivation & Emotion*, 1977, *1*, 331–346.

Schieffelin, E. L. *The sorrow of the lonely and the burning of the dancers*. New York: St. Martin's Press, 1976.

Schieffelin, E. L. Mediators as metaphors: Moving a man to tears in Papua, New Guinea. In A. L. Becker & A. A. Yengoyan (Eds.), *The imagination of reality: Essays in Southeast Asian coherence systems*. Norwood, NJ: Ablex, 1979, pp. 127–144.

Schneider, B., Parker, S., & Upenieks, E. G. The perceptual basis of judgments of pitch differences and pitch ratios. *Canadian Journal of Psychology*, 1982, *36*, 4–23.

Schouten, J. F. The perception of subjective tones. Proceedings Koninklijke Nederlandse Akademie van Wetenschappen, 1938, *41*, 1086–1093.

Schouten, J. F. The perception of pitch. *Philips Technical Review*, 1940, *5*, 286–294.

Schouten, J. F., Ritsma, B. J., & Cardozo, B. L. Pitch of the residue. *Journal of the Acoustical Society of America*, 1962, *34*, 1418–1424.

Seashore, C. E. *The psychology of musical talent*. New York: Silver, Burdett, 1919.

Seashore, C. E. *Psychology of music*. New York: McGraw-Hill, 1938.

Seeger, C. *Studies in musicology, 1935-1975*. Berkeley: University of California Press, 1977.

Serafine, M. L. A measure of meter conservation in music, based on Piaget's theory. *Genetic Psychology Monographs*, 1979, *99*, 185–229.

Shepard, R. N. Circularity in judgments of relative pitch. *Journal of the Acoustical Society of America*, 1964, *36*, 2346–2353.

Shepard, R. N. Geometrical approximations to the structure of musical pitch. *Psychological Review*, 1982, *89*, 305–333. (a)

Shepard, R. N. Structural representations of musical pitch. In D. Deutsch (Ed.), *Psychology of music*. New York: Academic Press, 1982, pp. 343–390. (b)

Shower, E. G., & Biddulph, R. Differential pitch sensitivity of the ear. *Journal of the Acoustical Society of America*, 1931, *3*, 275–287.

Shuter-Dyson, R., & Gabriel, C. *The psychology of musical ability* (2nd ed.). London: Methuen, 1981.

Siegel, J. A. The nature of absolute pitch. In E. Gordon (Ed.), *Research in the psychology of music* (Vol. 8). Iowa City: University of Iowa Press, 1972.

Slawson, A. W. Vowel quality and musical timbre as functions of spectrum envelope and fundamental frequency. *Journal of the Acoustical Society of America*, 1968, *43*, 87–101.

Smets, G. *Aesthetic judgment and arousal*. Louvain: Leuven University Press, 1973.

Spelke, E. S. Exploring audible and visible events in infancy. In A. D. Pick (Ed.), *Perception and its development*. Hillsdale, NJ: Erlbaum, 1979, pp. 221–235.

Spinoza, B. *The ethics* (R. H. M. Elwes, Trans.). New York: Dover, 1955. (Original work published 1677)

Stevens, S. S. Tonal density. *Journal of Experimental Psychology*, 1934, *17*, 585–592.

Stevens, S. S. The relation of pitch to intensity. *Journal of the Acoustical Society of America*, 1935, *6*, 150–154.

Stevens, S. S. A scale for the measurement of psychological magnitude: Loudness. *Psychological Review*, 1936, *43*, 405–416.

Stevens, S. S. The measurement of loudness. *Journal of the Acoustical Society of America*, 1955, *27*, 815–829.

Stevens, S. S., & Davis, H. *Hearing: Its psychology and physiology.* New York: Wiley, 1938.

Stevens, S. S., & Newman, E. B. The localization of actual sources of sound. *American Journal of Psychology*, 1936, *48*, 297–306.

Stevens, S. S., & Volkmann, J. The relation of pitch to frequency: A revised scale. *American Journal of Psychology*, 1940, *53*, 329–353.

Stravinsky, I. *Poetics of music.* New York: Vintage, 1956.

Surjodiningrat, W., Sudarjana, P. J., & Susanto, A. *Penjelidikan dalam pengukuran nada gamelan–gamelan djawa terkemuka di Jogjakarta dan Surakarta* [Research into tonal measurements of prominent Javanese gamelans in Jogjakarta and Surakarta] Jogjakarta, Indonesia: Universitas Gadja Mada, 1969.

Suzuki, S. *The "mother tongue method" of education and the law of ability.* Paper presented to the Japan Institute of Educational Psychology, 1973.

Swets, J. A. Central factors in auditory frequency selectivity. *Psychological Bulletin*, 1963, *60*, 429–440.

Terhardt, E., & Ward, W. D. Recognition of musical key: Exploratory study. *Journal of the Acoustical Society of America*, 1982, *72*, 26–33.

Tolman, E. C. Cognitive maps in rats and men. *Psychological Review*, 1948, *55*, 189–208.

Trehub, S. E., Bull, D., & Thorpe, L. A. Infants' perception of melodies: The role of melodic contour. *Child Development*, 1984, *55*, 821–830.

Tulving, E. Episodic and semantic memory. In E. Tulving & W. Donaldson (Eds.), *Organization of memory.* New York: Academic Press, 1972, pp. 381–403.

Tulving, E., & Thomson, D. M. Encoding specificity and retrieval processes in episodic memory. *Psychological Review*, 1973, *80*, 352–373.

Turnbull, C. *The forest people.* New York: Simon & Schuster, 1961.

Turnbull, C. M., & Chapman, F. S. (Eds.). *The pygmies of the Ituri forest.* Folkways 4457.

van Noorden, L. P. A. S. *Temporal coherence in the perception of tone sequences.* Eindhoven, The Netherlands: Institute for Perception Research, 1975.

Varèse, E. Poème électronique. Columbia MS-6146.

Vitz, P. C. Affect as a function of stimulus variation. *Journal of Experimental Psychology*, 1966, *71*, 74–79.

Vitz, P. C. Preference for tones as a function of frequency (Hertz) and intensity (decibels). *Perception & Psychophysics*, 1972, *11*, 84–88.

Wade, B. C. *Music in India.* Englewood Cliffs, NJ: Prentice-Hall, 1979.

Wallach, M. A., & Greenberg, C. Personality functions of symbolic sexual arousal to music. *Psychological Monographs*, 1960, *74*(7).

Walliser, K. Über die Speizung von empfundenen Intervallen gegenüber mathematisch harmonischen Intervallen bei Sinustönen. [The stretching of perceived intervals between sinusoids with respect to mathematical harmonic intervals]. *Frequenz*, 1969, *23*, 139–143.

Ward, W. D. Subjective musical pitch. *Journal of the Acoustical Society of America*, 1954, *26*, 369–380.

Ward, W. D. Absolute Pitch. *Sound*, 1963, *2*(3), 14–21, & *2*(4), 33–41.

Ward, W. D. Musical perception. In J. V. Tobias (Ed.), *Foundations of modern auditory theory* (Vol. 1). New York: Academic Press, 1970.

Warren, R. M., & Byrnes, D. L. Temporal discrimination of recycled tonal sequences:

Pattern matching and naming of order by untrained listeners. *Perception & Psychophysics,* 1975, *18,* 273–280.

Warren, R. M., Obusek, C. J., Farmer, R. M., & Warren, R. P. Auditory sequence: Confusion of patterns other than speech or music. *Science,* 1969, *164,* 586–587.

Warren, R. M., & Warren, R. P. Auditory illusions and confusions. *Scientific American,* 1970, *233,* 30–36.

Waterman, R. A. Music in Australian Aboriginal culture: Some sociological and psychological implications. *Journal of Music Therapy,* 1955, *5,* 40–49.

Weaver, H. E. Syncopation: A study of musical rhythms. *Journal of General Psychology,* 1939, *20,* 409–429.

Wedin, L. A multidimensional study of perceptual-emotional qualities in music. *Scandinavian Journal of Psychology,* 1972, *13,* 1–17.

Werbik, H. L'indétermination et les qualités impressives des modèles stimulants mélodiques [Uncertainty and the affective qualities of melodic stimuli]. *Sciences de l'Art,* 1969, *1–2,* 25–37.

Wessel, D. L. Timbre space as a musical control structure. *Computer Music Journal,* 1979, *3,* 45–52.

White, B. W. Recognition of distorted melodies. *American Journal of Psychology,* 1960, *73,* 100–107.

Wightman, F. L. Pitch and stimulus fine structure. *Journal of the Acoustical Society of America,* 1973, *54,* 397–406.

Williamson, M. C., & Williamson, R. C. The construction and decoration of one Burmese harp. *Selected Reports,* UCLA Institute of Ethnomusicology, 1968, *1*(2), 45–76.

Wilson, E. O. *On human nature.* New York: Bantam Books, 1981.

Winckel, F. *Music, sound and sensation.* New York: Dover, 1967.

Wittgenstein, L. *Lectures and conversations on aesthetics, psychology and religious belief.* Berkeley: University of California Press, 1966.

Wollheim, R. *Art and its objects: An introduction to aesthetics.* New York: Harper & Row, 1968.

Woodrow, H. Time perception. In S. S. Stevens (Ed.), *Handbook of experimental psychology.* New York: Wiley, 1951, pp. 1224–1236.

Wyatt, R. F. The improvability of pitch discrimination. *Psychological Monographs,* 1945, *58*(267).

Yeston, M. *The stratification of musical rhythm.* New Haven: Yale University, 1976.

Young, R. W. Inharmonicity of plain wire piano strings. *Journal of the Acoustical Society of America,* 1952, *24,* 267–273.

Zajonc, R. B. Feeling and thinking: Preferences need no inferences. *American Psychologist,* 1980, *35,* 151–175.

Zajonc, R. B. On the primacy of affect. *American Psychologist,* 1984, *39,* 117–123.

Zenatti, A. Le developpement génétique de la perception musicale [The genetic development of musical perception]. *Monographies Françaises de Psychologie,* 1969, No.17.

Zwicker, E., Flottorp, G., & Stevens, S. S. Critical bandwidth in loudness summation. *Journal of the Acoustical Society of America,* 1957, *29,* 548–557.

Zwislocki, J. J., & Kletsky, E. J. Tectorial membrane: A possible effect on frequency analysis in the cochlea. *Science,* 1979, *204,* 639–641.

Index

253

ACADEMIC PRESS
SERIES IN COGNITION AND PERCEPTION

SERIES EDITORS:

EDWARD C. CARTERETTE
MORTON P. FRIEDMAN
Department of Psychology
University of California, Los Angeles
Los Angeles, California

Stephen K. Reed: *Psychological Processes in Pattern Recognition*

Earl B. Hunt: *Artificial Intelligence*

James P. Egan: *Signal Detection Theory and ROC Analysis*

Martin F. Kaplan and Steven Schwartz (Eds.): *Human Judgment and Decision Processes*

Myron L. Braunstein: *Depth Perception Through Motion*

R. Plomp: *Aspects of Tone Sensation*

Martin F. Kaplan and Steven Schwartz (Eds.): *Human Judgment and Decision Processes in Applied Settings*

Bikkar S. Randhawa and William E. Coffman: *Visual Learning, Thinking, and Communication*

Robert B. Welch: *Perceptual Modification: Adapting to Altered Sensory Environments*

Lawrence E. Marks: *The Unity of the Senses: Interrelations among the Modalities*

Michele A. Wittig and Anne C. Petersen (Eds.): *Sex-Related Differences in Cognitive Functioning: Developmental Issues*

Douglas Vickers: *Decision Processes in Visual Perception*

Margaret A. Hagen (Ed.): *The Perception of Pictures, Vol. 1: Alberti's Window: The Projective Model of Pictorial Information, Vol. 2 Dürer's Devices: Beyond the Projective Model of Pictures*

J. B. Deregowski: *Illusions, Patterns and Pictures: A Cross-Cultural Perspective*

Graham Davies, Hadyn Ellis and John Shepherd (Eds.): *Perceiving and Remembering Faces*

Hubert Dolezal: *Living in a World Transformed: Perceptual and Performatory Adaptation to Visual Distortion*

Gerald H. Jacobs: *Comparative Color Vision*

Trygg Engen: *The Perception of Odors*

John A. Swets and Ronald M. Pickett: *Evaluation of Diagnostic Systems: Methods from Signal Detection Theory*

Diana Deutsch (Ed.): *The Psychology of Music*

C. Richard Puff (Ed.): *Handbook of Research Methods in Human Memory and Cognition*

Raja Parasuraman and D. R. Davies (Eds.): *Varieties of Attention*